Ego Psychology II

Psychoanalytic Developmental Psychology

Ego Psychology II

Psychoanalytic Developmental Psychology

Gertrude and Rubin Blanck

New York
Columbia University Press

Library of Congress Cataloging in Publication Data
Blanck, Gertrude.
Ego psychology II.

Bibliography: p.
Includes index.
1. Psychotherapy. 2. Psychoanalysis.
3. Ego (Psychology). 4. Developmental psychology.
5. Mahler, Margaret S. I. Blanck, Rubin,
joint author. II. Title. [DNLM: 1. Ego.
2. Psychoanalysis. 3. Psychotherapy. WM420.3
B641e]
RC480.5.B585 616.8'917 78-10956
ISBN 0-231-04470-4

Columbia University Press
New York Guildford, Surrey

Printed in the United States of America
10 9 8 7 6

Clothbound editions of Columbia University Press books are
Smyth-sewn and printed on permanent
and durable acid-free paper.

Frontispiece

One dislikes the thought of abandoning observation for barren theoretical controversy, but nevertheless one must not shirk an attempt at clarification. It is true that notions such as that of an ego-libido, an energy of the ego-instincts, and so on, are neither particularly easy to grasp, nor sufficiently rich in content; a speculative theory of the relations in question would begin by seeking to obtain a sharply defined concept as its basis. But I am of opinion that that *is just the difference between a speculative theory and a science erected on empirical interpretation. The latter will not envy speculation its privilege of having a smooth, logically unassailable foundation, but will gladly content itself with nebulous, scarcely imaginable basic concepts, which it hopes to apprehend more clearly in the course of its development, or which it is even prepared to replace by others. For these ideas are not the foundation of science, upon which everything rests: that foundation is observation alone. They are not the bottom but the top of the whole structure, and they can be replaced and discarded without damaging it.*

—Freud, 1914, p. 77.

Contents

Foreword

Freud's work, so intrinsically valuable as it stands alone, is also seminal. Many theoreticians have proceeded with ongoing elaboration of his psychoanalytic discoveries. One thinks here of Anna Freud, Hartmann, Jacobson, Kris, Greenacre, Spitz, Loewald, and many others. My own work that led me to certain conclusions about early childhood development is built upon Freud's discoveries and is consistent with the complementary contributions of these other theoreticians. Through the more contemporary investigations, psychoanalysis as a psychopathology became expanded into a normal developmental psychology as well. Thus, contemporary Freudian theory—from Freud's structural theory, through Anna Freud's elaboration of the defensive function of the ego, Hartmann's elaboration of theory in his collaborative work with Kris and Loewenstein, Jacobson's description of the process of differentiation of self and object representations, and Spitz's and my work on direct observation of children—became a body of knowledge known as "ego psychology."

This ever-expanding body of knowledge that ego psychology represents has become a most important and fundamental theory upon which many clinical and theoretical works have been based in recent years. But it remained for the Blancks, with their thorough knowledge of Freud and of the psychoanalytic literature as a whole, combined with their by now well-known integrative talent, to bring out a book of such basic importance as the present volume.

In *Ego Psychology: Theory and Practice,* Gertrude and Rubin Blanck presented an integration of how these theories may be technically useful in the treatment of the borderline conditions. Because theory construction is continuous, the burgeoning developments since publication of that volume provide greater specificity to theory, but also necessitate clarification of some long-held assumptions. In their new volume, the Blancks rest their position upon the concept of ego itself as organizing process. This is not new. It pursues Freud's thoughts about the Gesamt-Ich, which were elaborated by Loewald. What is new, however, is the use to which the Blancks put that concept, blending it with developmental theory and deriving technical implications from that combination. Thus, narcissism and the borderline conditions emerge as disruptions along the continuum of development, that is, as deviant directions in the organizing process.

Also presented is psychoanalytic developmental diagnosis in a manner that preserves the concepts of development and organization, thereby providing a sense of the ongoing nature of the developmental process and how pathology can ensue in the form of impairment of development and organization. Yet they avoid the pitfall of making simplistic linkages between the clinical picture in adulthood and specific developmental failures or inadequacies of the early developmental phases.

On the theoretical side, the Blancks challenge the traditional interpretation of drive theory, using Freud's last statement on the drives to elaborate their own position. Significantly, as the Blancks' research discloses, Nunberg (1931) and Hartmann (1939) have also touched upon this concept of the drives. Even though many readers will find the chapter on drive theory and affect theory highly controversial, it is my opinion that the Blancks have highlighted a much needed revision of the dual drive theory. The direction in which they propose to take us promises to relieve our science of the terminological babel into which it has fallen with regard to these theories. It is necessary, as the Blancks point out, that the bipolar drive theory and the multifaceted affect theory be pried loose from each other.

Technical approach to the "less-structured personalities" deservedly receives attention by many these days. Here, the Blancks propose a unified treatment approach in which transference, defense, and resistance are viewed as phenomena deriving from the level of structuralization achieved in the developmental process. Building upon the bedrock of the standard works on technique—Freud's fundamental papers, and the texts by Glover, Fenichel, Sharpe, Menninger, Greenson, and others—they integrate and update the theory of technique to include the implications of developmental theory.

Especially important is the consideration of those pathologies in which oedipal and preoedipal features are intermingled. That essentially neurotic organization may be impaired by inadequate experiences in the subphases of the separation-individuation process is one of the most important diagnostic and technical issues which we have to consider today. The Blancks' clarification of it and their suggestions for dealing with it therapeutically would, standing alone, make this book important.

Overall, the Blancks provide an integration of psychoanalytic developmental psychology as it has evolved from Freud's work. The summary and recapitulation of theory and technique make this volume a sine qua non for psychoanalytic psychotherapists and theoreticians alike. The volume contains many important and timely contributions which, in my opinion, elevate the entire opus to the status of a classic.

—MARGARET S. MAHLER, M.D.

Preface

In *Ego Psychology: Theory and Practice* we summarized the works of the major ego psychologists, those heirs of Freud who carried theory construction forward in the direction in which Freud took psychoanalysis by his proposal of the structural theory in *The Ego and the Id* in 1923. Since 1975, theory building has accelerated, fueled to a large extent by Mahler's extensions of theory derived from her observation and research protocols published in her book (with Pine and Bergman) *The Psychological Birth of the Human Infant* (1975).

Mahler's work organizes developmental theory. The 1975 publication represents the theoretical conclusions that she and her coworkers drew from their many years of study of mother-child pairs in an experimental setting. Although she had proposed that there are three phases of development—autism, symbiosis, separation-individuation—long before, in her numerous papers and in her earlier book, *On Human Symbiosis and the Vicissitudes of Individuation* (1968), the profound and exquisitely detailed conclusions of the later volume cap off an era in ego psychological theory and, simultaneously, usher in a new one. Our book dwells only briefly on the theories put forth by the predecessors of Mahler—Hartmann, Kris, Loewenstein, Jacobson, Spitz, and others. Those are the theorists whose works we have already summarized. Here we intend to step into the era ushered in by the newer contributions. While coextensive with the work that went before, they extend also far into the future, providing a culmination in theory construction and, simultaneously, a point of departure for future theory construction. It is this coincidence of bringing together past, present and future that we have termed *an organizing principle* (1977).

There have been several such organizing principles in the evolution of psychoanalytic theory. First, Freud's monumental *Interpretation of Dreams* in 1900 established psychoanalytic metapsychology; then Freud's discovery of unconscious oedipal fantasy which formed the basis for the psychoanalytic theory of neurosis; his explication of infantile sexuality in the *Three Essays on the Theory of Sexuality* in 1905; his proposal of the structural theory in *The Ego and the Id* in 1923 which laid the basis for modern ego psychology; his revision of the theory of anxiety in *Inhibitions, Symptoms and Anxiety* in 1926; Anna Freud's *Ego and the Mechanisms of Defence* in 1936 which radically revised the theory of the technique of psychoanalysis; and Hartmann's revolutionary work *Ego Psychology and the Problem of Adaptation* in 1939 (first published in English in 1958) which changed psychoanalytic theory from a psychopathology only to include a normal developmental psychology as well. It is in such tradition that we view Mahler's work, utilizing as it does that which has gone before, yet adding a dimension that transcends past theory. We demonstrate its immediate effect upon the techniques of psychoanalysis and psychoanalytically oriented psychotherapy, and we think it fitting to give the extension of theory from which our proposed techniques will be extrapolated a new designation, *psychoanalytic developmental psychology* (first proposed by Sandler and Joffe, 1969) in recognition of the fact that *ego psychology,* as it has grown in sophistication, emerges as a broad theory of development.

This book is intended as the companion volume to *Ego Psychology: Theory and Practice* and it is assumed that the reader will have familiarity with the works of the ego psychologists summarized there, with the special techniques of psychotherapy proposed, as well as with the standard texts on the technique of psychoanalysis. Technique alters in the course of practice as the result of experience and increased knowledge. Since knowledge is never complete and must be continuously validated, a book such as this can only represent an arbitrary pause in ongoing development of theory and practice, a stopping point where past knowledge, observation and new premise can usefully be combined. Our technical suggestions will add to those already established without discarding that which has been validated by experience. For the psychotherapy (and sometimes psychoanalysis) of the borderline and narcissistic conditions, we do not yet have techniques which have stood the test of time and validation. Here we remain on pioneering ground as new theory suggests techniques to be tested. Our purpose is to show the impact of psychoanalytic developmental psychology on the classical views of certain technical issues. We expect our thinking to grow and change as those who proceed beyond us provide more knowledge.

We use the first chapter to present our plan. It is not an outline in the strict sense, but rather a reflection of our wish to give the reader an overview of our thinking and to show how we shall develop the next logical steps in bringing ego psychological thought into congruence with the theoretical proposals that have flowed recently from the seminal theories of the early ego psychologists.

A *theory* of technique is more useful than are specific "how-to-do-it" instructions. It leaves room for the individual practitioner to apply the theory creatively and to develop a unique style. Although both authors are in general agreement about theory, our practice styles differ. Mahler herself has not undertaken to suggest techniques. Those that seem to us to be dictated by her discoveries are our own, and we take responsibility for them. We are indebted to all of the ego psychologists for having provided so profound a base for elaboration of their theories and extrapolation of techniques.

New York, 1978

Gertrude Blanck
Rubin Blanck

Acknowledgments

As was true of our earlier volume, our first debt is to the theorists whose works preceded ours and provided the fundamental theories from which we were able to evolve our own thinking. Beyond that, we have found that teaching responsive and intellectually challenging therapists stimulates ideas that otherwise come slowly or not at all. And so we are once again grateful to our students for their part in a mutually rewarding intellectual and, at times, emotional experience.

Informal discussions between us and among colleagues served to sharpen our thinking on many issues. In particular, we wish to thank Dr. Margaret S. Mahler for our many talks together, as well as Dr. Nathaniel Ross and Dr. Joan Fleming. They were also most helpful in reading our manuscript and in providing the encouragement that authors yearn for before venturing publication.

The patients whose therapeutic needs challenged us to elaborate techniques deserve special mention but, of course, must remain anonymous. Once again, we hope we have helped them in our own process of discovery.

We also wish to thank the Faculty of the Smith College School for Social Work for honoring us with the 1978 Lydia Rapoport Distinguished Visiting Professorship, thereby enabling us to complete the research for this work.

Mrs. Barbara B. Frank was most patient in typing our many revisions of the manuscript.

Ego Psychology II

Psychoanalytic Developmental Psychology

CHAPTER 1

Psychoanalytic Developmental Psychology: An Overview

Examination of the issues with which psychoanalytic thought has been concerned in recent years reveals overriding interest in several areas which come logically to the fore as psychoanalysts and psychotherapists encounter patients with pathologies that do not conform to formal diagnostic classifications. These patients present problems that are rooted in the vicissitudes of the early months and years of life before structure is attained and therefore before true neurosis can be organized. Whether these issues come to our attention because more disturbed patients are presenting themselves for treatment or because clinicians are more alert to structural modifications is difficult to decide without statistical data. Some clinicians suggest that the general population consists of more disturbed persons than heretofore; others that we are becoming sharper in diagnostic recognition of these disturbances. Loewald (1974) believes:

> . . . that we see fewer classical neuroses than we used to, is in good part due to the fact that our eyes and ears have been sharpened so as to recognize ego deficiencies far more clearly than in earlier

> times when we did not have the benefit of analytically informed child observation . . . as well as of a more refined theoretical understanding of ego development [p.187].

In the absence of statistical data, we have only the experience of those clinicians who have contributed to recent discussions of a number of issues pertinent to this question. These, gleaned from recent journals, panel discussions, symposia and like sources are: 1) reconsideration of the concept that is rather globally termed *transference,* as clinicians and theorists search for more precise information about the many ramifications of that phenomenon;[1] 2) reconsideration of the long-held position on the infantile neurosis, questioning especially whether such a formation is possible in early childhood and whether it is, indeed, a precursor of adult neurosis;[2] 3) exploration of the nature of the less-than-neurotically-structured personalities, the so-called borderline and narcissistic conditions;[3] and 4) reconsideration of the very concept of neurosis itself, how it is organized and how it may be resolved.[4]

The classical definition of neurotic structure, that of an unmodified ego that has foundered on the oedipal conflict, that defends and regresses along psychosexual lines mainly, has been enlarged, as indicated by the proliferation of new terms that have had to be coined to account for clinical phenomena that suggest that such structure is not found invariably in all analyzable patients. Some necessarily awkward terms that have begun to creep into psychoanalytic communications are: pathological neurosis versus normal neurosis; neurosis with borderline or narcissistic features; analyzable borderline states; less-than-optimally neurotic structure, and the like. Opinion is divided along several lines. Some hold firmly to the concept of a "pure" neurosis in order to maintain a clear distinction between neurosis and the borderline states; others regard "borderline" features as inevita-

[1]Paul Dewald (1976); Manuel Furer (1976); and Samuel Lipton (1976).

[2]Humberto Nagera (1966); Marian Tolpin (1970); Hans Loewald (1974); and Samuel Ritvo (1974b).

[3]Otto F. Kernberg (1975, 1976) and Heinz H. Kohut (1971, 1977).

[4]Margaret S. Mahler (1973) and Samuel Ritvo (1974a).

ble concomitants of every neurosis; still others believe that narcissistic pathology is a split-off part of an analyzable neurosis, with special techniques required to heal the split. Our own view, that development is continuous, asserts that pathology is a consequence of malformation that can occur anywhere along the developmental continuum and that techniques have to be designed to address the locus where impediment to development distorts the ongoing process of organization.

These differing views of pathology represent more than mere semantic confusion. They reflect the fact that theory construction is proceeding and that we are in the midst of change. Let us consider two of the many matters about which changing views are reflected by temporary terminological unclarity. *Narcissism* is now regarded by many as an aspect of normal development and, at the same time, as a phenomenon that may take a pathological turn. Freud (1914) thought of secondary narcissism as the reinvestment of the self (then termed *ego*) with libido, the result of disappointment in the external world, therefore a phenomenon of borderline or psychotic pathology. Mahler (1975) now uses the term *sound secondary narcissism* to refer to self-valuation that is the outcome of normal development. Similarly, the term *preoedipal* is used to refer globally to all of the profound development that takes place before the Oedipus complex, but the processes of psychic organization that take place in the first three years of life are so crucial to development that they must be definable in their own right in terms of precisely designated phases and subphases of development before psychological birth.

One can speculate, for the most part unsuccessfully, on why the development of the child from birth to approximately three years of age was of so little consequence to the early psychoanalysts. Clearly, they were absorbed with the fascinating ramifications of the vicissitudes of neurosis and with discovery of its core conflict, the Oedipus complex. Psychoanalysis as the "talking cure" relies upon verbal communication and, in its early days especially, had as its purpose uncovering repressed fantasies. Inevitably therefore, verbal life was valued as the source of psychoanalytic material. Some psychoanalysts still hold the view that since preverbal experience is subject to infantile amnesia, not to repression, it is unrecoverable except as it may be included in condensation with later experience. Many have found, however, not only that aspects of preverbal life are recoverable but that such recovery is essential to the complete treatment of most patients. Reconstruction has always been a part of psychoanalytic treatment. But its very nature is different these days, guided as it is by the important information about early life provided by developmental theory.

The history of psychoanalytic investigation of early childhood begins with Freud's study of infantile sexuality (1905b). Afterward, in his preface to the fourth edition of the *Three Essays on Infantile Sexuality* (1920) Freud said that those essays would not have had to be written had mankind been able to learn from direct child observation. To many contemporary theorists and clinicians, the observational studies now available to us leave no doubt about the importance of very early childhood and its effect upon ego development. They confirm Hartmann's (1958) proposition that the development of the human infant is shaped by the nature and outcome of the encounter of the child's innate endowment with the postnatal environment.

Modern ego psychology, as we have shown (1974), begins with Freud's introduction of the structural theory in 1923 and his revision of the theory of anxiety in 1926. From that platform, a number of theorists were able to embark upon investigations of ego (and superego).

Although Freud had thought of the ego as having to develop (out of the id), he did not pursue the vicissitudes of its development in minute detail. That task fell to the post-1923 ego psychologists. Thus, in 1924, Glover proposed that the ego develops in nuclei, that is, in islands of experience that are formed out of affect and memory traces; gradually, these nuclei coalesce to form the ego. Anna Freud (1936) elaborated on the defensive function of the ego and revised the theory of the technique of psychoanalysis to include attention to ego as well as to id aspects in psychoanalytic treatment. Hartmann introduced several propositions that form the backbone of modern ego psychology and that provide the theoretical base for the observational studies and for the theories that derive from them. We list Hartmann's propositions:

a. There is an undifferentiated matrix within which is contained the inborn endowment of each individual.

b. The ego and id exist, at first, in an undifferentiated state and separate out only after birth.

c. There are apparatuses of primary autonomy (potential) within the undifferentiated matrix which develop, also after birth, into ego functions.

d. The environment (mother and all else that impinges upon the neonate) is most desirably "average expectable," that is, reasonably nurturing in the psychological as well as the physical sense, for the infant to be able to use it maximally for adaptation.

e. Adaptation begins with the encounter of the neonate's inborn apparatuses with the environment, and from that point on, a most complex interaction between child and mother takes place which, for the child, results in a particular development of its inborn potential.

f. After separation of ego and id from the undifferentiated matrix, development of ego apparatus can proceed in a conflict-free sphere, that is to say that not all ego functions derive from conflict, but some develop outside the area of conflict.

g. Adaptation is defined as the reciprocal relationship of the organism and its environment.

Hartmann himself used his basic propositions for further elaboration of ego psychological theory (published in 1964) and collaborated with Kris (1945), with Loewenstein (1962), and with Kris and Loewenstein (1946, 1949) in a series of papers that delineated the nature of formation of psychic structure, the nature of aggression, and of superego formation. In all, this series provided a more solid basis for the theory construction that was to follow—for modern thinking about ego, superego, the dual-drive theory and especially the very nature of psychic structuring, for it is that intricate process of development that Mahler was to elaborate upon with such precision so many years later (Mahler, Pine, and Bergman, 1975).

Before Mahler, however, Spitz conducted his well-known studies in hospitalism (1945), in anaclitic depression (1946), his child observation that we have detailed in our 1974 volume, including his genetic field theory of ego formation which delineated the three stages of ego organization. It is from Spitz as well as from Hartmann that we derive our own concept of organization elaborated in chapter 2.

Upon the groundwork provided by the earlier ego psychologists, Jacobson (1964) based her theory of drive development, of the development of self and object representations, of selective identification, of superego formation and the functions of the superego, of ego ideal, all of which is also summarized in our 1974 work. We refer to these as we develop our theme in this volume, especially to show how the process of selective identification aids psychic structuring.

Thus ego psychology may be described not simply as a unification of the thinking of the several theorists, although it can be conceived in that unitary manner, but as an evolutionary process whereby one theory builds upon the one that preceded it, with considerable overlapping. It is in the context of evolution of theory that we see Mahler's discoveries as melding with those that were adumbrated alongside hers, but also as proceeding beyond them. In terms of chronology, Mahler's work has the advantage of being the most recent and so she has been able to integrate that which preceded it and to extend theory construction beyond where it had been before.

The steady progression of Mahler's work over a period of many years moved from study of child psychosis to normal development. It was in those investigations that she first delineated the three phases of early development. Later, she refined her findings to illuminate the four subphases of the separation-individuation phase. Study of these subphases led her to conclude that, "a major organization of intrapsychic and behavioral life develops around issues of separation and individuation" (Mahler, Pine, and Bergman, 1975, p. 4). It is this that we regard as a new organizing principle. In its turn, knowledge about the vicissitudes of development in the subphases of separation-individuation will undoubtedly propel significant new discoveries, possibly exceeding what Mahler has envisaged.

The focus of even more recent investigation (Mahler and Kaplan, 1977) is on the peripheral aspects in addition to the main developmental purposes of each subphase, with special attention to the peripheral needs of the practicing and rapprochement subphases. They introduce the term *subphase inadequacy* to describe some of the vicissitudes that militate against adequate completion of subphase tasks, emphasizing the normal narcissistic needs of the subphase toddler. Where narcissistic needs are not met, certain deficits accrue which affect later development. In the past, we used the term *subphase deficits* in an attempt to capture the unique aspects of pathogenicity in the subphase experiences as they might be reflected in the behavior or psychological makeup of the adult patient. As an example, we might cite the rather commonly encountered situation of the successful person whose accomplishments fail to bring elation, the affect that Mahler regards as the hallmark of the practicing subphase; Mahler and Kaplan found that elation cannot be experienced if there is inadequacy of maternal stimulation of narcissistic need at that subphase.

We now think that the term subphase deficit fails to grasp the essence of the developmental process and the problems that arise in the subphases. It is the *interaction* between the two partners in the dyad that determines the *outcome* or *resultant,* the form of organization of the psyche of the child participant in that interaction. As an adult patient, he appears before us, having already brought his inborn apparatuses (potential) to the dyadic encounter, having interacted with the environment by using what it had provided as well as encompassing what it had omitted, having organized experience into representations of the result of the interaction. Thereby he has become the unique person that he is, with adaptational arrangements as well as with pathology. Also, the process of development and organization *is* continuous. It begins, for the neonate, on day one. If the endowment is favorable and the environment reasonably growth-promoting, interaction with it brings that infant to psychological birth some three years later. With psychological birth, identity and psychic structure—the equipment necessary to cope with the tasks of later development—are attained.

Mahler regards the practicing and especially the rapprochement subphase as crucial, for it is the vicissitudes of those two subphases, especially rapprochement, that may determine whether development will proceed toward normal or neurotic formations, or whether it will be so impaired that more morbid forms of pathology will ensue. That it not to say that all subphases do not contribute to development and have their own effects upon the organizing process, but it is the rapprochement subphase that represents the decisive point in development where impairments from earlier subphases can become subsumed in the developmental thrust or can become exacerbated by organizational malformations added, in that subphase, to those that existed from earlier subphases. If the experience in the rapprochement subphase is unfavorable, ongoing development is hindered to a pathological extent even before neurosis proper can be organized. At best, pathology from the rapprochement subphase invades the neurotic formation, rendering its appearance and structure different from the classical neurosis. That subphase is critical, also, because it is there that the senior toddler is required to accept its separate fate; the toddler and mother no longer (and will never again) fit together as before. As one patient said, "The ball game was over." The writers of the Bible put it more poetically—Paradise is lost.

From the combined works of the ego psychologists, we are led to the proposals of an *organizing principle* in theory construction and of an *organizing process* in psychic development. Spitz described how the psyche is organized and showed that evidence of that organization is observable at certain intervals where indicators appear. Applying that concept to the process of theory construction by extrapolating it from its pertinence to individual development, we found that certain peaks of theory organization are observable at intervals in the history of psychoanalytic theory-building. It is these that we have termed *organizing principles*. The most recent organizing principle is Mahler's.

Upon reviewing Freud's thoughts about the ego, Hartmann's addenda, the contributions of Jacobson, Spitz, and others, and now including Mahler's organizing principle, we conclude that those combined ego psychological theories and their technical implications can be elaborated upon by addition of the following propositions:

1. That the ego is to be regarded as the process of organization per se. Consistent with that, we propose to amend Hartmann's assertion that the ego is defined by its functions. We suggest that the ego is defined by its function*ing* and explain how that better serves the therapeutic necessities of presently recognized pathology (see chapter 2).

2. That drive theory calls for clarification. In general usage, psychoanalysts have lapsed into confusing drive with affect—libido with love and aggression with hostility. Basing our position on Freud's last definition (1940) of the drives—that libido is the force that connects and seeks to establish ever greater unities, while aggression is the force that serves to undo connections (and thereby destroy things, Freud added)—we emphasize that aggression severs connections for the purpose of propelling growth (see chapter 3). Uniting the findings of the ego psychologists with this more circumscribed view of the drives provides an integrated theory of the drives operating in concert as well as in polarities to power the developmental thrust. Distinction between drive and affect promises to provide clarity not only to drive theory but to affect theory as well. Although there are many reasons why the psychoanalytic theory of the affects has languished, a major one is that affect is too often confused with drive. Thereby separate elaborations of both theories are hampered. It is also conceivable that the current controversy about psychic energy may be resolved in a new way when drive energy is no longer regarded as somehow involved with affect.

3. That diagnosis is more useful if it reflects the psychological makeup of the whole person, his adaptation as well as his pathology and symptoms. Therefore a fulcrum is described around which development pivots in the rapprochement subphase (see chapter 5). It is in that developmental subphase that structurali-

zation, internalization, and the progress of the organizing process itself becomes equipped, if all goes favorably, to encompass subsequent developmental tasks such as the oedipal crisis, latency, adolescence, and on through the life cycle.

4. That a reconsideration of discrete diagnostic terms such as normal neurosis, pathological neurosis, borderline neurosis, and the like is essential. These definitions have been bound to a definition of neurosis which does not encompass the intricacies of the organizing process. "Pure" or normal neurosis implies that the ego had not been subject even to slight modification or alteration in its progress through the subphases. Such an ego might not founder on the oedipal crisis.

It is almost unnecessary to say that there are differences, often profound, in structure formation; some patients have reached a relatively advanced level of organizing capacity while others have lagged in that capacity in varying degrees. Our diagnostic and technical proposals are based upon experience with analyzable patients who, nonetheless, required subphase reparative work in order to become equipped to deal with oedipal demands upon the organizing capacity, and with more disturbed patients who attained higher functioning levels and have even become analyzable through treatment of their organizational malformations. We mean to stress that the oedipal formation itself takes on different qualities with different organizing capacities. We have seen evidences of all kinds of oedipal processing, from relative resolution at best, to acting on incestuous wishes in the extreme.

The thrust of our effort is to understand the contribution to development of features of the innate endowment in interaction with the maternal side of the dyad and with the expanded environment (father and siblings), and to study the unique form and outcome of these interactions in each individual. In this we recognize that development is more than an ongoing process; it is a ceaseless one. Out of this recognition, discrete diagnostic designations appear to fail to reflect the pathological results of interaction in the primary dyadic or triadic relationships. Consideration of whether the organizing process has proceeded normally or in distorted forms in a given individual eliminates the constrictions of a static diagnostic scheme.

There are times when the demands of physical maturation must be brought into convergence with ego development. Spitz referred to these as "critical periods." It is the task of the maternal object to guide the coincidence of these two factors whenever her intervention is necessary to bring them into smooth concordance. Where this favorable coincidence fails to take place, certain ego functions may also fail to be quickened at the optimal time of ascendancy. Then they will not develop, thereby failing to join the maturational event. They become atrophied and irretrievable. This is consistent with the contention that the resonating effects of deviant interaction have an impact upon later development. In this instance, a capacity or function that does not come into existence cannot participate in development. This delimits the possibility of later repair of the atrophied function developmentally and therapeutically. Thus, for example, the psychotic ego may profit from learning better ways of management, but will not be brought to levels of functioning possible of attainment by individuals whose ego functions have been phase appropriately quickened, or by those whose functions have been at least "started up." In the preponderance of out-patient borderline conditions, we encounter moderate to severe impairment of ascendancy at worst, and so we believe that ego building techniques can be beneficial in such instances. Therefore, we include, later, description of clinical methods by which assessment of capacity for organization and reorganization may be carried out as an aspect of diagnosis; further included are technical interventions for repair of ego functions that have been quickened enough to make further progress in ego building a feasible technical goal.

5. That the basic assumption of developmental theory is that experience (the resultant of interaction between the innate and the surround) must become "metabolized" to form structure. Fleming (personal communication) suggests that such process precedes organization. In this analogy, the products of the interaction consist of small mobile units which lend themselves to organization into more complex units with stable structure.

Spitz (1972) asserts that a capacity for fundamental learning is laid down in the coenesthetic phase of development. The infant learns how to learn. That refers, of course, to the early "learning" that takes place within the primary dyad; it describes the child's developing capacity to learn how to deal with its own drives, affects, object images, and the like within the dyad. This fundamental education precedes acquisition of capacity for storage, which is acquired later, after the fundamental capacity to learn has been laid down. It is of more than passing interest to learning theory that cognitive learning is impaired if not preceded by the earlier learning.

Spitz also describes an action-reaction-action cycle to show how an ever-widening spiral of development results from the dyadic interaction. To clarify Spitz' meaning, we transcribe the continuing interaction. The first cycle appears as

$$A + R = AR,$$

or more precisely

$$A + R = AR^1$$

to indicate that the effect of the interaction is greater than the sum of its parts. The next cycle begins with the resultant of the preceding cycle:

$$AR^1 + R^2 = AR^4$$

Then AR^4 interacts with R^2, and so on.

We are left to wonder what "force" powers the kind of leap that uses experiences, preserves them by memory traces, and also creates new structures which, in turn, alter subsequent interactions by virtue of the fact that something more than simple memory retention enters into the next action-reaction-action cycle. It has been observed that ongoing experiences of gratification produce more than anticipation that these will be repeated. Infants contribute their part to experience; they "connect" with it in a way that tends actively to add to it. For example, they repeat the words they hear into the best replica of which they are capable, in the form of vocalization. As the mother responds to these, a new action-reaction-action cycle is begun.

6. That the instinctual drives (libido and aggression) serve the interrelated needs for connection and individuation. On the instinctual side of development, as Jacobson (1964) notes, the two drives, under the auspices of adequate mothering, differen-

tiate out of the matrix. Loewald (1972) suggests that psychic representations of instincts, the infant's own unique life and death instincts, are created out of the dyadic interaction. To that we add the postulate that one of the first effects of interaction is that symbiosis (libidinal connection) waxes, later to wane as the differentiating aggressive drive, in conjunction with maturing physical apparatuses, reaches temporary ascendancy. Ultimately, both drives operate in concert to propel separation-individuation, retaining object connection while psychological distancing proceeds. We (1977) have expressed our preference for considering the drives (connection and separation) as innate rather than as psychic representations that arise out of the interaction in the dyad, as Loewald suggests. That issue is resolved, however, if the organizing capacity is considered to be the innate factor. We describe that organizing capacity in chapter 2, and in chapter 12 show how this capacity, which derives from the apparatuses of primary autonomy, develops into a quality essential for the patient to bring to the therapeutic encounter.

7. Turning to the technical implications of the proposal that ego is organizing process, transference, resistance and defense are reconsidered in order to illuminate that these, too, reflect the levels of organization that each individual has attained. Thus we find it desirable to consider whether the organizing process has led to a degree of separation of self from object images that makes transference possible, and to distinguish that level of development and structuralization from those more primitive formations in which the continued search for narcissistic supplies rather than transference proper dominates the therapeutic situation. For the latter, we suggest that it is more accurate to view persistent search for replication of experience with the primary object as a phenomenon other than transference.

We are forced also to reconsider the concept of resistance in order to include it under the aegis of the organizing process. It is clarifying to distinguish the sophisticated defense that is responsive to signal anxiety from defensive behavior reflective of lesser levels of organization.

Also dictated by the developmental point of view is that

preverbal experience plays a vital part in the first round of development that leads to psychological birth, and to show that techniques for recovering these experiences in the treatment situation involve use of replication of object experience, dreams, persistence of maladaptive behavior, and the like.

Finally included are reflections of our experience with ego-building techniques in psychoanalysis and psychotherapy. Elaborations of techniques for the treatment of the less-structured personalities are being contributed by many. We present clinical illustrations to demonstrate the techniques that we suggest. These will undoubtedly be revised, elaborated, and refined in the future. At this point we have no vision of the end.

CHAPTER 2

Ego as Organizing Process

The basic proposition we wish to develop is that the concept ego, as it has evolved through its several definitions in the course of psychoanalytic theory construction, has become synonymous with organizing process. Hartmann (1964) notes, as he traced the development of the concept ego in Freud's work, that "we can hardly do justice to Freud's thought without an intimate knowledge of the remarkable growing power inherent in it, and of the ways in which this development came about" (p. 268).

Here, we shall review that development and proceed one small step beyond it. We feel inspired by the theory itself and by Hartmann's emphasis upon Freud's own attitude toward his work of "not being finished, of not having said the last word" (p. 268). Our proposal is certainly not the last word, but only a link in the chain of theory construction that, we hope, will suggest the link to follow it.

The germ of our concept of organization, including that pathology is the result of malformation in organization, may be found in Freud's writings as early as 1912. He says: "It must further be borne in mind that many people fall ill precisely from an attempt to sublimate their instincts beyond the degree permitted by their organization" (p. 119). And his developmental position is established in 1914 when he said: "We are bound to suppose that a unity comparable to the ego cannot exist in the individual at the start; the ego has to be developed" (pp. 76–77).

But, before he could come to define the ego, Freud himself had to go through considerable organization of theory itself. Thus, we see evidences of thought about the ego in his early clinical work as he recognized some of its functions such as perception, synthesis (secondary revision), and defense (1909). But compelling interest in the vicissitudes of drive development deriving from his clinical experience led him to investigate narcissism (1914a) and drive theory (1920) before he could turn to full-fledged consideration of the ego in 1923; only then did he define it: "We have formed the idea that in each individual there is a coherent organization of mental processes; and we call this his *ego*" (p. 17).

He continued to elaborate his thoughts about the ego in 1926 in *Inhibitions, Symptoms and Anxiety,* where he revises his theory of anxiety. There he says: "The ego is an organization. It is based on the maintenance of free intercourse and of the possibility of reciprocal influence between all its parts" (p. 98).

In 1937, in *Analysis Terminable and Interminable,* Freud reiterated his developmental concept of ego and provided the germ of Hartmann's 1939 proposal of an undifferentiated matrix out of which ego and id develop, and of inborn ego apparatuses. Freud says:

> But we shall not overlook the fact that id and ego are originally one; nor does it imply any mystical overvaluation of heredity if we think it credible that, even before the ego has come into existence, the lines of development, trends and reactions which it will later exhibit are already laid down for it. [p. 240]

Combining some of these thoughts, it is valid to think that an inborn ego apparatus (synthetic function) quickens at birth to power the formation of ego nuclei as the infant begins to organize extrauterine experience. Nunberg (1948) defined the synthetic function in 1931. He says:

> In the id there are accumulated various trends which, when directed towards objects in the outside world, lead to a union between these and the subject, thereby bringing into existence a

> new living being. These libidinal trends are ascribed by us to Eros, in the Freudian sense of the term. Our daily experience teaches us that in the ego also, there resides a force that similarly binds and unites . . . [p. 120].

Synthesis rather soon gives way to organization as the islands of experience coalesce. Hartmann (1964) uses this to enlarge upon the concept of the synthetic function:

> The term *organizing function* may fit the facts better than *synthetic function,* because in the concept of organization we include elements of differentiation as well as of integration [p. 62].
>
> An equilibrium between the various adaptive trends will finally, more or less successfully, be established by experience and by the integrative, or synthetic, or organizing function of the ego, which works on several levels and correlates aspects of mental functioning with each other and with outer reality [p. 254].
>
> The recognition of the synthetic function (not exclusive of, but in addition to, other regulations) made the ego, which had always been considered an organization, now also an organizer of the three systems of personality. This has rightly been compared with Cannon's concept of homeostasis or described as one level of it [p. 291].

Loewald (1977) also shows how the concept of organization existed in Freud's thought:

> The comprehensive title for such investigations became: analysis of the ego, i.e. of the graded levels of more or less coherent organization. Ego . . . was the title for the totality of these levels *considered as a comprehensive organization.* Freud at times spoke, in reference to this ego, as the *Gesamt-Ich* when he wanted to distinguish it from the ego considered as the counterpart to id and superego. Organization here means organizing activity as much as the totality resulting from such activity [p. 14].

Sandler and Joffe (1969), too, refer to the concept of organization. They point out that it is an integral aspect of the process of adaptation.

Thus, it has been understood and accepted in psychoanalytic thought that the ego is an organizer or has an organizing function. Implicit in that position is that this function is somehow of greater importance than other ego functions, that it stands apart, that the other functions are subordinate to it for the very reason that they are purposeless without it. Motility, perception, intentionality, reality testing, anticipation, judgment, and even synthesis itself require organizing to attain meaning and purpose. It is for that reason that one may say that organization is the very goal of these and the other functions.

The central position of the organizing function is especially emphasized by Hartmann (1964):

> But many misunderstandings and unclarities are traceable to the fact that we have not yet trained ourselves to consider the ego from an intrasystemic point of view. One speaks of "the ego" as being rational, or realistic, or an integrator, while actually these are characteristics only of one or the other of its functions [p. 139].

When Hartmann asserts that the ego is defined by its functions he meant to imply that there is no ego unless it functions. We agree with him here, for the ego can only be said to exist when it functions since it is to be regarded, as Freud intended, as a construct. Where he describes it in anatomical terms, that is a metaphor, as it has neither form nor locus, only function.

The developmental position suggests that the concept of organization be broadened even beyond the conclusion that ego functions alone call for organization. We would include the drives, the affects, the self and object images, the external world, as well as the resultant of experience within the concept of organization, for all of these must become organized in order to achieve competent internal representation as development proceeds. This repeats Freud's concept of a *Gesamt-Ich.* We are led to conclude, therefore, that the ego is better defined, not simply by its functions, but by its function*ing* as an organizer. From this it follows that ego qua ego *is* organizing process.

Organization can only take place in a manner consistent with the level of development. Organizational formations and malformations, then, represent given levels and qualities of development. Normalcy, therefore, is the result of organization and development, while pathology is the result of malformation in the organizing process.

Data for developmental theory are provided by the observational studies. Extrauterine life confronts the infant with adaptational demands which did not exist in utero. Postuterine physical maturational processes undergo a form of organization, resulting in the rooting reflex at one week. At one month the maturational crisis (Benjamin, 1961) reflects vastly increased brain wave activity. Visual tracking some weeks later indicates increasing coherence, all still in the coenesthetic phase. These are indicative of processes which take place in nuclear islands not yet interconnected but, nevertheless, unmistakable as forms of organizing activity.

Spitz' work, which we have summarized (1974), supports our thesis that ego is organizing process. In describing the organizers of the psyche he notes that there are observable features of a particular level of psychic organization, marked by the indicators—the smiling response, stranger anxiety, semantic communication. The first indicator informs us that the infant has cathected the external object world and that psychic development will proceed, henceforth, more and more in that direction. If this turn toward the object world is not taken or if it is impeded in its progress, then further development is deviant and distorted because it is closed off from the myriad opportunities possible only in continuing contact with the surround. Similar potential for normalcy or pathology rests in the development that leads to the second indicator of organization, that which establishes the specific object now cathected with special value who will become the catalyst of organization. When the third level of organization is attained, further development is enriched by the potential for object relations provided by the capacity for semantic communication. Thus Spitz describes successive levels of organization of mental processes, the higher deploying more functions of greater complexity and effectiveness. To Spitz, the early months of life represent a pre-ego phase, a time when the infant is in a state of coenesthetic sensing or reception, corresponding to the autistic phase and the early part of symbiosis described by Mahler.

Perception is in totalities, usually visceral, because organized levels of responses and the use of discrete ego apparatuses have not yet become available. Our postulate that ego itself is the organizing process suggests that there is no division between "pre-ego" and inception of ego. Even in the early weeks of life, evidence of the organizing processes is observable—rooting, increase in brain wave activity, visual tracking.

While the term *organizers of the psyche* correlates well with Freud's definition of ego, it is not immediately apparent that what Spitz was describing thereby was the form, method and content of the ego, its very process at various levels of organization. To identify one such level—the communication of memory traces of gratifying experiences connected with the vague perception of the Gestalt of the human face excites, in anticipation, almost all of the motor capacities which the infant possesses. Here the apparatuses of primary autonomy—memory, perception, thinking, motor activity, anticipation, among others—combine with drive and affect to produce, along with the specific reaction of the smile, an entirely new direction for future organization of mental processes, the ego at work. Each quantum leap in development follows a period of accumulation of critical mass, to borrow an example from physics. To illustrate: If the smiling response, which indicates that there is sufficient organization to establish inception of a "rudimentary" ego, is delayed, the very delay connotes that there is developmental lag, that preceding organizing processes that would have led to the smiling response must have been disrupted.

From Mahler, we use some significant sequellae of the conceptualizations she derives from her observational data for further exposition. Before proceeding to them, however, it is pertinent to note that her work, together with that of Spitz, goes precisely to the theoretical challenge Freud (1917a) left when he said that the "ego, its composition out of various organizations and their construction and mode of functioning remains hidden from us" (p. 415). Parenthetically it may be added that, as Freud predicted, we have learned more about the ego from the study of the narcissistic neuroses (the psychoses), for the early work of both these investigators was drawn from those severe forms of pathology—Spitz' from studying babies with anaclitic depression and marasmus, Mahler's from her pioneering studies of psychotic children.

We restate Mahler's organizing principle—major aspects of intrapsychic and behavioral life are organized around processes of separation-individuation. The infant's personality and structure develop in harmony with and in counterpoint to that of the mother. Mahler's descriptions of symbiotic unity and of the processes of separation-individuation have been available for some time. To these she adds (Mahler, Pine, and Bergman, 1975) the significant formulation that ego structure per se evolves out of these processes as they encompass the impact of the instinctual drives. Differentiation of self images from object images is an essential part of the process of ego organization. Also available from Mahler's study is information about the minutiae of specific aspects of the organizing process in her expanded description of symbiosis and the four subphases of separation-individuation. It elaborates that which Hartmann had already stressed, that the ego develops the function of object relations as ego structure derives simultaneously from object relations.

Psychoanalytic developmental psychology, with its emphasis upon the dyadic relationship, appears to be a simple object-relations theory in the sense that it describes the neonate as so dependent upon the environment. However, to Hartmann's postulate that there are inborn apparatuses, Mahler elaborates, from her observation, that the lion's share of adaptation rests with the infant. This alters the simple view of object relations as resting solely upon the maternal contribution to the dyad. Mahler was even led to conclude that paucity of capacity to extract from the environment could prevent the child from engaging in the dyadic interaction and, also, that certain endowment can impel an infant into precocious development of ego functions to the detriment of over-all organization.

Organizing process is most apparent when leaps in development show that a peak of organization has been reached, followed by a plateau for consolidation of that gain and for preparation for the next leap. Let us consider, for example, one of the most observable leaps, free upright locomotion. There can be no doubt about the impact of crawling, toddling and walking upon the child's psychic organization. It ushers in the practicing subphase proper. The child sees its body and the external world in new perspectives. Also enhanced by the upright position is potential for identification with the parents. Mastery over locomotion leads to elation, an affect that enormously promotes the sense of self-esteem and that propels a leap into the object world. Physiologically, the prerequisites for such a leap involve maturation of muscular and neurological capacities. Psychological preparation is of equal importance; the toddler must have sufficient phase-specific doses of frustration and other separation-promoting experiences to have prepared him for this giant step in individuation.

Mahler's addenda to theory provide specificity to understanding of processes of differentiation as they were proposed by Jacobson. By way of brief example, the separating-individuating child requires phase-specific doses, that is, some, but not too much, frustration and absenting of mother to be able to accelerate development. Such elaborations and refinements of the child's experiences in the phases and subphases show how these constitute the bottom layer, influencing development of later levels of organization such as the Oedipus complex.

The observational studies bear out also that psychic structure develops sequentially; each phase of undifferentiation is superseded by differentiation, which then leads to a new level of integration; in turn, each integrated level provides the platform for new differentiation. Processes of differentiation and integration proceed to ever-higher levels beginning with differentiation of ego and id from the common matrix, of inside from outside, of psyche from soma, of self images from object images, of the two drives one from the other, and of affect from drive. Confirmed also is that psychological development proceeds, desirably, in parallel with physiological maturation, converging at critical periods. Freud's (1940) last reference to the instinctual drives as serving to create connections (libido) and to undo them (aggression) is significantly affirmed.

We suggest, out of this brief review of the observational studies, that a number of hypotheses can now be combined into a unified statement: there exists an innate capacity to organize mental processes into coherent form; such organization takes place, at the outset, in affectively charged islands of experience employing whatever apparatuses are at the time available; with organization, cumulation of experience results in qualitative change and becomes observable at points in development when certain peaks in organization are attained.

Having looked at the early phases of life, we turn now to a phase when there is yet another leap in development, from living in the interpersonal experience to living in the structure. Lichtenberg (1975) finds it useful to distinguish the term *self images* from *self representations,* using the former term to denote the mental impact of immediate experience (following Sandler and Rosenblatt, 1962), reserving *representations* to connote internalization leading to structure formation. What is it that changes an image at the experiential level into a structured representation? Rapaport's (1959) definition of structure is useful here: configurations—abiding patterns with a slow rate of change. May we not say that when structuralization reaches such point, the organizing process has attained not only coherence but stability as well? This stresses once again that the task of organizing experience into reasonable coherence is the very purpose of the ego. For example, an ego that is capable of grappling with the conflicts of the oedipal crisis must have reached sophisticated levels that indicate that a quantum leap in organization has taken place with integration of the many disparate faculties into a truly cohesive whole.

Diagnostic and technical advantages flow from conceiving of ego as organization. Let us take as an example a common and well-understood diagnosis such as "obsessional neurosis with depressive features." Although psychoanalysts feel on familiar ground with the structure, dynamics, economics and genesis of obsessional neurosis, the specific etiology of a particular depression or depressive mood is not reflected in the diagnostic statement. Mahler shows that the rapprochement subphase is one of particular vulnerability to predisposing to depression. But how do we know whether the patient described by a diagnostic phrase suffers from depression of one etiology or another? Further, how can we tell from it whether the obsessional neurosis represents, developmentally, arrival at the phallic-oedipal phase and regression therefrom with or without undercurrent of subphase inadequacy? One would have to consider whether the depressive features are caused by the cruelty of the superego alone or whether the superego is joined by predisposition to depression because of rapprochement inadequacy.

As to the technical advantages of defining ego as organizing process, it serves first to reinforce evenly suspended attention by broadening the analyst's purview of what is going on in the patient, deterring the analyst from settling upon the familiar. Close attunement to communications and associations cue into opportunities to employ ego-building devices where these are needed. Attunement is heightened to undercurrents of earlier developmental inadequacies as they have become integrated and organized into later phases of development. Subtle manifestations of phase and subphase inadequacies have to be sought in the forms in which they have invaded a third or fourth layer of development—the Oedipus complex, for example.

We do not wish to leave the impression that the attuned therapist or analyst can know, in most instances, precisely where there was subphase inadequacy in early life. Major biographical facts, known to the patient, are uneasy guideposts. These may tell us something about which phase or subphase might have been disrupted. But we have made the point that the adult patient is not at the same developmental position as he was in early childhood—that the interaction, or object relationship, produces a resultant within the individual, that even that resultant of experience becomes organized, first at its own developmental level and then at later levels. Therefore, the adult patient we see before us presents far more than the original subphase experience and his static (in the developmental sense) response to it. We are obliged to search for the malformation in the totality of organization incurred by the phase or subphase inadequacy, and especially are we to be guided by Mahler's discovery that inadequacy in a single subphase may sometimes be subsumed normally in the long pull of development.

Therefore, where early history is available, we have to assess the specific impact of the experience upon the individual patient and use that as a hypothesis only, searching out corroboration from the patient's behavior and using, especially, his own organizing function to direct our interventions. In many, perhaps most instances, biographical data are lacking, and there the therapist is totally reliant upon behavior in the treatment situation, be it transference or something that we must, for the time being, refer to awkwardly as "pretransference" or search for replication of early experience, and upon the directions from the patient which certain interventions elicit. The therapist is in a role resembling that of the artilleryman responding to messages from the forward observer to correct the range and lateral position of the trial shells as they test the accuracy of the sighting.

We present a case that illustrates severe malformations in the organizing process. Our purpose is to illuminate the clinical utility, diagnostically and technically, of the proposal that ego is organizing process.

As for diagnosis, this case shows how impossible it is to fit patients with such severe malformations into distinct categories, especially where the individual is able, apparently inexplicably, to function. It is, of course, simple to state that this is a borderline condition. But such a diagnostic statement omits consideration of the balance of conflict-free functioning, adaptation, malformation, and how all of these have worked their way into overall organization. In the conflict-free sphere, the patient was fortunately endowed with an unusual artistic talent. Adaptively, she was able to use this in bringing together form, ideas, color, configuration—in other words, to organize. In her manner of search for therapy, one finds capacities for reasoning and judgment (she had investigated some of the many fads) and even a modicum of search for object connection, since she chose individual treatment. This latter was useful in bringing her to treatment and later enabled the therapist, in the course of treatment, to help her turn from promiscuity to life with a consistent partner.

The malformations were quite compelling. There was paucity of cathexis of self and object images. Lacking there were the affective ties that Kernberg (1975) suggests form the links that make for object connection. There was serious regressive potential on the psychosexual as well as the ego side, represented by the recurring symptom of nocturnal enuresis. Especially depicted in the dialogue to follow are negative anticipation in object seeking, hypercautious rage, and yet a modicum of identity formation despite all of the above-described deficiencies.

The patient is in her middle thirties and has been in four-times-a-week psychotherapy for six years, during which time the symptom (which brought her to treatment) diminished and even disappeared for several years. Major advances in other areas of life also took place. She was able to terminate masochistic relationships with men friends and with employers who took advantage of her uncomplaining compliance. Overwhelming anxiety in the form of night terrors diminished and shaded into a semblance of signal anxiety. She became more active in the exercise of ego functions as passivity diminished but, as she continued to extend her scope of activities, infantile symptoms returned.

The following recounts part of a typical session that took place in the fifth year of treatment:

Patient: As usual, I can't remember anything. The moment I left yesterday it all went poof! Gone. When I close the door here, it's as though my mind closes too.

Therapist: Well, now you are back and if we give you a chance, you may be able to open that closed door of your mind. (Therapist aids the cognitive function in making distinction between the door and the mind.)

Patient: It's funny. As I sat down just now I remembered sitting down here yesterday. But that's all that comes back to me.

Therapist: All right, sitting down is all you can remember and that doesn't seem like much to you at the moment. But I think we might be more appreciative of your ability to remember *something,* that the door of your mind did open, if only a crack.

Clearly, the therapist is dealing not with repression, but with relative paucity of self-object image; experience is not bound by affective ties. The organizing process, therefore, cannot proceed because it does not include self image, object image, and affect, all of which are required to organize experience into memory. The therapist supports the highest level of functioning of ego organization.

Patient: As we talk, a bit more returns. Oh, yes, we were talking about . . .

Therapist: (Later) What do you suppose helped you remember? (Here therapist wishes to help the ego exercise its functioning, both by making the patient aware of the very process of remembering and in the hope that, when this function is understood and exercised it will be moved in the direction of secondary autonomy.)

Patient: It's hard to say. It just came back as suddenly as it usually goes away. (The ego is still passive; the organizing process cannot yet encompass the task presented.)

Therapist: You don't think that our being together had any effect? (Therapist wishes to capture whatever meager affective tie might be in the air.)

Patient: I know that it must. But I have to add that I don't feel it. What I feel is poof, it's gone, or poof, it's back. In my feelings you don't exist, so you have nothing to do with it. Sometimes, on my way here, I try to remember what we talked about yesterday, or in the last few sessions, but *you* don't ever enter into it. (Here we see how the object images fade. The hypothesis is that interaction in the primary dyad was too meager to effect establishment of enduring cathexis of object representations.)

Therapist: You don't anticipate that I will try to help you? (Therapist tries to introduce object connection and anticipation in the hope that these will broaden her repertory of ego functions.)

Patient: Are you kidding? I never anticipate anything good. Sometimes when John (her husband) comes home I look at him and go through an almost unconscious process of saying (to myself, of course), "Oh, yes, I know you, you're my husband, John, I remember you." Sometimes I touch his face to remind myself of his features.

Here she tells that she can anticipate only repetition of negative primary experiences. She manages to use her organization, even at such a primitive level, to recapture a "good" experience—tactile contact. Then she can remember better. Largely still, however, the memory function regarding objects remains outside the purview of her organizing capacity because there is so little object cathexis and anticipation of gratification. This patient's ego disorganization is also evident in her inability to remember her childhood, a rather common and clinically observable phenomenon in such pathology. It cannot be accounted for by the ubiquity of infantile amnesia. The normal or neurotic can remember events from early life in isolation before continuous memory is attained.

We have said that the patient is passive in Rapaport's sense of ego passivity. As a child she had always done exactly as she had been told, working in her parents' store and caring for her younger siblings. She believes that she never objected (had not reached the level of Spitz' third organizer). She did not play with other children or cannot remember childhood friends.

What, then, made it possible for this patient to function at all—to grow to adulthood, complete her education, marry, come for therapy, function successfully in a demanding and highly competitive field in a large city? What saved her from psychosis? She had a superb artistic talent, a better-than-ordinary feature of her inborn ego apparatuses. Presumably, also, despite inadequacy on the maternal side of the dyad, the patient had enough capacity to extract from the environment to have averted psychosis. Interestingly, the very failure of the parents to encourage her talent enabled her to attain a degree of separation-individuation, although organized in a distorted direction. Thus, she established some modicum of identity. Although her current work has won prizes, it never crossed her mind to want to show it to the therapist, as a more object related patient might. The following recounts the therapist's attempts to build a higher level of object relations:

Patient: We have talked so frequently about what went on, or didn't go on between my mother and myself, of which I remember so little. But over the weekend I was cleaning out an old, old mess of stuff and came across a sketch I made, probably in high school. Would you like to see it?

Therapist: (Noticing that patient does not have anything with her.) I would indeed. Thank you for your offer.

The sketch was brought to a later session. It depicts a teen-age girl punching a larger woman. The patient cries throughout the session. To the therapist, it indicated that, even as late as adolescence, there was still ambitendency (Mahler) in the simultaneous rage and attempt at tactile contact. This was in operation in relation to her husband as well. When ambitendency gives way to ambivalence, we know that a whole object is cathected. This patient had not reached that level, but perhaps is going in that direction when it occurs to her that the therapist might be interested in her work, that is, when her level of organization can encompass that he has a positive interest in her. Then she can respond positively, too, instead of automatically anticipating a bad experience. In that sense, she was able to risk showing the sketch after good experiences within the therapeutic alliance turned around negative-object expectation. It is also hardly an accident that she showed a sketch depicting the core of her self-maternal object problem—that she could not touch her mother with love, but that she needed the contact nevertheless.

In summary: this patient began treatment with severe malformation in the organizing process. Distortions arising from inadequate self-object experience combined with superior endowment militated toward uneven development, including incomplete self-object differentiation, precocious ego development, negative-object expectation—all organized into a "borderline" structure. The therapist's objective was to repair self-object expectation (replication) to bring this severe inadequacy in self-object relations to higher levels that would promote reorganization of the newer (therapeutically induced) structures with the already existing conflict free functioning.

We have used the very manner in which psychoanalytic theory has developed into the form in which we know it today to show how definition of the ego as organizing process derives logically from the history of the evolution of the concept ego. In arriving at our conclusion, we have followed Freud, Hartmann, Spitz, Jacobson, and Mahler to show how these giants of theory construction, each in turn, have led theory to new levels. To regard ego as organization opens yet more avenues toward the discovery of ego processes still unknown to us. It also contains broad implications for diagnosis and technique and possibly for a new approach to the question of psychic energy. We deal with diagnosis and technique in subsequent chapters, but we must leave the important issue of psychic energy to be pursued at a later time, perhaps by others. Here we can only point the way by suggesting that the requirement that psychoanalytic energic theory conform with twentieth-century physics (Applegarth, 1971, 1977; Holt, 1962; Wallerstein, 1977; Rosenblatt and Thickstun, 1977; Horowitz, 1977; Gill, 1977; Swanson, 1977) imposes unnecessary demands upon the clinical utility of a metaphorical proposition; that when the undifferentiated matrix is regarded as central to modern theory construction, one might conceive of a source of psychic energy within it; and, finally, that when drive and affect are regarded as separately derived from the matrix, concepts such as neutralization are bypassed since separation of drive from affect obviates the necessity for a theory of transfer of energy from drive to ego.

CHAPTER 3

Drive Theory Reconsidered

Certain theoretical and technical problems arise from the historical fact that drive theory was first a libido theory. Anna Freud alluded to this at the 27th International Congress of Psycho-Analysis held in Vienna in 1971, where the subject of the Congress was *Aggression.* She pointed out that the aggressive drive, added later to construct a dual drive theory, is now presumed to follow the same progression as libido through the psychosexual phases.

Interestingly, affect theory, too, was inadvertently influenced by this addendum to drive theory. Perhaps this accounts for the fact that psychoanalysis, despite valuable contributions by Rapaport (1953), Bergmann (1971), Ross (1975), Kernberg (1974, 1977), Altman (1977), and others, does not yet have an internally consistent affect theory. Clarification of drive theory promises to pave the way toward evolution of an adequate affect theory as well as toward clarification of energic concepts. Certainly drive theory is ripe for reconsideration, and a most promising direction is provided by inquiry into the relationship between ego maturation and drive maturation.

The undifferentiated matrix may be thought of as analogous to the periodic chart of the elements proposed by Mendeleev when fewer elements were isolated than is the case today, but were nevertheless so predictable that the periodic chart of the elements could leave room for them to be discovered later. Hartmann (1958) conceives the matrix as the source of the undifferentiated id and ego, similarly leaving room for more. That concept made it possible for Spitz and Jacobson to suggest that also undifferentiated before birth are psyche and soma, inside and outside, self and object representations. To that, Jacobson added the significant proposal that libido and aggression are also undifferentiated at first, and differentiate after birth under the auspices of adequate mothering. To these extensions of the nature and content of the matrix, we add only that the affects, too, are not yet differentiated there.[1] As we presently know it, then, the undifferentiated matrix contains potential ego, id, drive, affect, psyche, soma, inside, outside, and still more to be discovered.

Drive theory can now be broadened to include Freud's last thoughts about the drives as he noted them in *An Outline of Psycho-Analysis,* published posthumously (1940). This was the last of the several revisions of his own theories that Freud undertook. As is well known, he revised his first theory of anxiety, his theory of the actual neuroses, of the reality of the traumatic etiology of neurosis. Until Hartmann reviewed the increasing sophistication of Freud's thoughts about the ego as they evolved in Freud's work, it was little known how the concept ego changed gradually in Freud's thought from a vague repressive force in 1900, through many intermediary stages, to a coherent organization of mental processes in 1923. We find it interesting that Freud's 1940 restatement of drive theory has not had much influence upon theory or technique. Rather, most analysts, in their writings and verbal communications, use the 1920 theory as their reference point, although many reject the death instinct, considering it to be a philosophical rather than a theoretical concept, preferring to replace it with *aggressive drive.*

[1]In one of his last papers, Spitz (1972) suggests that affects are the bridges that span the chasm between psyche and soma, thereby offering a new approach to solution of the mind-body problem.

Jacobson (1954) presents a particularly lucid discussion of the nonessentiality of the death instinct to psychoanalytic theory.

Strachey (1957) notes that Freud was long dissatisfied with instinct theory. Only in his last work does Freud clarify the purposes of the drives.[2] There he appears no longer to have been thinking in sharp polarities. He comes remarkably close to a unitary concept of the drives, later to be elaborated by the ego psychologists. Freud (1940) says:

> The aim of the first of these basic instincts [Eros] is to establish ever greater unities and to preserve them thus—in short, to bind together; the aim of the second is, on the contrary, to undo connections (and so to destroy things.) Parentheses ours. [p. 148].

The Vienna Congress on *Aggression* took place thirty-two years after Freud's death, yet the aggressive drive was discussed there without consideration of Freud's 1940 explanation of the purposes of the two drives. For the most part, the aggressive drive was considered at the Congress in affective and behavioral senses, as hostility or rage, with destructive aims only. Thereby, the discussion confused two different derivatives of the undifferentiated matrix and contradicted the very concept of differentiation. It also promoted a basic fallacy, for affect is not drive. To refer to aggression as drive and aggression as rage, to libido as drive and libido as love blurs important distinctions. Freud's

[2]That this clarification of drive theory was already foreshadowed is shown by the following, excerpted from Hartmann's *Ego Psychology and the Problem of Adaptation* (first given as a lecture in 1937 and published in German in 1939). From the English version (1958):

> *Differentiation must be recognized, along with synthesis, as an important function of the ego. Spitz's (1936) recent lecture on differentiation and integration is relevant in this connection. Since we somehow connect the synthetic function of the ego with the libido . . . it is plausible to assume an analogous relationship between differentiation and destruction, particularly since Freud's (1937) recent inferences about the role of free aggression in mental life. Once again, I cannot discuss either the well known or the possible relationships between these developmental processes and the instinctual drives [p. 54].*

Hartmann's statement about differentiation is paradoxical. Although he recognized that differentiation is an important ego function, he was not yet able to dissociate it from destruction. It was only when theory construction had progressed to the point where the aggressive drive is regarded as powering separating processes that the paradox could be reconciled.

assertion that there are life and death instincts left room for destructive aims only so far as the death instinct is concerned and was consistent with his then emphasis on polarity. His 1940 statment, however, presents the possibility that the drives may operate in concert.

Stein (1972) classifies current psychoanalytic thinking into four groupings with regard to the manner of viewing the aggressive drive. There are analysts who accept a death instinct contraposed to libido; those who postulate two kinds of energy, libidinal and aggressive, neither accepting nor rejecting the view of a primary destructive instinct; those who view aggression (here regarded primarily as an affect) as a way of doing things, or extrinsically motivated; and those who do not find the energic model useful.

In pointing out that affect and drive are not the same, we do not confine ourselves to the aggressive drive, but assert as well that the libidinal drive does not connote love. Accustomed as we are to the interchange of aggressive drive and aggressive affect, we are somewhat less likely to realize that libidinal drive and positive affect are also confused in our communications. How much of the literature refers to an infant's love object when what is actually meant is a need-gratifying object? Some of this confusion results from the fact that Freud, in his early writings, struggled to distinguish between ego libido and sexual libido, without much success. This was an intermediary stage in his thinking. Nevertheless, some unclarity still lingers, perhaps more in the minds of physicians and other laymen who refer to libido as a sex drive. It is presumed further, and still within the confusion between sexual libido and ego libido, that infantile sexuality refers to psychosexuality. The very term lends itself to that error. It would be far more accurate to refer not to infantile sexuality, nor even to maturation as proceeding through psycho*sexual* phases, but rather to infantile need organized around the particular erotogenic zone when many needs, such as need for object connection and for separation, exist simultaneously. Such view allows room to recognize libido in the broader sense of a drive to unite rather than the narrower one of a sexual drive and, as we shall develop shortly, to regard the aggressive drive as a drive to separate rather than to destroy.

To distinguish drive from affect does not alter the fact that affective reactions pursue drive aims; love seeks union. It is also true that need for union makes love possible as drives and affects become organized on increasingly higher, more complex levels. Aggressive drive derivatives may be observed as they appear in self-assertive behavior, often accompanied by affect as well. As we point out again somewhat later, separation-serving behavior may be performed lovingly or with hostility. This does not justify designating the affect as the drive. Love may be *used* for union; similarly, hostility may be used for separation. When need is excessive, affects tend to attain direct discharge (impulsivity) and thereby impede orderly growth processes toward separation-individuation and psychological birth.

Object relations order the drives and seek out specific channels for drive gratification at various levels of development and maturation. Simultaneously, object relations influence the development of new and higher levels of ego functioning. Hartmann (1964) designates object relations an ego function, describing the progression from primary narcissism, through need gratification to object constancy; and adds: "while the development of object relations is codetermined by ego development, object relations are also one of the main factors that determine the development of the ego" (p. 105). For example, object relations organize affects and the development of ego functions such as perception, judgment, anticipation, intentionality, reality testing, semantic communication, and even the level and quality of the ego's capacity to employ defense. A need-gratifying object deals with the requirements of both drives. The "good enough" mother (Winnicott, 1953) addresses her efforts to the need for separation as well as to the need for union. This asserts that development proceeds best when there is optimal frustration as well as optimal gratification. Increasing levels of distinction between drive and affect, therefore, are factors of differentiation and development. Infants before differentiation of affect from the matrix do not have graded affects such as love, hate, envy.

Loewald recognizes the necessity for integration of drive theory with contemporary ego psychology. His conclusions (1972), however, are somewhat different from ours:

> Instincts are, to my mind, in the light of the work of Mahler (1968), Spitz (1965), Winnicott (1965), and many others, no longer to be conceptualized as internal stimuli impinging on a psychic apparatus, nor yet as forces enclosed and immanent in the primitive psyche of the newborn, psychic forces which would first find discharge in autoerotic-autoaggressive activities and then turn to the outside. We assume that at such early stages, inside and outside are not differentiated, that there is no subject-object split. Anything we can call instinctual drives, as psychic forces, arise and are being organized first within the matrix of the mother-child unitary psychic field from which, through manifold interactional processes within that field, the infantile psyche gradually segregates out as a relatively more autonomous center of psychic activity [p. 241–42].

Loewald retains the concept of the death instinct in his theoretical position and proposes also a reformulation of the concept of instinctual drives to include environmental influence:

> It is suggested that instinctual drives, understood as psychic forces, are to be conceptualized as becoming organized through interactions within the primitive mother-child unitary psychic field rather than as constitutional or innate givens. This would imply that the prevalence of self-destructive forces has something to do with particular interactions with the primitive environment; that organism and environment in their interactions and differentiation from one another produce, as it were, the individual's life and death instincts and their relative proportions; their origins and vicissitudes are not primarily independent of the caring persons [pp. 244–45].

While we, too, place emphasis on the importance of the early interaction with the environment, we agree with Hartmann and Jacobson in regarding the drives as features of the undifferentiated matrix, quickened by experiences with the environment indeed, but not originating in it. While we can agree with Loewald that disturbance in the mother-child psychic field may lead to imbalance in drive distribution—tendency toward destruction and violence—we account for such extreme affective phenomena without relying upon the concept of a death instinct. As already indicated, excess of affect before the ego becomes able to organize it competently can lead to impulse discharge. This accounts well for destructive phenomena.

This attempt to distinguish drive from affect confronts us with a number of problems, not the least of which is that, throughout the literature, aggression as a term is used interchangeably as affect and as drive. There are innumerable allusions to hostility, anger, rage, destructive wishes and acts, as aggression, while careful reading suggests that it would be more accurate to regard these as affective manifestations. Parens (1973) attempts to rectify this by proposing that there is a spectrum of aggression, with nondestructive aggression at one end and destrudo at the other. This remains closer to Freud's concept of the death instinct, but it does not offer a solution because it continues to blur the distinction between drive and affect. It also leaves us with some rather awkward assertions that remain difficult to support. For example, is an eight-month-old infant capable of love when one observes that it has cathected the libidinal object? It seems clear that its need is rather to establish connection with the important object in its life; that development has not yet proceeded to the point of capacity to love that object.

From Mahler's work it is known that the trend toward separation and individuation becomes dominant with waning symbiosis. We find this consistent with Freud's statement that the aggressive drive serves to undo connections. At this important phase of development, aggression operates as the force that thrusts the child onward in the long journey toward psychological birth. Not only is it unnecessary to use the identical term, aggressive, to connote both separation-individuation movements *and* hostility or rage, but the different implied meanings of the same term confuse our scientific communications as well.

Spitz notes (1965):

> In the literature this function of directed activity, or actions as such, in promoting development during the first year of life has not been duly considered. We speak often enough of the aggressive drive; it is rarely spelled out that the aggressive drive is not limited

> to hostility. Indeed, by far the largest and most important part of the aggressive drive serves as the motor of every movement, of all activity, big and small, and ultimately of life itself [p. 106].

It is of extraordinary clinical value to try to determine, when a patient wishes to interrupt treatment, for example, whether the patient is motivated by anger or by the acquisition of a more individuated self image. Such an important clinical distinction remains blurred if both phenomena are alluded to as aggression. Or, when the patient wishes to move closer, perhaps to intensify the frequency of sessions, one must determine whether these movements represent need, dependency, love, resumption of connection, guilt, or reaction-formation. It is also to be considered, depending upon diagnosis, that such movements may represent search for fulfillment or completion of subphase needs. In such cases, where separating-individuating behavior is continued (not repeated) in the therapeutic encounter, the to and fro movements most resemble those of the subphase toddler who moves toward and away from alternately and even simultaneously. To cite a brief but frequently encountered clinical example, the patient who wants to terminate today, perhaps even in rage as well as propelled by the separating feature of the aggressive drive, is deprived of the opportunity to return tomorrow unless the therapist is alert to alternation in drive-powered movement. We remain seriously cognizant of the widespread use of the terms aggression and libido to connote affect. Yet we hold the conviction that drive theory and affect theory must go their separate ways before a more unified theory can be constructed.

Since Mahler's and Spitz' work, there is agreement that, while birth alters the infant's physical state dramatically, it does not change the psychological conditions significantly. The need for connection exists, since infants cannot survive without mothering, but libidinal drive cannot as yet be understood as psychological need within the primitive organism. Only as awareness of an outside dawns upon the infant can it be said that innate drive has differentiated sufficiently to achieve psychological status. Then later affect, too, begins to play an important role. Because of the life serving need for connection, libido remains the dominant drive during the early period of life. In the sense that we refer to libido as the drive that seeks connection, it is also the force that serves symbiosis.

For the human infant, as for many mammals, connection (libido) is essential for survival. At the earliest and most primitive levels of development, when survival depends upon provision of external supplies, the neonate's intaking apparatuses are phase dominant. The mouth and the faculties of touch, hearing, and visual perception are subsumed within the oral phase of psychosexual maturation. As survival becomes more assured and distinction between inside and outside begins to be made, the anal (and later the phallic) erotogenic zone achieves temporary phase dominance in the order of a biological timetable. Simultaneously, developing levels of object relations propel the shift in drive organization from coenesthetic to diacritic modes. By the time of the smiling response, while libidinal connection is still in the oral phase, auditory and visual perception directs the infant toward the periphery of the external object world and thus begins to provide added impetus to differentiation processes.

The dominance of libido wanes with maturation of physical apparatuses and with differentiation of libido and aggression. The thrust toward separation-individuation begins there. Thereafter, if conditions are favorable, the two drives will operate more or less in concert. At phase-appropriate times one or the other of the drives will achieve temporary dominance, but in the long pull of development balance of both drives is essential. Over and over again, in early development, libido will seek connection while aggression will seek and maintain separation and individuation. In adolescence, the separating needs are served by still another temporary phase-dominant aggressive thrust, to be followed by libidinally powered search for connection with a new, contemporary object.

What about the very observable infantile rages then? Infants scream, turn red, kick, hold their breath. Spitz (1965) even describes how infantile "rage" must run its course by perseverance. Once overcome by "rage," the infant cannot accept the nipple if it is introduced before the affect is spent. These events are generally cited as evidence of an innate destructive drive, usually designated as aggression.

An alternate explanation, based upon the familiar concept that the ego is the seat of anxiety, leads to the question of what occurs before an organizing capacity (ego) exists. The infant is thought to be vulnerable to massive or overwhelming or annihilating anxiety. Interestingly, as early as 1952, Mahler notes "the young infant is readily thrown into affectomotor storm-rage reactions which, if not relieved by the mother's ministrations, may result in a state of organismic distress" (p. 286). Organismic distress in the psychophysiological being is the precursor of anxiety. This adds precision to understanding the affects for, as the organizing process reaches to ever higher levels, affect differentiation proceeds as follows:

1. At the level of nondifferentiation there is either acute organismic distress or its opposite, the dozing state.

2. At a later level there is alternation of pleasure and unpleasure.

3. Ultimately, a broad and many-hued spectrum of affect develops ranging from love to hate and, including within that spectrum, anger, joy, ecstasy, pleasure, sorrow, sympathy, grief, to mention a few of the many affective shadings that are part of the human repertory.

We find it significant that Mahler used the term *affectomotor storm-rage reactions* to describe the distress of the ungratified infant, as she saw this phenomenon in her early observations. Although she said this so many years ago, the tendency persists to refer to such behavioral manifestation as evidence of aggression. Rather, it appears to support our thesis. It is no accident that that careful observer of infants omitted connotation of drive in the term *affectomotor storm-rage reaction.* She used it to describe a nondifferentiated state involving affect and movement, diffuse organismic distress. To regard such reactions in this way fits very well within the postulate of the Nirvana principle. Stimuli which impinge are unwelcome. Distress is the result of failure of elimination of the stimulus within the infant's brief tolerance.

With the turn to the surround and the inception of object

awareness, distress shades into unpleasure; pleasure has its inception as memory trace and anticipation become organized. When the object is "for," gratification and pleasure ensue; when it is "against," frustration and displeasure are the consequences. From here on, object relations have a direct effect upon the establishment of myriad shadings of affect development. We present an illustration from a somewhat later period of life. The toddler, seeking to establish connection, perhaps in the rapprochement subphase, will tug at mother's leg or skirt. Affect will differ, depending upon whether she responds or fails to respond. In the first instance there might be joy, in the second disappointment, anger, and, if the frustration is not relieved, even violent rage.

Separation of affect from drive is already tacitly assumed in much psychoanalytic thinking. The concept of fusion, for example, while originally regarded as referring to fusion of the drives, has become broadened to include the developmentally determined fusion of images of the gratifying and frustrating object. It has long been recognized that the realization that these are representations of the same person marks a milestone in the infant's increasing levels of object relations and paves the way for ultimate capacity to love. Mahler (1971) and Kernberg (1975), in referring to the splitting of object images into all "good" and all "bad," imply that affect rather than drive is involved in that the "good" object is preserved (a precursor of love), while the "bad" object is hated. When rage occurs at such an early stage of undifferentiation, the so-called "bad" object image is externalized, that is, expelled prematurely. Cruelty, absence, neglect, or illness and pain, experienced in the symbiotic phase when optimal closeness is needed, lead to premature differentiation of self from object images. Pathological development proceeds, at best to a borderline state if there has been a modicum of symbiotic gratification, at worst to propensity to act on objectless violence. It is out of such deviant development that destructive behavior may be precipitated because of the absence of phase-specific syntonicity between drive organization, affect differentiation and structural development.

As the many ego functions develop and as structuralization

proceeds, libidinal needs can be gratified in increasingly sophisticated fashion. Visual contact replaces tactile, semantic communication replaces silent understanding and oneness. In this way aggressive (independent) needs as well as libidinal are simultaneously gratified. Where, however, phase-specific growth is retarded, precocious independence from the environment without object connection to fill the void, ensues. Tendency toward affective discharge becomes more extensive and is more lasting and damaging. The converse experience, maintenance of symbiosis beyond its phase-specific necessity by parasitic overgratification also results in affective disturbance because it precludes differentiation; thus, to the extent that self images are formed at all they are impoverished, that is, insufficiently cathected with value.

Kernberg (1974) regards affects as the very links between self and object images which would otherwise remain split. The development of higher levels of object relations depends upon the affective experiences with self and object images. He suggests also that affects organize the drives. It is recognized that there are affective reactions to drive tensions and drive gratifications. Ross (1975) notes that the fundamental dichotomy of drive tension and release are indissolubly linked to the affects of pleasure and unpleasure. We think it useful to distinguish these links because it makes a vast difference whether accumulating drive tension produces organismic distress or ego-filtered anxiety. Ross quotes Fenichel (1941a) in support of the position that we share—that differentiation of drive from affect is dependent upon the level of ego organization. Fenichel says:

> We have seen that affects first of all make their appearance as a force alien to the ego in situations where the normal mastery of excitations by the reasonable ego fails; that then the strengthened ego learns to anticipate the affects, to apportion them, and to use them purposefully [p. 218].

Distinction of drive from affect also has relevance to concepts of drive-taming such as fusion, sublimation, and neutralization. These have not yet been reconciled and are regarded as different forms of harnessing the drives. Separation of drive from affect promises the opportunity to reconsider the theory of drive-taming and, at the same time, offers to relieve psychoanalysis of the awkwardness of valuing one drive over another. *Fusion* of drives involves the dominance of libido over aggression. Sublimation deflects drive discharge towards acceptable channels. Both are concepts which imply, in the first instance, that aggression is held in check by libido and, in the second instance, that one aim is indeed of higher value than the other. This direction of thought carries implication of value judgment. Neutralization, the transfer of energy from id to ego, remains blurred as a concept of drive-taming for the very reason that it does not clarify whether it is the drive or affect that is attenuated by that transfer. The position we take on drive theory—that the drives serve growth—throws into question whether drive attenuation is necessary. Affect attenuation comes about when "bad" experiences are proportionate to the capacity of organization to absorb them without overthrow of the affective balance. Ultimately, with fusion of object images into representations of whole persons and expansion of the affective repertory, the object relationship itself attenuates and modulates affect. As for energic transfer, this will have to be reconsidered in a new way within the totality of energic concepts, as we have already suggested.

Identification with the aggressor (A. Freud, 1936) is an example of how the two drives operate in concert. In this combination of defense mechanisms it is implied that libido and aggression also combine. Need for union still prevails at the phase-specific period when identification with the aggressor is first employed. In this need, libido powers the identification component while, simultaneously, the thrust toward independence is powered by the aggressive drive. Spitz elaborated upon use of identification with the aggressor to show how it facilitates acquisition of that level of object relations involving semantic communication. In his description of this attainment of the third organizer of the psyche the simultaneous operation of both drives is most elegantly illustrated. Even while the individual uses the aggressive drive to power separation-individuation by wresting the "no" away from the object and making it one's own, he uses libido to retain the object representations by adopting the very gesture and word that the object employed, the prohibition, and the word *no.* Thus the libidinal drive is in simultaneous operation with aggression in the object-retentive and communicative aspects of this level of development.

The concepts of bipolarity and conflict-borne development are elaborated upon and also somewhat altered by Hartmann's postulate of a conflict-free sphere. Rangell (1972) in his address to the Vienna Congress regarding drive theory, says, "I often wonder at the proclivity of analysts to be satisfied with polar dichotomies when only a unity of the most diverse components can explain the whole picture" (p. 7). Gillespie (1971) also deals with this issue by proposing that instincts are homeostatic and that libido and aggression cannot be considered in isolation one from the other. Freud's frequent allusions to a mixture of the drives (fusion) may also be regarded in that same direction.

Pursuing that view of aggression which holds that it serves separation-individuation and identity formation, Jacobson proposes that instinctual strivings charged with aggressive energy change in aim at the pivotal point in development when ambition begins to replace narcissistic, magical attempt to control the as yet undifferentiated object. Elaboration of Jacobson's point would suggest that ambition, almost by definition, contains separating, individuating, autonomy-seeking features fueled by aggressive-drive energy. Such aggression is expressed in competition with admired objects and replaces magical attempts to retain union with them. Jacobson (1964) says:

> As these trends develop, the child's desires to remain part of his love objects, or to make them part of his own self, will slowly recede and give way to wishes for realistic likeness with them. This goal can be achieved by virtue of selective identifications, based on mechanisms of "partial introjection" [p. 50].

Thus she describes a process of internalization which enables the child to cope more effectively with distancing needs while yet retaining connections. By this means, the ego is profoundly modified through a compromise between need to retain the object versus need to expand aggressive, narcissistic ego functions. Acquisition of certain characteristics of the object will lead, ultimately, to establishment of ego and superego autonomy. In this unitary manner the demands of both drives are met. As processes of internalization make the object representations part of the self representations, union is maintained in continuously mutative forms simultaneous with increasing autonomy. We regard this not as a compromise, but as the paradigm of development.

Implicit in the concept of differentiation is the assumption that undoing one type of connection gives way to reestablishment of connection at a higher level of development and with greater degree of structuralization and internalization. Indeed, maintenance of connection beyond phase-specific time is destructive of development. This restates Hartmann's view of internalization—inner connections are created as external ones are severed, thus making for greater independence from the environment. It is for that reason that the undoing of connections is a phenomenon quite different from destruction. Perhaps beginning with the severing of the umbilical connection, undoing of connections serves constructive, life-promoting, developmental processes. Borderline patients are arrested or regressed at low levels of development. They arrive, usually, with considerable anger as well as with need for connection which can simulate love. These affective qualities can be clinically deceptive if confused with drive. For the treatment of such patients, it is particularly important to emphasize how development proceeds, not only by means of progressive and regressive steps but in complementary sequences as well. The two drives, operating in concert, sever connections at one level only to resume them at the next higher level in an on-going spiral of development.

Jacobson's concept of the process of selective identification is particularly apt for our purpose because it demonstrates so clearly how both drives power the developmental thrust by transferring qualities of the object to the self representations. The very acquisition of such aspects of the object and her functions constitutes a major step towards acquisition of independence and identity. As development proceeds to even higher levels, the mediation of libidinally powered identification processes provides a balustrade which keeps the individual from losing contact with the object as aggression powers his ascent on the developmental ladder.

Imitation, the precursor of internalization, begins the process. A mother waves bye-bye to her infant. He waves back in imitation, attempting to verbalize something like "ba-ba" at the same time. Nevertheless, he cries in anger and despair at her departure because, although he tries to encompass the object loss by imitation, that archaic mechanism is not equal to the task. Constant mental representations of the absent object, which will begin to form later and will increase to object constancy, are not yet available to him. The identification process will have to proceed to the next higher level before he will become able to say goodbye with some certainty that the object exists in her absence. Then, imitation will have been superseded because the libidinal tie is now maintained by cathexis of object representations, while aggression has served its purpose in using imitation to wrest the separating gesture away from the object and make it one's own. Drive needs which have not been met produce tension and this can result in affective reactions which, depending upon the level of organization, may range from displeasure, through the affective spectrum, to outright rage. In contrast, we may regard the smoothly separating toddler as having experienced optimal gratification and frustration which have fulfilled the growth-promoting requirements of both drives.

It should be borne in mind, however, that separation processes are not intrinsically smooth. The optimal state of affairs is one in which the oscillation from despair to hope is rapid, and where internal representations are formed without interposition of formidable obstacles. Nonetheless, the infant or toddler is bewildered by his affects. Normally, however, adaptive processes provide much to ease the tension and disequilibrium, whereas, in pathological development, the sharp oscillation of affect is unsettling. With deprivation or overindulgence, for example, there results a marked imbalance between the libidinal and aggressive drives in one or the other direction. In both pathogenic instances, tension results from unfulfilled drive requirements and may lead to hostile discharge. Deprivation produces tension and affective disturbance, not only because libidinal drive requirements have not been met but because aggressively powered movement towards independence proceeds nonetheless, but in a pathological direction because they are unaccompanied by essential identifications, and so they outpace object retention. An affective imbalance produces ejection (splitting) of the ungratifying object representations resulting in a kind of object loss. As the imbalance is corrected therapeutically, the object representations are recathected. Overindulgence produces similar tension states and affective disturbances because optimal frustration has not been experienced; therefore aggressive drive requirements become submerged by excessive dependency.

The importance of distinguishing affect from drive is illustrated by the following: A patient who had experienced a barely adequate symbiotic phase began treatment largely in silence, frequently punctuated by angry outbursts. For the analyst to interpret both the silences and the outbursts as manifestations of the aggressive drive overlooks that libidinal needs brought this patient to treatment. When the behavior is regarded as affective reaction, there is opportunity to respond, not necessarily in the form demanded, but certainly in acknowledgment of the pressure upon him. The silence is understood as representing the libidinal requirement to be together without words, while hostility serves to defend against the symbiotic wish because it contains fear of loss of identity. The therapist's recognition of the need engages the patient in a therapeutic alliance which constitutes, in and of itself, a libidinal (connecting) phenomenon. An observing ego is born as the patient begins to grasp that the analyst is not the primary ungratifying object.

More traditionally, in psychoanalysis, silence has been seen as a resistance. Indeed, the silent patient is so baffling because so little clue is provided about what it is that is going on in the silence. We (1974) refer to a Panel of the American Psychoanalytic Association (1961) where the problem of the silent patient was, for the first time, considered to be not necessarily that of a resistant patient, or an angry patient (although these do in some instances obtain), but possibly one who wishes to be with the analyst in a regressed, preverbal state. This was before there existed as much knowledge as today about preverbal life, and it is therefore of more than passing interest that analysts were thinking in directions that recognized that there might be an impact from the preverbal era upon the very form of the therapeutic situation—a wish to establish or retain connection.

The knowledge that we have today adds to the clinical perplexity of the silent patient. How we decide whether the silence represents resistance, hostility, regression, or need for connection determines the direction of our interventions. To those issues must now be added consideration of subphase longing and whether such longing is more desirably gratified or to be interpreted without abandoning the abstinence rule. These interventions are decided by understanding the very nature of the residual subphase need and how the subsequent organization has proceeded. We describe the diagnostic considerations in chapter 12, but here we begin on the drive aspects of this most important diagnostic and technical issue.

Where drive has not yet completely differentiated from affect, the reality of the nonhostile analyst promotes ego dominance over affect, facilitating identification processes and opening the barrier that had hindered development, thus freeing both drives to begin the upward spiral. After an initial period of lovelike affective reaction by the symbiotically deprived patient, during which time some internalization takes place, one may expect hostile affect to resume. Couched within the framework of an ongoing libidinal relationship, the hostility resembles the negative tinge that Kris (1956b) described as heralding the "good hour." Actually, it is a manifestation of an attempt to undo connections on the next higher level. Thus it represents a new surge towards independence within the security of having first established a libidinal tie. Now, however, the aggressively determined developmental spurt can be maintained because libidinal requirements have been met. In this manner, the upward spiral proceeds as selective identification facilitates replacement of the real external object in ever greater degree by internalization. The reappearance of hostile affect indicates that a homeostasis has been attained as separating and uniting requirements are being met. The homeostasis serves also to prevent regression to symbiotic need. The analyst or therapist does not take on the role of a real object in this process, but acts as a catalyst of development by recognizing and encouraging each drive manifestation as it presents itself (Mahler, 1963). This use of drive theory makes it possible to treat the borderline conditions effectively, but it imposes the difficult task of deciding when gratification is appropriate and when it would be damaging.

We shall also discuss the role of the therapist as catalyst in chapter 12. Here we wished to illustrate how separation of drive from affect has clinical utility that extends the scope of therapeutic operations to low levels of structuralization formerly held to be untreatable, or treatable by intuitive therapists without a teachable conceptual framework.

CHAPTER 4

Normal Narcissism

Narcissism is an integral part of the organizing process and therefore is best understood when considered within it rather than as an isolated phenomenon. That was already inferred by Freud as early as 1917, for it was then that he hoped that "the analysis of the narcissistic disorders would give us an insight into the way in which our ego is put together and built up out of different agencies" (p. 428).

Much more than the concept of narcissism alone is modified by redefinition of ego as organizing process. Of special interest is the manner in which diagnostic assessment is affected by that new way of understanding the ego (see chapter 5). The traditional description of behavior and of symptom clusters becomes subserved to the evaluation of assets and deficits in the organizing process. With specific reference to narcissistic features, those which are familiarly designated as grandiosity, magical omnipotence, and the like are now more accurately thought to be behavioral manifestations of unfulfilled developmental tasks, as clinical evidences of phase and subphase inadequacies. In whichever phase or subphase inadequacies may have originated, the damage is to the organizing process itself, to the organizational forms that the individual becomes able to develop. This formulation is derived directly from Hartmann and indirectly from a study of Freud's ongoing struggle with the mystery of narcissism, with the difficulties he encountered as he pursued one pathway after another, often finding himself at dead ends. In fact, his major work on narcissism was entitled *An Introduction,* thus implying that there is much more to be considered. Strachey (1957) describes Freud's struggles with the concept narcissism and how he returned to the problem again and again without, however, adding a full-fledged elaboration of his introductory thoughts.

In his attempt to unravel the complexities of narcissism, Freud had at his disposal his clinical observations, which had taught him to look for conflict as reflected in symptoms and behavior and how to seek out the unconscious determinants. When he studied Schreber's memoirs (1911) he was inspired to search for the secret of narcissism in severe pathology. Since he was working with the only developmental theory available to him at the time, libido theory, he saw narcissism as normal when the progression of libido was from autoerotism to primary narcissism to object love, and pathological when libido was withdrawn from the object world and reinvested in the ego (as he then understood the concept ego). Thus, so-called secondary narcissism has long been thought to be the pathological core of the *narcissistic neuroses,* the then believed-to-be untreatable psychoses and borderline conditions.

Narcissism, as so much of Freud's thought, was conceptualized in polar form, with object cathexis at one extreme and narcissism at the other, as well as in economic terms—in love (libidinal cathexis of the object) narcissism is at a low ebb. He says (1914a):

> . . . we must recognize that self-regard has a specially intimate dependence on narcissistic libido . . .
>
> Further, it is easy to observe that libidinal object-cathexis does not raise self-regard. The effect of dependence upon the loved object is to lower that feeling: a person in love is humble. A person who loves has, so to speak, forfeited a part of his narcissism . . . [p. 98].

By 1914, Freud saw that the concepts *ego* and *narcissism* posed interrelated theoretical issues pertaining to the very beginnings of extrauterine life. As he continued his work he began to distinguish sexual libido from ego libido (the energy of the ego instincts) but he (1917b) still expressed continuing bewilderment about the ego: "But the ego, its composition out of various organizations and their construction and mode of functioning remain hidden from us" (p. 415).

Defining secondary narcissism as the recathexis of the (then) ego with narcissistic libido because of disappointment in the object world compounded the puzzle of the so-called narcissistic neuroses. Belief in their intractability rested on the supposition that libido had become immobile; once withdrawn from the object world it could not find its way back to it. This was explained by differences in innate dispositions and by fixations which were irreversible because they originated at early phases of development. Freud (1917a) was, nevertheless, quite optimistic about future conquest of the narcissistic neuroses "by coming to understand the ego" (p. 422), its disturbances and disruptions. He regarded this task as greater than that of understanding libidinal development, expressing "a low opinion of our present knowledge of the vicissitudes of the libido, which we have gained from a study of the transference neuroses" (pp. 422–423). To accomplish the greater task he says: "our technical methods must accordingly be replaced by others" (p. 423). Here Freud demonstrated his flexibility in turning from something as basic as libido theory, in this one instance, as observation provided data that did not fit the theory. When he saw that libido theory might not serve the purpose of understanding the narcissistic neuroses, he announces the shift in his thinking:

> Nor can I think that it would be a disaster to the trend of our researches, if what lies before us is the discovery that in severe psychoses the ego-instincts themselves have gone astray [p. 430].

The term *narcissism* has come to acquire a variety of meanings. In pathology it is a form of personality disturbance; in developmental theory it is a normal developmental line and an essential prerequisite for mental well-being. Freud attributed the term to

Näcke and to Havelock Ellis, both of whom used it to denote the taking of one's own body as a sexual object, therefore a form of perversion in which external objects play an insignificant role. By defining secondary narcissism as he did (libidinal cathexis of the ego)[1] Freud moved narcissism one small step away from a perversion. Nevertheless, we were left with serious theoretical problems. If we continue to define libido as sexual energy, then narcissism remains a perversion. If we use Freud's last definition of libido as the force that seeks to connect and to establish ever greater unities, what is being connected and to what?

We have already referred to Freud's early formulations on narcissism as involving shifts in libidinal cathexis from objects (or object images) to self (or self images). At that time in the history of theory construction, libido and love were not well distinguished one from the other, as exemplified by Freud's description of persons in love having forfeited part of their narcissism. A new direction in the theory began to appear when Freud realized that the entire phenomenon could not be explained by libidinal shifts alone, especially while libido was so broadly applied to sexual energy, to love, to attraction, and the like. A solution appeared in the form of distinguishing ego libido from sexual libido, the former to denote the energy of the ego instincts. Here is the beginning of the separation of ego interests from drive. The remaining ambiguity was clarified by Hartmann (1950a), who distinguished cathexis of the self from cathexis of the ego.

So long as narcissism remained bound to libido theory, it was necessary to retain concepts of primary and secondary narcissism to reflect investment and withdrawal of cathexis. Can this be one of the areas with which, according to Strachey, Freud was discontent? A solution became possible with Hartmann's introduction of the concept of the undifferentiated matrix, providing space for a developmental point of view. This concept enabled Jacobson (1954) to show that, before differentiation, there can be no self-cathexis (primary narcissism). Hartmann (1964) describes how

[1]Hartmann notes Freud's pre-1923 ambiguity in his use of the term *ego,* suggesting that self (or self-representations) is the more accurate term.

ego psychological thought broadens our purview of the problem of narcissism and its impact upon object relations:

> The earliest stages of these self-object relations have usually been described as steps leading from primary narcissism to object relation. Essential pathological features of schizophrenic regression could be elucidated from this angle. We know the role of narcissism in causing disturbances of object relation—and also the role of impaired object relation in augmenting narcissism. Since the twenties, when Freud redefined ego functions in terms of his later views, a more differentiated,—i.e., the structural—concept of ego-id relations has been more or less generally accepted among analysts, and the developmental description of object relation, on the one hand, and of the ego functions involved, on the other, became more concrete and specific. This broadens the range of our questioning, and also the access to the answers [pp. 186–87].

Thus narcissism shifted, in psychoanalytic thought, from a pathology to a line of normal development. With optimal development, Jacobson asserts, identity is formed as both self and object representations become equally endowed with value.

In conformity with Freud's (1923) statement that the ego is first and foremost a bodily ego, Nagera (1964) sees the beginning of the ego as an organized system with the acquisition of the body image. It follows from Freud's (1937) reference to innate ego constitution and from Hartmann's (1958) postulate of apparatuses of primary autonomy that formation of body image is the first result of ego organization. Sandler and Rosenblatt (1962) paraphrase Freud by stating that the self representations are first and foremost body representations. In this they suggest that it is the very processes of differentiation and structuralization that produce the capacity to experience the body image.

By such refinement in the theory of the very manner in which the ego acquires organization, one is forced to think that no longer does narcissism involve polarization of self and object cathexis, but rather that narcissism and object relatedness are two developmental lines, not polar but interlocking. This was already suggested by Hartmann and Loewenstein (1962) when they described how grandiose self images and idealized object images become absorbed into the normal ego ideal. The reconsideration of drive theory that we have proposed makes it possible not only to think of cathexis with either positive or negative value without confusing drive with affect (libido with love or aggression with hostility) but it also shakes narcissism loose from the restricting confines of libido theory and shifts it to the status of a developmental line that now leaves room also for another line—affect development.

The developmental point of view resolves the issue of whether narcissism involves libidinal connection to self rather than to object representations. Mahler describes sound secondary narcissism as the result of acquisition of healthy self regard. This does not represent libidinal self connection, but rather an affective state in which the self representations are cathected with value. Even when taken in Freud's terms of ego interest or ego libido, affective interests are implied. Continuing to think in developmental terms, one may say that the turn from the Nirvana principle to the pleasure principle is taken with the inception of developed affective capacities. While the Nirvana principle still dominates, the infant experiences either vegetative dozing or organismic distress. Thus, at the threshold of development, immediately after physical birth, there are simple precursors of two broad affective categories, pleasure and pain. But the affects themselves will only be experienced as they become differentiated within the totality of the organizing process, when the organizing capacity reaches the point where relief is associated with pleasure while frustration is associated with displeasure.

Spitz has described the process of affect differentiation. The early weeks of life, spent in the dozing state of coenesthetic sensing, are characterized by response to stimuli viscerally and in totalities because differentiation has not yet begun. Differentiation of affect begins at about the time of the one-month maturational crisis, the point where Mahler believes that the autistic shell cracks. Only then does the neonate begin to be able to distinguish between inside and outside, psyche and soma, pleasure and pain; at about the same time, according to Jacobson, libido and aggression also begin to separate out. Spitz noted the visual tracking of the moving face above the crib as clear evidence of interest that will lead shortly to the distinctly pleasurable smiling response. The quantitative difference between visual tracking and the smiling response illustrates how affect differentiation takes place. The unmistakable evidences of exuberance accompanying the smiling response are markedly different from the milder curiosity of the visual tracking that preceded it and vastly different from the even earlier presumably comfortable, dozing state of neonatal life.

Not yet differentiated, however, by the time of the smiling response, are libido and affect, as Spitz's experiments with the Halloween mask show. The connection (libido) is with the object world, while the concomitant affect (pleasure) is not yet differentiated from that drive. Equal pleasure derives from the mask or the moving face, while displeasure does not appear in relation to the presence or absence of either mask or face, but only when need requirements are not met. Where need does spring up, the infant, by the time of acquisition of the smiling response, also acquires capacity for brief delay without displeasure unless waiting becomes too prolonged. Objects who formerly served need gratification gradually begin to become associated with pleasure. Splitting has its inception when the "good" object who provides pleasure is experienced as separate from the "bad" object who fails to relieve distress. This division of "good" from "bad" object coincides with acquisition of the second organizer as described by Spitz—in his terms, the libidinal object proper. Adding the distinction between affect and drive that we have proposed, we would refer not only to the libidinal object but to the positively cathected object, thereby restricting libido to its status as a drive. While we believe it desirable to maintain clear distinction between drive and affect, their development is intertwined. We have shown that the concept of the undifferentiated matrix implies that all development is interrelated as it proceeds through innumerable grades of differentiation and integration.

With dim awareness that there is an outside, symbiosis begins if there is felicitous encounter of innate capacity to extract from the environment with a favorable enough environment. The thrust from autism to symbiosis requires libidinal energy to power it. If, by some unfavorable distribution of drive energy, aggression should differentiate prematurely and become dominant, then symbiotic union is precluded by the obstacle of the aggressive drive serving separation while the phase-specific requirement is for union. But if the libidinal drive is phase-appropriately dominant, symbiotic union is facilitated. Here is the point where normal narcissism, defined as cathexis of the self-object unit with positive affective value, has its inception.

As differentiation proceeds, further distinctions are made in the realm of affect development. Of particular importance to normal development is that experiences of "goodness" of self and object images predominate. Then self and object differentiation proceeds, accompanied by continuing endowment of each set of images with quantities of positive and negative value. Qualitative distinction is a next higher step in affect differentiation as shadings begin to appear. "All good" and "all bad" gradually acquire shadings such as pleasurable, happy, exuberant, loving—on the one side—and unpleasurable, disappointing, depressive and like shadings—on the other side. Thus we are obliged to speak of normal narcissism at different grades of self-object differentiation and with different shadings of affect differentiation. In the symbiotic phase, it is the unit that is valued. With entry into the subphase of separation-individuation, one thinks more in terms of degree of differentiation, as well as of qualities of cathexes of self and object images as these come into being.

In effect, normal developmental splitting includes four sets of images: "good" self, "good" object, "bad" self, "bad" object. While the self-object unit was valued in the symbiotic phase, thus constituting a particular kind of narcissistic unity with special qualities, the narcissistic formation changes in form and quality with entry into the separation-individuation phase. It is essential for development that the good self and object images be valued. This is accomplished by employment of the separation serving feature of the aggressive drive to maintain a set of bad self and object images apart from the good while the infant still needs a preponderance of goodness with which to linger until developmental strides make it tolerable to become aware that the all good and all bad object images refer to the same person. Then, the dual images of self fuse simultaneous with fusion of both kinds of object images. Ultimately, representations of whole persons are established (Sandler and Joffe, 1969; Lichtenberg, 1975), a process that involves complex interaction of drive differentiation and affect development.

A third grade of normal narcissistic development is reached with fusion of the sets of good and bad images. The first occurred during symbiosis, when it was the totality of the self-object unit that was valued. The second was characterized by cathexis of one of the two sets of good images. The third grade comes into being as the child becomes capable of cathecting whole persons, combining the good and bad self representations and good and bad object representations. Then we may speak of narcissism as positive cathexis of whole and relatively stable self representations. With this development, a sense of enduring self-esteem comes into being.

At some early point in development, a significant shift in the manner in which experience is registered takes place. In the early weeks of nondifferentiation (coenesthetic sensing) life is purely experiential. Processing takes place in experiential islands such as tension, tension reduction, accompanied by some form of memory registry. With the arrival of diacritic perception (Spitz), a more unified, centralized form of registry is instituted. Over-all organization includes drives, experience, affects, and capacities such as volition and motility, as in the smiling response. One may postulate that here rudiments of an inner world which will ultimately form psychic structure are established. Organization proceeds. The mind begins to come into being and the infant will live a bit more in it as growth proceeds, slowly shifting toward living a bit less in the body. As Lichtenberg (1975) puts it:

> Bit by bit the child acquires a growing inner world of experiential images, which reflect the developments in the nonexperiential realm of structured representations, and organized memory traces;

> he thus becomes able to evoke the image of the mother at will. The developing richness of his inner experiential life provides a critically significant compensation for the losses he incurs as part of the processes of separation and individuation. The child therefore begins to "live" a bit less in his body . . . ; he lives a bit more in his mind [p. 461].

With entry into the subphases of separation-individuation myriad opportunities exist for enhancement (or impairment) of self-esteem. The principal developmental function of each subphase is described, in part, by the subphase designations—differentiation, practicing, rapprochement and on the way to object constancy. The very experience of adequacy, that is, optimal fulfillment of the developmental purpose, adds to the sense of self-valuation. But the affective experiences which accompany the main developmental purpose contribute significantly to accumulation of self-esteem or to pathological narcissistic formations.

According to Mahler and Kaplan (1977):

> Each subphase makes its particular contribution to healthy or pathological narcissism; narcissistic reserves are still being built up, to a great extent, by subphase-adequate mothering in the later subphases. *The autonomous achievements* of the practicing subphase are the main source of narcissistic enhancement from *within*. Most infant-toddlers of the practicing stage show three contributories to narcissism at their peak. These are (in an exaggerated way and in individually different proportions): self-love, primitive valuation of their accomplishments, and omnipotence. During the rapprochement subphase, prior to and dependent on the resolution of the rapprochement crisis, narcissism (particularly omnipotence shaken by the coming of age of representational intelligence) is subphase-specifically vulnerable [p. 73].

The thrust into separation-individuation brings with it embryonic self cathexis arising from differentiating movement away from the mother's body in the first subphase.

Elation is the hallmark of the next subphase, practicing. There is now upright locomotion and the world is experienced omnipotently, with considerable valuation of accomplishment. The self, having so recently begun to differentiate from the symbiotic unit, continues to accumulate value in that mode—that is, by magical absorption of the larger world into its image. Self-esteem thus acquired is exceedingly vulnerable because it is so dependent upon magical omnipotence and is readily lost if not supported from without.

By the rapprochement subphase, a reversal begins to take place propelled, in large measure, by better reality testing. With it comes realization that the primary object can no longer be used to reestablish omnipotent dual unity. The rapprochement toddler is forced to more realistic discovery of the self and its capabilities, and of the object world and what can be expected from it. The delicacy of this subphase comes into focus as we understand the necessity for favorable balance of cathexis of self and object images to preclude surrender of independence and self esteem in favor of compliance or to preclude loss of object cathexis. Optimal frustration—not too much and not too little—is essential to maintain this balance.

It occurs to us here that the tendency to use the adjective *narcissistic* in a pejorative way arises from the counter-reaction we experience when we see the effect in an adult of insufficient frustration in the subphases as that deficiency peaks at the rapprochement crisis. Such an individual suffers from failure to have integrated realistic, object-related requirements with realistically evaluated self-esteem. There is a regressive trend toward the greater comfort of the magical omnipotence of the practicing subphase. As adults, such persons remain tyrants of the nursery. Where frustration has been optimal, however, the rapprochement subphase becomes the crucible for melding the two poles as Freud saw them—narcissism and object relations.

With rapprochement adequacy, the elation of independent mastery which had assumed magically omnipotent proportions in the practicing subphase is now laid aside as the "senior toddler" discovers the truth that he and mother no longer fit together as before, and that he now has to begin to rely on his own still-embryonic self-esteem for narcissistic supplies.[2] It is this radical

[2]Narcissistic supplies are defined as experiences which enhance self-esteem.

shift from reliance upon the external world and upon magical omnipotence that makes the rapprochement subphase so delicate and vulnerable. Although it will be a short while yet before psychological birth, the rapprochement subphase represents a quickening—a transition from the state of adaptedness which was so essential until this time to enable infant and mother to fit together (in Hartmann's sense) for psychological survival of the infant. By then, internalization will have gone a long way and with it, as Hartmann points out, greater independence from the environment will have been attained.

Adequate resolution of the requirements of the rapprochement subphase also accelerates the process of selective identification. With the discovery that the former omnipotent dual unity is no longer recoverable because neither partner can now find a comfortable fit in it, the child is forced ever more strongly in the direction of increased separation-individuation. The dramatic fights with mother which Mahler noted represent the toddler's defense against the depressive realization that the world, including the primary object, is no longer his oyster. With rapprochement adequacy, there is an accretion in self-esteem which Mahler designates as sound secondary narcissism. We suppose that she is referring to the shift, at this subphase, from the primary state of dependence upon the dyad for narcissistic supplies to greater reliance upon realistic and ever more securely internalized self valuation. This becomes possible as admired qualities of the object images are internalized into the ever-differentiating self images in the process of selective identification. Interpersonal interaction, while continuing in importance for a long time to come, begins to be replaced by intrapsychic and intersystemic transactions as the structure of the inner world is formed.

We return full circle to Freud's definition of secondary narcissism. In a sense, he was correct. Love (an affect) rather than libido (drive) is indeed turned upon the ego (self images). It comes about, not out of disappointment with the object world, not because a person in love has to forfeit a part of his normal narcissism, but because what has to be forfeited is participation in omnipotent dyadic unity. Freud already knew this in a certain sense in 1914 when he said that narcissistic love is, among other things, love of "someone who was once part of himself" (p. 90).

It is, therefore, the infantile narcissism which appropriately precedes the rapprochement crisis that must be forfeited to be superseded by object love. Freud sensed this, too, for he implied also that object love replaces the self-object love of the dyadic narcissistic unit, although he did not understand that developmental phenomenon in modern terms. He says: "but in the last resort we must begin to love in order not to fall ill, and we are bound to fall ill if . . . we are unable to love" (p. 85).

Mahler describes the special vulnerability of the rapprochement subphase by illustrating it as the fulcrum around which early magical narcissistic formations shift toward more realistic self-evaluation (see also chapter 5). With this shift, narcissism approaches the healthy state where it exists side by side with object love. This coincides with Jacobson's description of attainment of healthy self esteem when there is evenly distributed cathexis of both self and object representations. This arises out of developmental opportunity to endow the self images with positive value. It underscores the status of narcissism as a development within the concept of ego as organizing process, following the direction that Freud indicated in 1917:

> I have now led you into the region in which the next advances in the work of analysis are to be expected. Since we have ventured to operate with the concept of ego-libido the narcissistic neuroses have become accessible to us; the task before us is to arrive at a dynamic elucidation of these disorders and at the same time to complete our knowledge of mental life by coming to understand the ego. The ego-psychology after which we are seeking must not be based on the data of our self perceptions but (as in the case of the libido) on the analysis of disturbances and disruptions of the ego [p. 422].

Psychoanalytic developmental theory promises to fulfill Freud's hope that by studying the narcissistic disorders we will gain insight into the way in which the ego is put together. There is little doubt that narcissism must be studied within a developmental frame of reference, within the ego psychology that Freud was seeking. It takes its place among the multifaceted perspectives from which we view that extraordinarily complex structure, the human mind. It cannot be restricted to libidinal drive, nor can it be defined more accurately as we include the dual-drive theory in our consideration. It is broader than those. It reflects the normal aspects and the vicissitudes not only of drive development but of affect and structure. It is an aspect of the organizing process itself.

CHAPTER 5

Diagnosis in Terms of Organizing Process

In *Ego Psychology: Theory and Practice,* we discuss descriptive developmental diagnosis as an approach to understanding the patient in a manner different from the medical model of searching for disease entities. In medicine, often but not always, if a correct diagnosis can be made, the appropriate treatment is indicated and can follow. Sometimes even in medicine, however, treatment decides the diagnosis; if treatment cures a patient's complaints or symptoms, then the physician can reason backward that the patient suffered from a certain illness. The scientific mind is not content with such retrospective diagnosis and seeks to eradicate it as soon as better diagnostic methods become available. Yet, it is that imprecise method, so reluctantly employed, that more closely resembles the method of psychoanalytic diagnosis. Certainly that was true at the beginnings of psychoanalysis when Freud advocated a trial analysis to determine whether the patient could tolerate the cure. To this day, one hears about analyses that have had to be interrupted because the patient suffered an "ego breakdown." When the organizing process is considered as fundamental to diagnosis, then the analyst does not undertake to tax the ego beyond its capacity with techniques that it cannot endure.

Psychoanalytic thinking about diagnosis has long departed from psychiatric diagnosis, so much so that psychoanalysts are baffled by having to fit complex data into rigid psychiatric categories for statistical purposes. By now this is quite familiar, but calls for reemphasis here as insurance carriers, for example, ask questions not only about diagnosis but about the onset of the illness. To be truthful and thorough, one would have to reply that an "illness" seen in the sense of psychoanalytic developmental psychology has its onset wherever the organizing process has begun to veer in a deviant direction. As we take into account organization, development, internalization, and structuralization, the question about onset of illness can be divided into several parts: When did organization become distorted? What direction did that distortion take? How much structuralization and internalization have proceeded nevertheless? Where are the developmental lags? Has the Oedipus complex been reached with competent enough organization to encompass it? What innate apparatuses and other capacities aid organization despite its distortions? When illness is defined as malformation in the organizing process, it is to be regarded as having its onset anywhere along the developmental continuum. More likely, the question about onset, in the mind of the questioner, means when did the symptoms first appear, and that is another matter indeed.

Psychoanalysts learned the fallacy of diagnosing from symptoms as they began to see that so-called hysterics were often found to be psychotic; that persons with phobias were often suffering from borderline conditions rather than from anxiety hysteria; that obsessives were sometimes using those mechanisms to hold the line against psychosis rather than always as symptoms of obsessional neurosis. Even more baffling is that we now encounter asymptomatic patients, some neurotic and some borderline or even psychotic. Ego syntonic structures appear to be more prevalent today than heretofore, or we better recognize them as pathological, and so we are unable to report the time when a nonsymptom, ego syntonicity, began but must think in terms of structure (organization). Eissler (1953) points out the importance of consideration of the structure of the ego in which the symptom is imbedded, rather than the structure of the symptom.

Anna Freud (1963) took modern diagnosis a long step by introducing the concept of developmental lines. This approach to diagnosis advocates that each separate line of development has to be considered as contributory to the total diagnostic picture. Then, however, the diagnosis is no longer a brief statement or label, but a description of a total personality. We pursue this philosophy of descriptive developmental diagnosis in *Marriage and Personal Development* (1968) and in *Ego Psychology: Theory and Practice* (1974) by proposing that a diagnostic psychogram can be drawn by plotting the features of a given patient's development on a graph that will provide a picture of development, its lags, regressions, and progressions. There is much room for improvement in both these versions of the psychogram, especially as knowledge about development increases, and so we have not presented them as finite, but only as guides to descriptive developmental diagnosis. Especially, we wished to indicate the many features of development that have to be taken into account.

Of the several contemporary descriptions of the less-than-neurotically structured personality, we find Mahler's (1971) suggestion about the influence of the vicissitudes of the separation-individuation process most useful. She holds that attainment of neurotic structure necessarily lags if separation-individuation falls short of its first round of completion. With adequate attainment of psychological birth, at approximately three years of age, the child is "on the way to object constancy." While this is another beginning, not the end, of development, and there will be several, perhaps infinite rounds of separation-individuation throughout life, the first round is decisive to how secure subsequent rounds will be. Blos (1962) thinks that a second major development takes place in adolescence, but it is shorter lived and more successful if the childhood process has been adequate. We (1968) suggest that marriage can constitute another "round" in separation-individuation. Benedek (1959) describes parenthood as yet another developmental phase.

Analysts have long known and have treated, with modification of psychoanalytic technique where necessary, certain types of essentially neurotic structures with some borderline features. This type of structure is one that is less than optimally equipped to deal with the oedipal conflict. Mahler's attribution of this form of pathology to a failure in the rapprochement subphase of separation-individuation includes the consideration that such patients attain oedipal development with lower forms of ego organization than those who arrive at the oedipal position relatively less burdened by residual subphase inadequacy.

That subphase problems can persist in neurotic structure has been sensed for a long time without conceptualization. Mahler gave it substance in her description of the vulnerability of the rapprochement subphase, where, if there are inadequacies, the future neurosis may be invaded by unsatisfactory completion of subphase requirements. Many terms have crept into the literature and into papers presented but not yet published. Ritvo (1974b) follows Mahler's conceptualization of this matter in a discussion of "normal" and "pathological" neurosis, which terms distinguish the fully structured form of neurosis from the subphase-burdened form.

It is a moot point whether pathological neurosis is to be categorized as neurosis or whether it is more accurate to use Kernberg's (1975) designation of "high level" borderline, or, alternatively, whether to diagnose such a case as "neurosis with borderline features " or as "borderline with neurotic features." We are not debating these issues, but use them only to illustrate that categorization is less accurate than description. Our preference, while perhaps more awkward, is to describe such patients as having some neurotic features burdened by subphase inadequacy and, if possible, to designate where that inadequacy began to impose malformation in organization.

We illustrate a fulcrum of development (Figure l) to describe the prestructural situation, the long process of structuralization, and how adequate structure appears in a given patient. In this we follow developmental theory with special stress upon the importance of the rapprochement crisis in determining whether development will proceed beyond it relatively normally or with organizational malformations, or whether development will be so impeded by subphase inadequacy that fixation in severe borderline pathology precludes neurotic formation.

Lichtenberg (1975), in agreement on this matter, says:

> The normal child experiences the sixteenth to eighteenth month as a "*nodal* point of development," the height of the toddler's inflated sense of omnipotence. In the next eighteen months, this "ideal state of self" must become divested of its delusional increments [p. 465].

A preponderance of borderline outpatients have attained a modicum of structure and fall, diagnostically, somewhere between the two extremes of full structuralization and relative nonstructuralization. That is not to exclude the important fact that there is considerable movement, progression, status quo, and regression. Where the organizing process has approached the fulcrum, defensive measures not available to the more severe pathological formations are possible. This is of decisive importance to the treatment approach. Regression in defense against the anxiety of a fully organized oedipal conflict may appear, clinically, in a presentation that resembles a lesser level of organization. In such instances, the therapist may hear reverberations of subphase problems, even though they will have been adequately swept up by the ongoing march of generally favorable development. Because of this, regression in the service of the ego may be mistaken for the less controlled regressions of borderline states, or for the actual arrest or fixation that exists in those cases. To overlook the difference in the level of organization could lead to incorrect and even damaging intervention. Treatment would then be addressed to lesser organizing capacity, risking infantilizing the patient; the ability to endure anxiety, frustration and to exercise function would remain insufficiently taxed. We (1974) describe the distinction between regression and fixation in the metaphor of a jungle pathway. It is easier to retrace a preexisting pathway that has become overgrown than to establish a new one.

Subphase need often assumes the guise of heterosexuality if

patient and therapist are of opposite sexes or of homosexuality if they are of the same sex. Neither includes love, an illustration of the fact that sexuality, a maturational phenomenon, can be reached without the concomitant development of the object-relations line. Coincidence of sexuality with self and object esteem defines genitality as a psychosexual level of maturation with simultaneous valuation of the object. In the less organized structures, it may add clarity to dub these manifestations as sexualized subphase levels of relatedness.

A woman patient expresses romantic interest in her male therapist. This is not necessarily reflective of oedipal fantasies, although that is what comes most readily to the therapist's mind. One considers the life history, explores dreams as well as fantasies. In the case to be presented now, it was found that an oedipal father representation is absent. One way to affirm diagnosis is exploration of the quality of contemporary relationships.

Patient: I was with Jim last night and it was pleasant.
Therapist: What did you enjoy about it?
Patient: Well, he takes his time.
Therapist: What did he do?
Patient: He held me close and we cuddled.
Therapist: Was there intercourse, too?
Patient: Well, he wanted it at the end, so we did.
Therapist: How was it for you?
Patient: All right. I didn't mind it.
Therapist: Nothing more?
Patient: Well, no, but I didn't mind. It was so nice to be close to someone.

The therapist has had to press rather hard to ascertain that this was not truly a genital experience. It is rather commonplace for patients to gloss over these details, not because they wish to confuse or conceal, but because the true psychic emphasis is on needs disguised from the patient herself. Touching and cuddling can be preludes to the genital act or can, as in this case, substitute for it because the genital position has not been reached.

How can a fixation of this sort be distinguished from defensive regression? A thirty-seven-year-old bachelor is in treatment because, although many women are easily available to him, he loses potency when attempting intromission. His preferred form of sex is fellatio.

Therapist: What feels good about it?
Patient: Well, when she enjoys it.
Therapist: What about you?
Patient: I enjoy it, of course, but there are different qualities. When I see the pleasure on her face I like it best.
Therapist: What do you think that is all about?
Patient: I suddenly remembered my mother feeding Eleanor (sister three years younger).
Therapist: What brings that to mind now?
Patient: I begin to think I'm doing the same thing.
Therapist: How's that?
Patient: (Excitedly) Well, they were all so attentive to the baby and my father doted on her.
Therapist: Oh, your father is in that picture.
Patient: He used to scold me for wanting mother's attention.

In another session:

Patient: I felt at the end of the last session that you couldn't wait to get rid of me. That woman who comes after me was in the waiting room. (Therapist had ended the session on time and unhurriedly.)
Therapist: Why would I do that?
Patient: I'm so angry. I had a dream last night. You were in it. It was like a movie. I can't remember much, but it felt terrible.

Resistance heightens with negative transference. But it is clear that the clinical presentation of infantile sexuality represents regression in defense against oedipal guilt. In his sex life, this man uses repression, reversal, and regression. He becomes the baby and the mother who feeds the baby, while the stern father (superego) looks disapprovingly on his son's unconscious oedipal wishes, expressed in regressed oral form; the presence of the paternal representation is an important clue that object relations are triadic despite the manifest appearance of a dyad. Also, considerable internalization and structuralization have taken place; there is a superego, depicted in the form of a disapproving father.

Figure 1 illustrates how some of the primitive features of development proceed, with differentiation, integration, structuralization—in short the entire organizing process—to higher forms. It is not intended to be accurate in the sense of all-inclusive, nor is the following description of the organizing process, for the same reason. Differentiation, proceeding from the matrix, is so complex and multifaceted that no single feature of the whole can be isolated without doing violence to the orchestration of the myriad features proceeding simultaneously, interrelatedly and in parallel. The higher levels of organization are, almost by definition, so much more complex than those preceding them that neither diagram nor description can provide more than an approximation of these processes. If description is so circumscribed in effective exposition of the organizing process, it is clear why diagnostic nomenclature serves that purpose even less. What we propose, instead, is that psychoanalytic developmental diagnosis is a marriage of our present knowledge about infant and child development with evenly suspended attention. The latter keeps the entire patient in focus and also provides fertile ground for more diagnostic discoveries. The thrust is to find and to keep landmarks in mind to be of use in compressing our many disparate clinical impressions into a diagnostic whole.

Figure 1 uses the analogy with a fulcrum that pivots developmental movement as it proceeds in normal progressive and regressive shifts. It is designed to show that normally, in the long pull of development, progressive thrusts are predominant even though there are regressions as well. As Hartmann (1958) puts it:

> I refer to what might be termed *progressive* and *regressive* adaptations. The term progressive adaptation is self-explanatory; it is an

FIGURE 1.

The Fulcrum of Development

AUTISM SYMBIOSIS SEPARATION-INDIVIDUATION

Differentiation Practicing Rapprochement On the way to object constancy

A. Living in the body .... ▶ .... Living in the mind (structure)

B. Interpersonal interaction .... ▶ .... Intersystemic and intrasystemic operations

C. Primary process thought .... ▶ .... Secondary process thought

D. Undifferentiated self-object .... ▶ .... Differentiated self with gender identity

E. Direct impulse discharge .... ▶ .... Ego as mediator

F. Fear of annihilation ..... of loss of object ..... of loss of love ..... ▶ ..... of castration .... Superego

G. Organismic distress ..... use of external soothing ..... use of self soothing ..... ▶ .... Signal anxiety

H. Defensive capacity not organized .... ▶ .... Capacity for defense and resistance

I. Simple affects "for" and "against" .... affect differentiation .. ▶ .... Full affective repertory

J. Ambitendency .... ▶ .... Ambivalence

K. Split self and object images .... ▶ ..... (fusion) ..... Whole self and object representations

L. Need gratification .... object love .. ▶ .... Self and object constancy

M. Search for primary object experience (replication) .... ▶ .... Capacity for transference

N. Dyadic relationship .... expanded object world .... ▶ .... Oedipal object relationships

> adaptation whose direction coincides with that of development. But there are adaptations—successful ones, and not mere unsuccessful attempts—which use pathways of regression. I do not refer only to the well-known fact that the genetic roots of even rational and adapted behavior are irrational, but rather to those highly adapted purposeful achievements of healthy people which . . . require a detour through regression [p. 36].

One way of regarding pathology, then, is to consider whether regression overrides progression and expecially whether it moves below a regressive floor that renders too difficult resumption of progressive strides. Such a floor might be visualized to exist somewhere at the left side of the diagram.

A diagram gives the impression of stillness, while the attempt is to depict the continuity of development—continuous in its movements in both forward and backward directions. We have tried to indicate that movement and, especially, to emphasize that development produces a marked qualitative shift somewhere around the rapprochement subphase when higher levels of development bring about a turn inward, that is to say, when internalization and ego organization normally reach relatively stable levels which will continue in their onward progress but will no longer be so vulnerable to regressions to lower levels of the totality of organization. The following describes the fulcrum:

A. The infant lives at first in the body, before psyche and soma undergo the long process of differentiation of one from the other. Before differentiation, the human infant is a psychophysiological organism. Soon after birth, under the auspices of adequate mothering, as Jacobson puts it, differentiation begins. Still living "in the body," the child also lives in the immediacy of the interaction in the dyadic experience as self and object images remain merged. The separation-individuation process whereby major aspects of psychic structuring take place, coincides with the gradual sorting out of self from object images and of gradual selective identification, the process by which attributes of the object images become transformed into parts of the self images. By the time the later subphases of separation-individuation are reached, considerable structuralization will have taken place.

Then one might say that the psyche is born as specialization of psyche and soma turn the organism into less of a psychophysiological being. Normal and pathological psychosomatic regressions probably always continue to take place, however, and psyche and soma are never so sharply divided, nor would that be desirable; unity of self images includes the body image as an essential feature of the self representations.

B. After autism and continuing through symbiosis and the subphases, self-object negotiation is largely interpersonal in nature. With structuralization, however, that diminishes and distance or independence from the object is attained by means of internalization. While selective identification precludes object loss, the structured psyche now negotiates among its three agencies as well as within each of them. The interpersonal interaction becomes less influential, giving way to "living more in the mind," that is to say, in the structure. Experiential negotiations with an external object will continue for a long time, but the ego as mediator of intersystemic negotiation takes on greater prominence.

C. With organization, secondary process thought gradually supersedes the primary process as the dominant mode. The primary process, however, is never lost, remaining part of the unconscious. It is especially operative in dreams, in esthetic experience, in sexual intimacy, in fantasy life and is deliberately summoned by the analyst who uses free association to bring it into operation in psychoanalytic treatment. The very fact that the secondary process is attained tells us, by a kind of rule of thumb, that use of free association—the technical device by which primary process thought is encouraged—is useful only with those patients whose development has shifted to the right side of the fulcrum.

If, in a given patient, that shift has not taken place firmly enough, the therapeutic task is to further that development. Use of free association is incompatible with that goal, since thought processes are already too much in the primary mode. This brings up a technical precept in the treatment of borderline structures for free association, inappropriately transposed from treatment of neurosis to treatment of less developed structures, promotes fragmentation of the thought processes already vulnerable and in need of cathexis of the secondary process. If this technical necessity is well enough understood by the therapist, there need be less fear of decompensation, for the technical thrust will be toward encouraging ever-higher levels of development.

The so-called obsessive mechanisms come into play as structure builds because they are useful in binding secondary process thought. Thus, careful differential diagnosis is in order. The obsessive mechanisms of the borderline structure, struggling to retain a foothold in the secondary process, are not the same as neurotic obsessional symptoms. Appropriate diagnostic distinction between the two is aided by consideration of all the conjunctive aspects of the fulcrum of development and dictates appropriate treatment—building structure and aiding the defenses in the borderline patient; psychoanalysis of the dynamics of the symptom in neurosis with true symptom formation.

D. The long and interesting evolution of the human child from a psychophysiological being to an undifferentiated self-object unit to a differentiated self with a distinct body image and distinct awareness of gender identity is perhaps best described by Jacobson. She traces this developmental process through ever-increasing degrees of differentiation of self from object images as it proceeds in conjunction with ever-increasing levels of internalization.

We might stop the continuity of the action here to examine a point in this developmental progression where middle-range borderline pathology exists, whether because of fixation or regression; usually we are dealing with a combination of both.

Such patients would experience themselves (unconsciously) as part of a self-object unit. They would, perhaps, seek continuous union with other persons and tend to experience them as part of themselves; or, if we wish to use the example of interpersonal interaction, they would not yet deal with the other person as a separate being, but as part of the self. If the other person does not cue in or fit the unconscious script, there might ensue bewilderment, frustration, rage. Probably all therapists are familiar with this phenomenon. One tends to report the outcome (behavior) as inappropriate. And indeed it is when viewed from outside. From the point of view of the patients, however, it is quite appropriate (although unconscious) that they would seek to complete themselves by union with another.

This describes in Jacobson's terms the same phenomenon discovered by Mahler—that during symbiosis and the early subphases of separation-individuation there is not yet an individual from the subjective point of view, but only one who experiences himself as part of another, gradually separating and individuating (or differentiating as Jacobson would put it) until psychological birth brings the first awareness of separateness to the fuller realization that one is a whole individual and that the object is another.

Not all borderline patients at this level of self-object differentiation necessarily enter treatment in active search for union. Some defend against fear of loss of identity in such wished-for union, and so they appear to be aloof. We describe in more detail how such defenses are always to be respected (see chapter 12). Others have formed a narcissistic pseudo-self-sufficient union with a fantasied other who, of course, very much resembles the self. This is a terse description of pathological narcissism (see also chapter 11). These patients are the most inaccessible of the three types here described because the self-sufficiency is relatively impervious. What we wish to emphasize at this point is that all three types of patients, whose clinical presentations appear so different, are fixated or regressed to similar levels of self-object differentiation (see Figure 2).

Figure 2 attempts to reflect, pictorially, the movement from the autistic phase through symbiosis and into the subphases of separation-individuation and the accompanying development of affective cathexis. The symbiotic phase, which comes into being with some dim awareness of affective ties with an object, contains the first representation of affect, here depicted as + signs; negative affect (− signs) are shown, outside the symbiotic orbit.

FIGURE 2.

Self-Object Differentiation

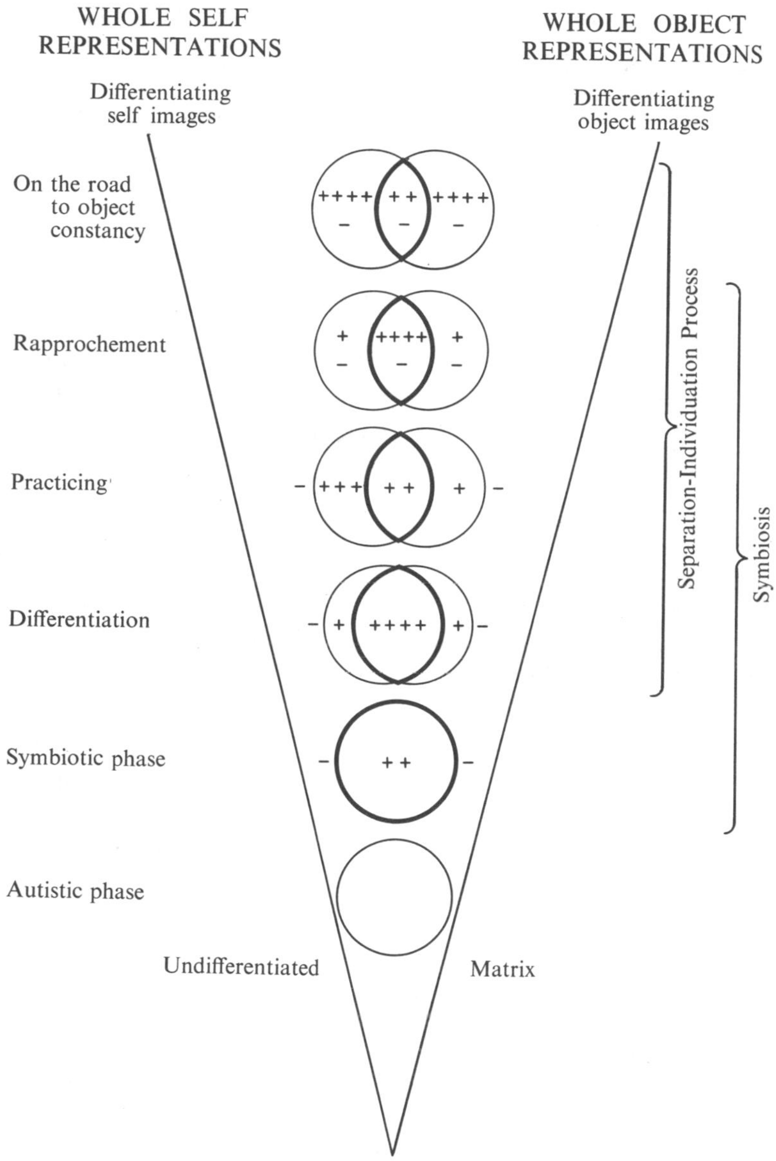

The attempt is thereby to depict splitting, that is, maintenance of negative cathexis outside the positively cathected self-object unit.

As differentiation proceeds, positive affective charges are contained mainly in the undifferentiated part of the unit at first. By the practicing subphase, positive cathexis of the self representations increases. At the rapprochement subphase, there is a temporary imbalance; the still-less-than-differentiated part of the unit is once again strongly cathected. As normal development proceeds, evenly distributed cathexis of self and object representations reflects normal narcissism and normal object cathexis, in other words, self and object constancy.

E. Before there is a functioning ego as mediator, discharge of stimuli, whether from internal or external sources, tends to be direct. While there is still relative absence of differentiation between psyche and soma, discharge tends to be to the inside, that is, upon the soma; this accounts for psychosomatic phenomena. With gradual differentiation, discharge is turned outward. The feature of directness is similar to stimulus-response phenomena and often results in action. If hostile impulses are acted upon, the action may be destructive. Need for union may also be acted upon, either in hostile or in loving ways. These are often confused with acting-out (Blanck and Blanck, 1974).

With increasing degrees of differentiation and structuralization an organized structure gradually becomes more effective and purposeful. Among its many functions is defense in response to anxiety. Probably use of anticipation, judgment, and delay are the first signs that the ego is beginning to operate as a mediator. With this event, discharge is no longer direct, but depends upon the ego's capacity to control behavior based upon its unconscious assessment of danger, anxiety, affective response, appropriateness of action, anticipation of result.

F. The human infant is one of the most helpless of animals at birth and would perish without physical and psychological care (Spitz, 1945). It is poorly endowed, at first, with an archaic and ineffectual means of adaptation—fear of annihilation. The only way available to the infant to alter that situation is to cry. Survival depends upon whether the sound succeeds in summoning a person to administer physical and psychological care, unless there is a caring adult to anticipate that the infant needs tending. With the dim awareness of an outside that arises at the outset of symbiosis, fear of annihilation gives way to fear of loss of the object; as the object becomes cathected with value the fear becomes that of loss of the love of the object; with internalization proceeding to ever-higher levels, there is thought to be fear of castration as the consequence of phallic-oedipal strivings; ultimately, with superego formation, it is the superego that regulates behavior.

G. Closely allied to fear of annihilation is organismic distress, the response in totalities to displeasure or disequilibrium. Gradually, the neonate who is soothed, that is, relieved of distress, builds up memory traces of the "good" experiences and becomes able, at first with the aid of hallucination, to delay response in conjunction with development of capacity for anticipation of remembered relief that will again be provided within a familiar rhythm of gratification and frustration. The dim awareness of the outside brings with it acceptance of external soothing. Later, by means of selective identification and creation of the transitional object, means for self soothing are internalized. When the ego as mediator becomes functional, capacity to experience anxiety as a signal and to employ defense is acquired. With this shift around the fulcrum, neurotic or normal solutions to conflict become possible.

H. The acquisition of signal anxiety requires deployment of effective defenses. Since Anna Freud's (1936) groundbreaking discussion and organization of psychoanalytic thought on defenses, they have been thought of as reflective of the ego's level of structuralization. Thus, some defenses are considered primitive, others middle range, on up to the most sophisticated forms, such as repression. Our own diagnostic psychograms (1968–74) follow this progression.

However, with ongoing conceptualization of normal growth, including continuing studies of infant behavior, questions arise about some processes considered to be defenses. These—denial, projection, introjection and splitting—are discussed in chapter 9. At this point we need only raise question as to whether these are indeed defenses or whether they indicate early levels of structuralization with consequent limitations of capacity. The effectiveness of the defense also reflects the level of organizational structure. Obviously, ineffective defenses denote structural lags and deficits. Progression in structuralization, therefore, leads to capacity to use effective defenses.

I. The affects, we have proposed, derive independently from the undifferentiated matrix and have a development of their own. With differentiation they separate out from ego, id, drive, soma, and gradually from one another. Early in their differentiation they appear in primitive form. Then objects are experienced globally as "for" and "against," "good" and "bad." It takes many years for the full affective repertory to develop, especially because these abstractions are more difficult for the infant to conceptualize than are concrete thoughts. The extent of the affective repertory is a guide to diagnosis.

We suggest that the concept *neutralization* is limiting because it refers to drive-taming in traditional confusion of drive and affect. With the proposal that affects follow a separate line of development, the range of affects that the patient has at his disposal is of diagnostic interest because it reflects degree of differentiation. We search for whether true affective shadings have developed. Joy, glee, enthusiasm, passion, depression, sadness, grief, sorrow, exemplify how affects are shaded. The affect *guilt* occupies a special position because it is a sign of high-level structuralization, of tension between ego and superego denoting thereby that superego formation has been accomplished. Before true superego formation, when there is fear of loss of the object or of loss of the object's love, the organization is still operating in the realm of interpersonal negotiation. Where guilt is present, even if unconscious as it is much of the time, intersystemic negotiations are taking place. Guilt signifies that there is conflict. There can also be peace. It is well to be wary of a patient's designation of affect. "I feel guilty" does not always reflect true feelings of guilt imposed by the superego as regulator of behavior. It may connote a lower level of organization, of compliance to external stricture, of having been taught that one *should* feel guilty about certain acts or even of thought. Thus, the patient names an affect; the therapist has to ascertain whether that truly expresses what the patient feels.

A first step in affect differentiation is taken when the object and the experience provided by the object are equated. A much larger step is taken when object and experience are recognized as two different matters. The movements toward and away from the object in the differentiation, practicing, and rapprochement subphases are simultaneous or almost so. In the differentiation subphase, movement toward and away from can already be observed as the infant-still-in-arms envelops the mother's waist with its legs while stretching its torso away from her. By the time of the second subphase, practicing, there is upright locomotion and the child enters into the well-known "love affair with the world" (Greenacre, 1971). This is the period of elation; the toddler explores everything, only apparently oblivious of the mother (Mahler). The toddler uses visual perception to bridge the distance between self and mother with the eyes.

The rapprochement subphase comes about because one more return to home base is necessary to locate the mother firmly among the mental representations in order to make possible retention of a mental image of her. That is to say, one more libidinal connection precedes the concerted thrust toward object constancy. The rapprochement subphase has already been described as vulnerable because the child and mother no longer fit together. The unattuned mother may also disappoint. Mahler observed that disappointment in the rapprochement subphase constitutes a predisposition to depression, compromising the organizing process by rendering it less competent to deal with the Oedipus complex.

J. Mahler terms the "toward and away from" movements *ambitendency.* They can occur simultaneously as well as alternately. The movements are precursors of ambivalence, which supersedes ambitendency as development proceeds to the level where there can be representation of a single whole person. This is accomplished if the good experiences predominate over the bad so that the child's reality testing can enable him to absorb the fact of the wholeness.

A temporary illusion first of an omnipotent and later of an idealized object is necessary to the child's firm acquisition of his sense of the adult's power and ability to protect him, and later to identification with it in order to acquire a sense of his own power. This is essential to self esteem and to superego formation (Jacobson) and to sound secondary narcissism (Mahler). If disappointment or disillusionment in the object is too bad or too abrupt or too severe, the comfortable gradualness of detection and tolerance of parental flaws is lost. Then fusion of the good and bad images is slowed or altogether precluded. With fusion of object images, however, the self images also fuse and then there is cohesion (self and object constancy). A very large leap in development is accomplished, therefore, with the capacity to fuse the disparate images into a single object representation. This supersedes splitting and brings with it capacity to tolerate mixed affect toward a single, whole person.

K. The foregoing follows upon Mahler's observation that the developing subphase toddler needs time to stabilize the experience of goodness by splitting the object (and self) images into all good and all bad while these experiences are not yet firm enough to support further development. As we (1974) put it the child "buys" developmental time thereby. In normal circumstances, the child can begin to tolerate parental flaws gradually and can then begin to fuse the self and object images into whole representations.

Both Mahler and Kernberg regard the capacity to repress as a desirable consequence of fusion of the formerly split self and object images. This appears to us to mix the separate albeit often simultaneously occurring developments. We think rather that the capacity for repression is the result of development of the defensive function (Items G and K). Splitting and fusion of the object images is a phenomenon of development along the line of object and self relations.

L. The neonate and young infant need the object first for survival and later for gratification of need as well. As the child becomes first dimly and gradually more clearly aware of its separateness and that the object is other than the self, affect differentiation also proceeds. There is envy and also appreciation and gratitude. With development, these lead to capacity for identification as envy employs the aggressive drive for selective identification and as capacity to love grows out of gratitude.

M. While living still in the immediacy of the interpersonal experience and while there are not yet whole self and object representations, the child becomes accustomed, gradually, to similarities in experiences with the same person and adapts to them by patterning responses which become relatively fixed, constituting an aspect of character formation. This patterning is the resultant of myriad interactions which shape the responses to anticipated next experiences. The adult borderline patient, still living more often in the experiential realm than in the structure, comes to the treatment situation with the patterned expectations which constitute, in effect, a search for replication of primary object experience. This we distinguish from true transference, reserving that term and concept for the clinical phenomenon presented by those patients who have attained self and object constancy. Then experiences, affects, attitudes, and behavior toward the primary object can be displaced to the person of the therapist precisely because these experiences were with whole object representations. Here we might paraphrase Jacobson: Before differentiation of self from object representations, what can be the meaning of transference in a merged self-object unit?

The capacity for engaging in transference, then, is another developmental consequence of successful negotiation of the fulcrum. Transference and resistance are of such major technical importance that they require chapters of their own (see chapters 6 and 9).

N. Progression in levels of object relationship from dyadic to triadic begins as the object world expands. Father and siblings make important contributions to the child's development by providing object experiences wider in scope from that of the dyadic one, thereby encouraging progress through the subphases of separation-individuation. Greenacre (1972) describes the father's role in orienting the subphase child in time and space, in promoting idealization by bringing the mystery of the wider world to the child's awareness, thus making the wider world more attractive than the primary dyad. Although the child will still need the dyadic experience for a long time, its interests broaden and encourage the "love affair with the world" of the practicing subphase.

Abelin (1971) added important observations about the role of the father in establishing triangular relationships long before oedipal development. Again we find a developmental precursor to a phase-specific phenomenon that will come about successfully once the earlier development is conquered. The Oedipus complex proper is reached as the second phase of a triadic relationship that begins in the subphases. The ego organization becomes more competent to deal with the vicissitudes of the oedipal crisis if the object relationships that precede it provide firm support for that next level of organization.

Identity formation, including gender identity, is furthered by the discovery of one's capability for functioning autonomously as well as by genital interests. Jacobson says (1964):

> In the beginning oedipal phase, the child's identity formation gains a strong impetus from his increasing genital interest, which centers the self- and object-directed cathexes about images of others' and his own genital organ [p. 70].

This task is somewhat easier for the boy than for the girl for, Jacobson adds (1964):

> . . . The little boy establishes his phallic position and hence his sexual identity more easily and readily than the little girl, who needs more time to form a realistic image of her genital, to accept it, and hence her feminine identity [p. 71].

Nevertheless, we agree with those who have questioned the postulate that there is a phallic phase in girls. That view of female psychosexuality was based on the assumption that the psychosexual maturation of boy and girl proceeds for both through a phallic phase (Freud, 1905b). But it is no longer tenable in the light of the present view that there exists a primary femininity in girls (Galenson, 1978).

Therefore, a position that is not based solely upon anatomy would include psychological development as well as physical maturation. Then, discovery of the genitalia *and* of autonomous functioning can be seen as constituting determinants of identity formation and simultaneously as furthering the separation process, the complementary track of the individuation process. From this we may conclude that interest in one's genitals at the so-called phallic phase represents, for both sexes, a beginning culmination of the connection to the symbiotic object and to symbiotic need. It is at this point in development that aggressive drive comes into dominance as a separating and individuating force. That part of the anatomy that will later be used by the libidinal drive to seek connection is used also by the aggressive drive to preserve ego boundaries by establishing gender identity and gender difference.

If libidinal connection with the primary object is still sought beyond the phase-specific time the child will become the victim of anxieties which include 1) engulfment by the mother of symbiosis, 2) castration, and 3) loss of autonomous functioning. The third cause of anxiety has not yet been accorded sufficient importance with respect to its role in the resolution of the Oedipus complex. Indeed, consideration of this role may contribute to better understanding of the puzzle of the resolution of the Oedipus complex in girls. We suggest that the redirection of heterosexual strivings toward contemporary objects is powered by autonomous functioning that involves both gender identity and the physical apparatus in the adolescent thrust toward the world outside the family. This formulation is applicable to both sexes and supersedes the awkwardness of attributing a phallic phase to girls. A term and concept such as *genital interest,* constituting a precursor to true genitality, includes normal narcissistic cathexis of one's own genitals in boys and girls, and constitutes a psychosexual-developmental phase that paves the way for the genital phase proper.

It is not our intention to convey an impression that the therapist need memorize all the features of development around the fulcrum and search these out with every patient. They are interrelated and often simultaneous phenomena that occur early in life. For example, fusion of the object images into whole object representations and the beginning capacity for signal anxiety and sophisticated defense have been described as occurring simultaneously in time and have even been regarded as the same phenomenon. We think it is more accurate to regard them as two separate aspects of a unified developmental thrust. The point we wish to emphasize is that the adult who arrives for consultation differs from the developing child in that organization, with the flaws and malformations that derive from early life, has proceeded through later developmental phases. The minute aspects of development can no longer be retraced step by step. Therefore, as organizational malformations are presented, we consider where and how development around the fulcrum might have been impaired. This helps to acount for the pathology and begins to organize the diagnostic exploration (and the treatment) around a unified theory of development. The clinical companion to this theoretical position on diagnosis is discussed later (see chapter 12, subsection "Identification of Malformations in the Organizing Process").

CHAPTER 6

The Capacity for Interpretable Transference

We are constrained by use to discuss transference (including transference neurosis) and transference-like phenomena within their generally understood meanings and definitions. According to Moore and Fine (1967) transference is:

> The *displacement* of patterns of feelings and behavior, originally experienced with significant figures of one's childhood, to individuals in one's current relationships. This *unconscious* process thus brings about a repetition, not consciously perceived, of attitudes, *fantasies* and emotions of love, hate, anger, etc. under many different circumstances [p. 89].

The precision of technique, we find, gains by distinguishing *interpretable* transference from ubiquitous transference phenomena. On highly organized levels, object need can propel an individual to seek to reproduce the past with a contemporary object, with an idealized authority figure, or with one who represents a figure in fantasy isolated from reality testing. But the decisive factor that renders transference interpretable or uninterpretable is the level of organization as a whole. All transference phenomena, at whatever level of organization, may be regarded as disoriented ego states. These result not only from persisting object need (which may be normal or pathological) but from unresolved developmental tasks, from traumatic events, or from combinations of these. The degree of ego disorganization *and* the ability to recover reality testing are decisive to whether transference is interpretable. We prefer, therefore, to consider transference as an attempt at mastery which may be adaptive or maladaptive. In so doing, we include the features of seeking unconscious gratification by repetition and also of attempting to find solution and resolution of conflict and of subphase inadequacies at lesser levels of organization.

Whether organization exists predominantly at the left or at the right hand side of the fulcrum determines recoverability of reality testing and therefore interpretability. Thus, that which we would term *interpretable transference* refers to the fact that regressive need to distort and misperceive contemporary objects is reversible by interpretation. By so suggesting, we are obliged to consider that another term is needed for the phenomena of developmental lags and organizational levels where distinction of self from object images is so meagerly attained that search is for an object with whom to interact in the immediacy of the experience. We reserve discussion of those phenomena for chapter 7 and proceed now to consider how the concept transference evolved historically and why it requires amendation now.

The earliest definitions had a certain specificity that, as Anna Freud (1936) observes regretfully, becomes lost if used too loosely or too broadly to refer to the totality of the therapeutic relationship. In Freud's first experiences with transference in the therapeutic situation, he (1905a) describes it as a replacement of some earlier person by the person of the physician. That gave it a most circumscribed meaning. As he continued his therapeutic work, he began to use the concept transference in a diagnostic sense as well. He divided pathology into two broad categories: the transference neuroses, which were treatable by the method of psychoanalysis precisely because the individual with such pathology, by virtue of mobility of cathexis and capacity to displace from past to present was capable not only of transference but also of reliving the entirety of the infantile neurosis in a transference neurosis; and the narcissistic neuroses which he believed to be untreatable because capacity to form a transference neurosis was lacking. He (1917c) says:

> Thus in general a man is only accessible from the intellectual side too in so far as he is capable of a libidinal cathexis of objects; and we have good reason to recognize and to dread in the amount of his narcissism a barrier against the possibility of being influenced by even the best analytic technique [p. 446].

and adds:

> Observation shows that sufferers from narcissistic neuroses have no capacity for transference, or only insufficient residues of it. They reject the doctor, not with hostility, but with indifference [p. 447].

When Loewald described the therapeutic action of psychoanalysis in 1960, he observed that transference is virtually synonymous with object cathexis. Since then, there has been an ongoing reexamination of the concept transference. The most recent panel discussions on that subject were held in Paris in 1973 at the International Congress of Psycho-Analysis, in New York in 1974, and in Beverly Hills in 1976, the two latter at meetings of the American Psychoanalytic Association.

Reconsideration is timely once again because contemporary analysts continue to find, as did Freud, that there is a patient population whose pathologies do not conform to the long-familiar transference neuroses. The less-than-neurotically structured personality, whether designated as borderline, narcissistic, pathologically neurotic, is still regarded as unanalyzable by those who continue to adhere to Freud's position that a major criterion of analyzability is the capacity to engage in transference and especially in transference neurosis. That implies that the more severe pathologies are not analyzable and, indeed, that view has prevailed over many years of the history of psychoanalytic technique. While there is now controversy about whether such patients are analyzable, it is necessary to avoid the fallacy of equating unanalyzable with untreatable. The more severe pathologies are treatable, whether by analysis or by analytically oriented psychotherapy.

We (1972, 1974) discussed the philosophies of the widening versus the narrowing scope of indications for psychoanalysis. In recently reviewing these two apparently opposing philosophies as they are represented on the current analytic scene, Stone (1975) follows up on the conclusions he summarized when he was moderator of the Symposium on the "Widening Scope of Indications for Psychoanalysis" in 1954, necessitated at that time because of the very problem we are here still considering—namely, that persons whose structures do not make it possible for them to develop a transference neurosis present themselves for treatment, and therapists are responsible for finding appropriate techniques. The conclusions that Stone drew in 1975 acknowledge a "crisis" in existing psychoanalytic thought and reflect opposing views in the following polarities: on the one hand, there is a "plenitude of untapped resources to offer as a science and therapy as the parent to other therapeutic methods" (p. 367). On the other, there were "unfounded dreams of panacea" (p. 367), as though psychoanalysis as a treatment modality was reaching the end of the road.

The widening and narrowing scopes are mutually exclusive positions only if one holds to a rigid line of demarcation between the analyzable transference neuroses and some of the less-than-neurotically structured personalities. In the developmental view, therapeutic intervention can build structure to cross that line, or fulcrum, as we describe it in chapter 5. Many patients remain unanalyzable because too-early affront to development is irreparable, because innate endowment was unfavorable, or because of a combination of both. Although we (1974) suggested that it is useful to preserve the distinction between psychoanalysis and psychotherapy as techniques, there remain forms of pathology that are treatable first by psychotherapy and later by psychoanalysis. Thus the widening and narrowing scopes are not irreconcilable in the absolute sense—that is to say, there are types of pathology that are unanalyzable when patients present themselves for treatment but become analyzable after application of developmentally oriented psychotherapeutic techniques shift the ego towards higher levels of organization.

The issue of capacity to engage in transference is central to elaboration of techniques for effective treatment of such cases. Loewald has already called attention to the fact that the character of transference is different where ego boundaries are not clearly established. This gains new emphasis by Mahler's later findings concerning the specifics of ego development in the subphases. The difficulties in achieving unimpaired negotiation of the fulcrum are highlighted by consideration of the highly complex and individually unique form of the organizing process.

Despite so much reconsideration, the concept of transference has not been revised. It is still based on Freud's assumption that the analyzable patient comes to the treatment situation with an intact ego or, as we would put it now, organization, arising from a developmentally favorable early life coupled with favorable innate endowment. This implies that neither inadequacy nor conflict was encountered to a disabling degree until the oedipal conflict arose. The technique needed in such cases is mainly interpretation. Most of the analytic work is devoted to dealing with defense and resistance in order to uncover fantasies, conflict, and, according to Kris (1956a), patterns as well. So far as transference is concerned, a full-blown transference is permitted to develop in order to "capture" and treat the infantile neurosis that is revived thereby. An informal survey shows that the very concept of infantile neurosis is shadowy in the minds of many analysts. Tolpin (1970) finds it surprising "that a concept so deeply rooted in psychoanalytic thinking still requires . . . clarification" (p. 273). She defines it as:

> the outcome of progressive libidinal and ego development along more or less normal developmental lines, without decisive impairment, so that the child experiences . . . the complex conflicts of the phallic-oedipal stage and is faced with the intrapsychic task of mastering the conflicts [p. 277].

She adds that unimpaired attainment of the phallic-oedipal phase implies that the ego has become a coherent organization, a concept of the ego somewhat different from that of ego as organizing process per se.

With increasing knowledge of development, analysts no longer consider revival in the transference neurosis to be simple recapitulation of a neurosis completely formed in the infantile period around the Oedipus complex and then awakened in adult analysis as though, like Sleeping Beauty, it had lain dormant in unaltered form. We now know that probably a full-blown neurosis is rarely, if ever, organized in childhood, that the latency period does not put a halt to development, and that adolescence and probably early adulthood as well are periods of accelerated development and reorganization. Loewald (1974) regards the infantile neurosis as an analogue to the latent dream thoughts. Thus "the infantile neurosis, as reconstructed from the manifest neurosis, partakes of an order of psychic reality which can be discovered only in a psychoanalytic investigation" (p. 188).

In 1960, Loewald assailed the long-held position that the psychic system is closed, thereby not only posing serious question about the existence of a primary infantile neurosis that can be revived in the transference neurosis, but adding also the radical idea that the analyst, as a real object, can enter the structure in order to alter it. (We deal with that issue in chapter 7.) If Loewald is correct, what is it that is revived in the transference neurosis then? Freud first wrote about the repetition compulsion in 1905c and, in 1920, defined it as the tendency of organic matter to return to the inorganic state—the death instinct. Analysts continue to employ the concept of repetition, discarding the death instinct. This leaves open the question of the exact nature of the compulsion to repeat. As is well known, it often serves mastery. This is quite familiar in the tendency to repeat trauma, to seek out the familiar. Although it occurs every day in the experience of every analyst, it is always a source of wonder and surprise how a patient can seize on an aspect of the analyst's personality or of the therapeutic situation that might faintly resemble a person or event from the past and, employing the primary process, make whole cloth out of a single thread reminiscent of the past. This accounts, then, for the distortions that appear as failures in reality testing in intact ego organization. These distortions resemble a dream which also, of course, employs the primary process. They result from regression in the service of the ego in the analytic situation. Interpretation of transference is most useful to the intact ego which can observe as well as experience (Sterba, 1934).

Because we encounter more or better recognize patients with far less than this optimal capacity, we are forced to approach the matter of transference in a new light and to see within it complexities which challenge long-established definitions. For the time being we confine our discussion to the so-called positive transference which includes the capacity to love in its broadest sense. Developmentally, object love becomes a concomitant of self love as differentiation of self from object images proceeds to the point of evenly distributed affective cathexis of self and object representations. Love for the analyst, considered broadly, implies that there is the capacity to displace onto another whole person in the present positive object cathexis from the past. It is in those in-between situations of neither full-blown neurosis nor severe borderline pathology that we experience greatest difficulty in determining what is transference and what is blurring of self and object images; what is love and what is need; what is the Oedipus complex and what incomplete and distorted earlier development disturbs full attainment of the phallic-oedipal position and elaboration of a genuine neurosis. If organization has reached the point where there is the capacity to bring to the analysis the very desirable state of affective cathexis of self and object representations, a so-called positive transference is possible. Greenson (1965a), recognizing that the relatively healthy neurotic does not engage solely in transference in the restricted sense of dealing with the analyst as an object from the past only, observes that there is also a real relationship and capacity to work with the analyst toward a common goal, terming this the *working alliance.* Something similar, the *therapeutic alliance,* was observed by Zetzel (1956). Freud (1914b) already knew this, as is evident from his observation that the transference neurosis "is a piece of real experience" (p. 154) albeit provisional, and that one must treat the illness as "a present day force" (p. 151), not as an event of the past, but real and contemporary, to be analyzed by tracing it back to the past. Loewald believes that there is neither reality nor a real relationship without transference.

Sterba's (1934) concept of the therapeutic split was useful at the time he proposed it, but unfortunately confuses the issue now. Only in part can this confusion be attributed to his use of the word *split,* which has so many other connotations. Sterba's meaning of split refers to the capacity of the ego both to experience and to objectify. While part of the ego experiences, the so-called observing ego allies itself with the analyst in the common goal. Freud had already used the term *splitting* to describe a defense particularly employed in fetishism. Now it is used to refer to failure to fuse "good" and "bad" object images (Mahler, Pine, and Bergman, 1975; Kernberg, 1975). Since love, or object esteem, is interwoven with self esteem even before individuation, capacity for transference is affected by the quality of the early self-object experiences and by progressive and regressive shifts in degree of individuation and organization. Sterba's concept of the therapeutic split refers, therefore, to the capacity of a person with a high level of organization to regress in its own service (Kris, 1952) and to recover from such regression or, to put this in developmental terms, of already differentiated self and object images to merge, to differentiate once again, and to retain identity while paradoxically surrendering it temporarily.

A patient was in the fifth year of psychotherapy which became an analysis when organization reached the point where the structure was able to tolerate it. She was the kind of patient that Freud may well have declared unanalyzable. At the outset of treatment she was recently divorced and, although functioning, was dissatisfied with her accomplishments especially as she compared herself with colleagues and friends. It was the analyst's view that this dissatisfaction was powered by internal forces; the patient was restless because she was far more gifted intellectually than she appreciated. She was functioning below capacity, although well enough for a person of average gifts. Her marriage had failed because her level of object relations was without much capacity to love a separate, whole person. This would have represented an insuperable obstacle to early classical analysis because a transference neurosis would not have been possible. She was mildly depressed and desperately promiscuous.

One day the patient began to express concern about the analyst's emotional stability. She was certain that there were lapses in the analyst's behavior in the last several weeks. To the analyst, this was a sign that the patient's ego could now tolerate the knowledge that her mother had been psychotic. This is an example of intrasystemic, as contrasted with external, confrontation. It may be regarded as a transference phenomenon only when the analyst is certain (and correct in that certainty) about his sanity. It was, of course, in the context of an improved level of object relations and trust in the analyst built up over many years of treatment that the patient could risk facing her darkest knowledge. But why in that form and with such absolute certainty that the analyst was deranged? Why not as a memory of the mother's bizarre behavior? True, transference is thought to be a way of bringing such memories into the analysis by reliving. But in this instance of mistaking the present for the past, the patient did not bring feelings, attitudes, affect, or memory. She was not even aware that she mistook the analyst for her mother.

This does indeed resemble the ordinary, temporary lapse in reality testing by the experiencing ego thought to occur in the transference neuroses. But part of the very question we wish to raise here is whether, where conviction overrides reality testing so thoroughly, we can deal with the ego as though it is capable of functioning on the highest level of organization. We think, rather, that such lapses represent an ego regression to an undifferentiated point of contact where self and object images unite. In this case, the point of union with the maternal object was attained by sacrifice of otherwise competent reality testing because it was that very ego function that was deficient in the mother. Loewald said that, where ego boundaries are not clearly demarcated, primitive and massive transference phenomena appear. These are indicative of regression toward undifferentiation and are not to be mistaken for withdrawal of libidinal cathexes from objects.

Why does this matter? Every analyst would interpret the obvious transference phenomenon. Timing is of the utmost importance. Such interpretation can only be made within the context of a secure therapeutic alliance and of trust built up over many years of experiencing the analyst's reliability and steadfastness. In this instance, the interpretation was made in the form of a question, "Do you think your mother had these sorts of lapses at times?" This gives the patient food for thought and also leaves room for her to negate if the "interpretation" is not yet tolerable.

This case illustrates the very dimension that we are trying to add to the concept of transference—namely, that malformations in the organizing process reveal themselves in the analytic situation and have to be recognized as such in order for the analyst to be able to distinguish between intact structures and those in which failure in earlier levels of organization burdens oedipal development excessively. In the latter, the unresolved earlier needs have to be dealt with first. This patient would not have been able to engage in analysis of her oedipal conflict before the dyadic longing was resolved. The case described bears out Mahler's dramatic conclusions about the influence of the rapprochement and earlier subphases on later development. She (Mahler, Pine, and Bergman, 1975) says:

> The persistence and degree of the rapprochement crisis indicate premature internalization of conflicts, developmental disturbances that were precursors of infantile neurosis, but may even decisively stand in the way of the development of infantile neurosis, in the classical sense [p. 104].

Interestingly, as Tolpin points out, analysts have tended to overlook the fact that Freud knew this in a certain way. Quite early, he referred, in the terms of the day, to the fact that the Wolf Man did not experience a normal phallic-oedipal phase because earlier pathology had affected ego organization adversely.

With Mahler's confirmation and elaboration of Freud's

thought, one may see this patient as having had to carry the larger burden of subphase need as a toddler. Since the mother was psychotic and unattuned, the child reached out by uniting with the mother in mutual incompetent reality testing. The specific nature of this lapse in the treatment situation, where reality testing was otherwise relatively sound, leads to the assumption that this was a circumscribed failure in differentiation which distorted the organizing process at an early level. A less gifted person might not have been able to extract from the environment even in such distorted form, and this would have made for more severe pathology.

Technique gains from such specific understanding of the complexities of transference phenomena. We learn that organization has to be aided and how to seek out the precise developmental area where therapeutic attention is required. These are the kinds of cases that fail in traditional psychoanalysis because the oedipal crisis is impossible of resolution by an ego that lacks high enough organization to meet the demands of that developmental phase. Whether the patient be male or female, a shift from the dyadic relationship to the triadic, and ultimately to love of the parent of the opposite sex, cannot be successful while persistent subphase longing and distorted organization make an approach to the phallic-oedipal position weak and uncertain. Kernberg notes that, conversely, if oedipal development is stimulated prematurely, it can only evolve in distorted form because there will be condensation of genital and pregenital conflicts. To him, this is characteristic of a category of pathology that he designates as borderline personality organization.

Another patient experienced an affront when he had emerged from symbiosis into the subphases; a sibling was born when he was fourteen months old. We consider, in such rather common events, that the mother is aware of her pregnancy some seven to eight months before the next child is born and that her feelings, whether positive, negative or ambivalent about being pregnant again impinge upon the phase-specific experience of the first child. Since the patient was not psychotic, it is assumed that he had adequate endowment and an adequate symbiosis. We date the developmental affront to five to seven months, when differentiation had just begun, and we speculate that regression to the haven of symbiotic closeness was inevitable. Finished with childbearing at the time of the patient's oedipal phase, the mother resumed closeness with him belatedly. This is not unusual and is often confused with maternal seduction, as though the patient was at the oedipal level with both feet, so to speak. It seems, rather, that he welcomed a regressive, out-of-phase closeness that impaired the full organization of the capacity to deal with oedipal strivings at this point. Revived in the transference, it took the form of sexual interest in his female analyst. But instead of fear of the oedipal father, he felt intense fear of the preoedipal mother. This phenomenon finds new explanation beyond the classical one of defensive regression from castration anxiety. As he envisioned the sex act per se, he saw himself losing not his penis but his total self. In other words, the fantasy of sexual union with the oedipal mother quickly gave way to anxiety about loss of identity in the wished-for merger with the mother of symbiosis. Such transference phenomena alert us to the fact that the oedipal position was reached with too much contamination of needs from preceding phases and subphases; thus it failed to become the core of neurotic organization. The clinical clue that the transference did not reflect the triadic oedipal relationship lay in the absence of a father representation in dreams and fantasy.

Mahler (personal communication) proposes three criteria of a viable Oedipus complex:

1. Self and object constancy achieved by the end of the rapprochement subphase
2. A level of object constancy that facilitates triangular relationships cathected with neutralized libido and aggression
3. Along psychosexual lines, a degree of the narcissistic genital phase

When it was a hard and fast rule that analysts think of themselves solely as transference figures, they needed only to ponder which primary object they were representing at a given moment in the analysis. Now they have to think not only about whom they represent but whether they represent the primary objects in the sense of displacement only. We are led to conclude that the ego organization of some patients does not make for such transference capacity. This very issue perplexed the panel at the Congress of the International Psycho-Analytical Association in Paris in 1973. Arlow (1974), in summing up the question, asks:

> how much ego development has to take place before persistent organized unconscious conflict is structured into the psyche; this is decisive for the future nature of the transference [p. 320].

We elaborate on that question: At which phase or level of organization does capacity for interpretable transference become possible? Obviously, such questions did not have to be raised before we knew that the infant, from symbiosis on through attainment of self and object constancy, is engaged in the process of gradually distinguishing self from object images until relatively distinct and separate representations of each become constant. Constancy has to be thought of as relative for there are normal fluctuations in individuation and dedifferentiation.

To begin to answer the question we have raised: Where there is impairment of ego organization; level of object relations; degree of internalization; development of autonomous ego functions; then it follows that neurosis proper cannot be organized. In that condition, there is impaired capacity to receive and utilize interpretation of transference. Where the therapist is perceived as a potential gratifier of symbiotic need, for example, or as narcissistically perceived parts of a self-object unit, then long-held formulations of transference do not apply in the traditional way. Often, the analyst is neither a true transference object nor a real external one, but only a potential gratifier of subphase need.

It would be hazardous and misleading to propose a sharp line of demarcation to designate the precise point where capacity for appreciation of the analyst as a whole person and to absorb transference interpretations becomes possible as the result of organization. We think, rather, of a hazy line with fluctuations to the left-hand side of the fulcrum. One would have to take into account the myriad aspects of development and the precise nature of the organizing process in each case. Because of individual variation in the innate givens with regard to capacity to adapt to and interact with the environment, and of the infinite variations in the organizing capacity as well, no two individuals develop similarly, especially in terms of a timetable. Lest this appear too broad and therefore discouraging to the therapist, we might add that there are nevertheless definite patterns and, beyond that, firm guidelines in the totality of psychoanalytic developmental psychological theory.

Capacity to receive transference interpretation has to be seen in the form of a spectrum. On one end, we can expect to find a person relatively well oriented to reality, capable of engaging in a transference because there is sufficient separation of self and object representations to make it possible for him to recognize, with an observing ego, that he experiences the analyst as a whole displaced object. On the other extreme are those whose persistent subphase needs and inadequacies cause them to seek objects who will gratify those residual needs. Since such needs are no longer age-appropriate, contemporary objects are most likely to perpetuate the disappointment. More often, persons whose subphase interactions have resulted in distorted self-object perception tend to attempt to repeat the distorted self-object relationship—that is to say, they no longer seek gratification of residual needs. Rather, the very absence of phase-appropriate gratification has created a malformation in organization. Powered by the compulsion to repeat, replication of the pathological relationship is sought. The therapist is experienced in a distorted form, a far cry from what the primary object really was and certainly from what the therapist really is.

Having discussed the important criteria of borderline versus neurotic development, it becomes evident that wherever the border may lie, the capacity to transfer from past whole objects to the present is intimately involved with those criteria. There is no gainsaying that transference and transference neurosis are indispensable concepts in the theory of psychoanalytic technique. Indeed, we are indebted to Freud not only for his genius but also for his courage in venturing into an area where others (such as Breuer) feared to tread. Without Freud's discovery of the nature of transference phenomena, the technique and probably even the theory of psychoanalysis would have languished. The centrality of transference and transference neurosis to technique need not be emphasized for those who employ these concepts in their daily work. But our advancing theory now demands that they be reconsidered to include assessment of capacity not only for interpretable transference in certain borderline conditions but also for redefinition of the technical role of the analyst with respect to this capacity on the part of the patient with such pathology.

Probably the single term transference without modification does not do justice to the range and variety of object relatedness in the therapeutic situation that have to be considered as we undertake to treat the more severe pathologies as well as neurosis with more precision. While a certain consistency in level of object relations can be expected in neurotic structures because these share the common feature of self-object constancy, the wide fluctuations in this feature of development in pathological neurosis and in the borderline conditions demands that the analyst be ever alert to variations in the presentation of interpretable transference as contrasted with transference-like phenomena that refer to subphase levels of undifferentiation of self from object images.

This brings us once again to our base questions which can now be rephrased: When is the analyst real, when is he truly a transference figure, when is he experienced as part of a self-object unit fantasied to be a potential gratifier of unfulfilled need? There is vast experience with transference in the psychoanalysis of neurosis with regard to needs on regressed levels of psychosexual maturation. Now it is necessary to add that the analyst may also be experienced as potential gratifier of symbiosis, differentiation, practicing, rapprochement—the needs of early subphases of ego organization.

Furer (1976) applies Mahler's findings to the understanding of nontransference aspects of the relationship with the analyst of the true neurotic by tracing features of the therapeutic alliance to their origin in the practicing and rapprochement subphases. The capacity for empathy, he contends, originates in these interactions and communications and constitutes a precursor of the therapeutic alliance. He suggests that patients who confuse transference and reality lack the capacity to accept substitutes for the mother of the practicing subphase. This is an extension of Mahler's theoretical formulation similar to our extrapolation of its technical utility. The distinction we make between capacity for formation of an interpretable transference and one in which the patient is unable to accept that the therapist is not the primary object derives from experience with adult borderline patients who cannot make such substitutions.

Before attempting a final and more complete answer to the repeated question about how capacity for interpretable transference originates, the so-called negative transference requires discussion. It was thought, early in the theory of psychoanalytic technique, that both sides of the ambivalent feelings toward the primary objects are revived in the transference. Greenacre (1954) questions the tidiness of the view that transference takes first one form and then the other. She thinks, rather, that both aspects of the primary object relationships are revived in a more haphazard manner in the analytic situation, that alternation in attitude and affect are often seen even within a single session. Rather than positive and negative transference as entities, Greenacre proposes that "active-transference-neurotic manifestations" might better reflect the rapidly shifting qualities of affect often encountered within a session and from one session to another. But when she speaks in terms of polar or shifting transference qualities, she is still adhering to the assumption that the patient has reached the level of object relations where ambivalence obtains. Mahler's observation that ambitendency precedes ambivalence forces us to consider the transference implications of this earlier level before separation when the child moves alternately and sometimes even simultaneously toward and away from the object.

Movement away from is a feature of development. As such, it cannot be considered negative or undesirable. It employs the aggressive drive in the service of separation to power the thrust toward a higher level of development, not as an act against the object. For the kinds of uses of aggression that serve growth we need a designation that does not have the connotation of negative or hostile. While we seek one, it is useful to bear in mind that not every movement away from the analyst anymore than from the primary object is necessarily negative. Distinction must be made between anger and progressive developmental thrusts. These exist at every level of development and have important technical implications at every stage of treatment, even of the most analyzable neurosis where autonomous functioning is greatest.

The back and forth movement in the subphases reflects the fact that libido seeks union while aggression serves separation (to sever connections). It is such phenomena that are often mistaken for positive or negative transference, that is, for affective instead of drive expression. If accompanied by action, they are likely to be designated, equally incorrectly, as acting out. Although they are neither positive nor negative in affective quality, this oversimplifies; in usual development they are likely to be accompanied by affect. This iterates that affect and drive coexist but are not the same. An aggressive developmental thrust may be carried out angrily, or it may be performed playfully and lovingly. These behaviors, whether aggressive or libidinal, are positive in the developmental sense.

As structure builds, affective reactions are to a whole person, and then one may speak of ambivalence and therefore of negative and positive transference. Here we may begin to think about capacity for conflictual neurotic rather than borderline solutions. Capacity for forming an interpretable transference may have its roots at this very place in development where organization accelerates. This also clarifies why we encounter so much diagnostic controversy about adult pathologies that originate here. If one looks at the neurotic symptoms, one diagnosis is made; borderline behavior, also present, dictates the other. Since this is the place where development begins to cross the border, it seems correct to designate it as borderline until treatment has furthered structure building and organization. Then such patients shift more toward the neurotic side of the diagnostic fulcrum. The line to be drawn to delineate borderline and neurotic organization cannot be absolute. It resembles the boundaries of states of the United States where no border guards are stationed. A house and land on the border between, let us say, Massachusetts and Vermont, may span both states and be subject to dispute over which state receives the taxes and provides the services, just as analysts dispute about whether the diagnosis is borderline condition with neurotic features or neurosis with borderline features.

In reconsideration of the concept transference, Lipton (1976) expresses doubt about whether one can accurately reconstruct early life experience in the analytic situation, arguing that the phenomena of early phases and subphases are not confined to their initiation but repeat in modified form later in life. He maintains that we cannot be sure, therefore, in treating an adult, that we are dealing with the earliest layer. Was he not thus reiterating the well-known fact that development proceeds throughout life and that the thrusts and counterthrusts of early development are repeated on new levels of organization each time? The very point about transferential reflections of early experience is confirmed and strengthened by Lipton's observation, for we never see precise repetition of genetic experience in an adult, but only the complex elaboration thereof, built upon many layers of integration of the first round of these experiences with later ones. This is but an extension of Kris' (1956a) contribution to the technique of recovery of childhood memories; the adult does not remember an event as it actually occurred, but only as it has become telescoped into patterns combined with later experience. Spitz, too, cautioned against misperceiving adult behavior as analogous or homologous to infant experience. And certainly our own proposal regarding the organizing process would deter us from making a simplistic reconstruction of early experience.

The historical development of the concept transference is intertwined with the design of psychoanalysis as a therapy for the treatment of drive regression caused by the pitfalls of the oedipal conflict—the nuclear problem in the transference neuroses. Freud had full conviction that the analyzable neurotic has, by definition, an intact (unmodified) ego which may be relied upon in the psychoanalytic compact to respond to a process of uncovering unconscious conflicts and fantasies. This sound ego can then perform the tasks of working through and synthesis, leading eventually to a capacity for instinctual discharge along appropriate channels. Freud had equal conviction about the intractability of the "narcissistic neuroses." He predicted their conquest as a future possibility which would be brought about by understanding the ego, its mode of organization and functioning. We have reached the theoretical position that Freud predicted and so we may return for final reconsideration of the fundamental question about where in development capacity for interpretable transference is attained and this time we deal with it in the negative. Where the therapist is perceived as an attenuated symbiotic object, as narcissistic functions of a self-object, as potential gratifier of subphase inadequacy, there cannot be such capacity, for the therapist is not a true external object perceived in the same way as by a person who has relatively distinct and whole self and object representations.

In discussing this matter, we pursue the route that Freud took in an effort to designate where there is sufficient ego organization to make correct technical use of the concept transference. These reflections produce the following thoughts about transference phenomena: Mistaking the present for the past (Fenichel, 1945), that is, misperception of the object in the transference neuroses, is based upon a theory of instinctual drives and instinctual regressions in a sound ego and superego structure beset by unconscious incestuous conflicts. We need a new term, therefore, to connote the introduction into present interpersonal relationships of unfulfilled needs incurred in the earlier periods of life when ego organization has not yet been completed or has been disrupted. The rationale for our position rests on the proposition that there is a point in development where experiential interaction begins to be supplanted by organized mental structure. At such point there is thought to be "ego filtered longing" (Mahler, Pine, and Bergman, 1975, p. 75) as the ego builds in the process of organizing the tasks of separation-individuation. Where the ego succeeds, development proceeds toward capacity for interpretable transference. Where it fails, the residual longings will be reproduced in the therapeutic setting. There an object is wished for to provide not instinctual gratification, as in the more structured patient, but narcissistic (ego building) supplies. Thus the terms and concepts *transference* and *transference neurosis* are best preserved for the well-organized ego, while a term that describes longing for replication of the self-object unit in fulfillment of experiential needs in the immediacy of the dyad might more precisely describe the unfiltered longings revived in situations where subphase inadequacy persists without intervening structure. We do not yet have terms for two grades of differentiation within the self-object experience. At the earlier level, it is gratification of *need* that is longed for; at the next higher level, the *object* as part of the self is desired. The closest we have been able to come to something communicable is "search for replication of early self-object experience." We suggest the abbreviated forms *need replication* or *object replication* for the time being.

CHAPTER 7

The Real Object

The literature reflects changing views about the role of the analyst and the nature of the therapeutic interaction. Those trends were reviewed at the 28th Congress of the International Psycho-Analytical Association in Paris in 1973 and were summed up by Dewald (1976):

> the conceptual understanding of the role of the analyst in the psychoanalytic process has undergone a continuing expansion away from the image of the neutral, passive, non-participant mirror who merely provides the patient with insight through interpretations. Increasingly, the psychoanalytic situation is seen as an active and evolving process between two participants in which each is responsive and reactive to the input from the other [pp. 215–16].

Dewald believes that the very climate of the analytic situation, such as empathy, absence of judgment, kindness, attunement, availability, reliability, and the like provide a new experience of a "good parent" [quotation marks his, p. 218] which is inevitably more growth-promoting than the primary experience. That issue was more sharply drawn in 1946 when Alexander and French proposed that the analyst could provide a "corrective emotional experience." It was an idea whose time had not yet come. Alexander and French did not have the sophisticated theory of psychoanalytic developmental psychology and so could not provide a rationale for their procedure. They could only propose an interpersonal experience which included manipulative measures to an unfortunate extent. That proposal had to be rejected by analysts who adhered to the established position that the intrapsychic arrangement is impervious to interpersonal intervention; thus the corrective emotional experience as a term and concept fell into bad repute. That was in another era, however. Now, with knowledge that was not then available, the concept of the analyst as a real object is being reconsidered in many quarters.

Loewald (1960), for example, does not regard psychic structure as impervious to interpersonal experience. He believes that structural change is contingent upon the relationship with the analyst. Thus, while the manipulative aspects of the Alexander and French technique, such as varying the availability of the therapist and the frequency of the sessions to attenuate the transference remain unacceptable to most analysts, the concept of a corrective or reparative experience is being seriously discussed in a new theoretical framework. Fleming (1975) asks: "Is it possible that the structural changes we hope for from the psychoanalytic experience can be facilitated by responses from the analyst other than interpretation in the usual sense of the term?" And she answers that psychoanalytic experience led her more and more insistently in that direction for "object need in many adults reproduces in many ways the functional relationship between mother and child" (p. 749).

Of particular value is precision now available from the organizing principle—that the organizing process takes place around processes of separation-individuation. From that, we derive information about the specific features of the developmental processes as the fulcrum is negotiated. In addition, the revolutionary discovery that certain seemingly neurotic formations are germinated, not at the phallic-oedipal level, but in the subphases, begins to alter our view of the very theory of neurosis and suggests rather strongly that, even in the psychoanalytic treatment of neurosis, subphase inadequacies play a role more significant that was heretofore believed.

For clarity we find it preferable, at this stage of our experience as well as our knowledge, to retain the view that, in normal neurosis, intersystemic conditions dominate the analytic picture and that, while the realistic features of the patient-analyst relationship are not to be denied, they attain their fullest importance in the final phases of the analysis when transference and transference neurosis have begun to be dissolved. Then, as Loewald (1962) describes in another paper, processes of internalization which resemble the initial selective identifications of early development resume, now with the realistic qualities of the analyst that the patient will make his own in order to be able to terminate treatment.

Eissler thought, in 1953, that the ideal neurotic formation could be analyzed by means of interpretation only. We refer to this as a point for measured departure since no patient in reality matches that ideal model. With sharpened awareness of the fact that ego organization is at least as important as are the psychosexual and drive aspects of neurosis, technique has to deal with dimensions which have only in the last decade or so begun to be considered seriously (G. Blanck, 1966). While it remains useful to think that, in neurosis, regression is along psychosexual lines mainly, now ego regression is a factor to be considered as well. Especially is this so in neuroses with subphase inadequacies, a complexity that was not conceptualized before Mahler presented it in 1973. Perhaps these were overlooked in the past because they are not as dramatically patent as are the ego deficiencies of the more seriously disturbed patients. Competent enough for ordinary functioning, the ego in neurosis nevertheless can be observed to be faulty in some aspects of organization. Analysts are familiar with discrepancies between an individual's level of functioning and his maximum potential in terms of neurotic inhibition. Freed of conflict by analysis, the individual becomes capable of working more effectively, for example.

It is worthwhile to expand the long-held view that diminution of function is the outcome of inhibition or conflict only. In addition, a valid goal of analysis is to promote development of ego apparatuses from the conflict-free sphere if these have been "started up" in early life, but not encouraged to develop to the fullest extent. We think here of neurotic as well as borderline patients whose capacities such as anticipation, initiative, and curiosity—to cite only three of many—have been suppressed by parental indifference or even opposition. The exploring practicing subphase toddler, for example, may have been an inconvenience to a mother who could have been too busy with other children, or pathologically unable to tolerate the child's burgeoning locomotion and curiosity. Absence of curiosity can result in learning difficulties, long thought to be the consequence of neurotic inhibition because of suppression and repression of sexual curiosity.

In adult neurosis such matters are usually treated on the basis of the same premise—drive components are in conflict with superego prohibitions. Little attention has been paid, thus far, to the reasonable observation that suppression of an ego function can be the consequence of parental neglect in the subphases originating, therefore, developmentally earlier than superego prohibition. In addition, the qualities of the innate endowment contribute to facilitating or burdening the dyadic interaction, with consequent effects upon the progress of organization. This asserts that pathology with similar appearing symptomatology can result not only from conflict, not only from failure on the maternal side of the dyad, but from the endowment that the child brings to the dyad and also from combinations of these. Further, competent or even gifted inborn apparatuses can fail to be quickened when the infant with these apparatuses encounters a less-than-average expectable environment. A person such as this is usually described globally as not living up to his potential.

A patient, the youngest of five children, was told rather cruelly that he had not been wanted. He had experienced only the most meager contribution to development from the maternal side of the dyad, especially in the subphases. The family had a high middle-class income and could afford many luxuries. Cultural customs, nevertheless, dictated that there could be only minimal household help such as a once-a-week cleaning woman. So far as our patient was concerned, this left him in the care of a mother who was not much attuned to him while she busied herself with the daily cooking and the like for her moderately large family. He appeared, nonetheless, to have had a good enough symbiosis and was able to extract more than minimal supplies from the environment. He became the unique child of his mother. According to Mahler (1968):

> It is the specific unconscious need of the mother that activates, out of the infant's infinite potentialities, those in particular that create for each mother "the child" who reflects her own *unique* and individual needs. This process takes place, of course, within the range of the child's innate endowments [p. 19].

He described what he could remember of his toddling years as being always underfoot while his mother went about her own work. He appears, as an adult, to have pathologically narcissistic features, reflecting Mahler's view that development of sound secondary narcissism requires appropriate maternal response at every subphase. The parents already had three older sons and a daughter who preceded the patient in the small-town school where, when his turn came, he had the same teachers. All were proud of the intellectual achievements of the four older children. The mother decided, long before he reached school age, that the patient was her dull child. While physically well cared for in his preschool years, there was little emotional or intellectual stimulation. He could not recall that anyone, not even his older siblings, ever played with him or read to him. He fulfilled the role that he sensed was demanded of him unconsciously by his mother and became, in his words, mother's dolt. The teachers expressed surprise, as early as the first grade, that he came from the same family as the very bright siblings they had taught.

This man did attain a neurotic structure, but one heavily burdened by pathological narcissism and much rage at his objects because of their taunts. In his analysis, a central diagnostic question was how much of his low intellectual functioning derived from innate endowment, how much was involved in conflict and anger, and how much because he had merged his self images with maternal images at subphase levels in the mother's need to have him her dull child. Rapprochement as well as practicing needs could not have been met in full measure by so unresponsive a mother and, as was repeated in the analytic situation, the patient "extracted" her attention by doing things that distracted her enough from her other tasks to respond to his "stupidity." It was necessary, in the analysis, to interpret this layer before interpreting conflict-borne inhibition of function. The oedipal wishes, interestingly, were contaminated with the maternal need for an incompetent child. Just as he could do nothing right in his subphases, he developed potency problems in adulthood. In fact, the presenting problem was that he was an incompetent lover. Technically, prior attention to the subphase inadequacies, especially with regard to self esteem, brought the treatment to the Oedipus proper so that it could be analyzed at that level of organization without the weight of the problems that preceded it.

This patient had little ambition for himself beyond the niche of a minor civil servant, which fulfilled his parents' aspirations. The broadened horizons of experience with the analyst as a representative of a larger world intrigued him. For example, he remembered having liked music as a child, but was not encouraged to develop this gift. The analyst's office is close to a major music center, and so ultimately the patient asked him whether he ever goes there. It would have been an error to have misused the abstinence rule by failing to answer. The analyst's "yes" revealed not the analyst's particular likes or dislikes but only that the larger world is there and available to the patient as well. He became intrigued with attending concerts and even learning to play an instrument. The analyst did not direct these interests. This is an example of the effect of the analyst as a real person, not imposed upon the patient but noticed by him. It did not at all involve intimate revelations about the analyst, whose very presence and obvious difference from the parents were enough to convey that. Neither did the analyst impose his particular penchants. Ultimately the patient chose a new profession, not that of the analyst, but in combination of identification and independence, an example of selective identification by an ego competent enough to take the next higher step away from the object.

Another example of subphase influence on neurosis is the case of a woman whose subphase development was adequate enough for her to have attained a full-blown neurosis, but barely so. Even the peripheral interaction of most of the subphases seemed to have taken place adequately, by and large. The mother valued intellectual achievement and taught the child to read very early. The quality of subphase inadequacy is encapsulated in the mother's leaving the child to watch "educational" programs on television without regard for their phase-appropriateness or timing of the needs for aloneness or for object connection. This subtle removal of herself at times when connection was needed left the child to cathect the television screen as a part object, thus impairing acquisition of optimal self-object constancy. As an adolescent and adult, television remained a source of comfort and companionship over and beyond the average use of it. She would watch "any old program" when lonely or awake during the night.

In the therapeutic interaction (which we shall not for the timebeing describe specifically as transference) there was a slight tendency to withdraw from a real object (analyst) when she felt displeased. The analyst thought that the ready availability of television as object obviated the necessity to deal with a real person in uncomfortable situations. This made it possible for her to retain a "good" object without conflict. For a long time she maintained that her subphase mother was only good. She reported that she was soothed, read to, and the like, which appears to have served to quicken her apparatuses. The anger at being left too much to be entertained by a machine had to be elicited before this gifted young woman became able to develop the rich potential of her inner world. In this case, because there was structure, the analyst was mainly a transference object, except in the single area where the primary object had failed to provide sufficient object connection. The specific technique that departed from the classical was to suggest waiting for thoughts to come before turning on television automatically. Gradually, the patient found herself so interested in her own thoughts and fantasies that she forgot to turn on the external "soother."

This technique succeeded only because self-object constancy was good in other respects. Therefore, the analyst was convinced that, with her intellect, the patient would not have been "alone" without television. In other cases, where there is less internalization, one would not risk object loss but would wait for the organizing process to include higher levels of object relations before making such suggestion. Better still, in such instances, when self-object constancy is reached, the suggestion is often made by the patient rather than by the analyst.

Suggestion has a mixed history in the technique of psychoanalysis. Seen as closely allied to the hypnosis of the prepsychoanalytic era, it fell into disrepute as psychoanalytic technique acquired more sophistication. The connotation that the analyst, in his greater wisdom, can *suggest* to the patient remains unsavory. Yet, somewhat later than the hypnotic era, Freud found it necessary to deal with phobic patients by insisting (at a time deemed optimal) that they face their phobias in order to deal with the anxiety and thereby to conquer it, presumably with a stronger ego than existed when the phobia was formed. Interestingly, Freud did not work directly with ego-building techniques, yet he recognized that the stronger ego of the adult could cope better with anxiety than the ego of the child or of the adult patient whose phobias were formed by the ego in childhood. Eissler terms Freud's suggestion in that regard a *parameter*, but Eissler's definition of parameter includes the requirement that it be eliminated before the analysis can be concluded. That is because, in the psychoanalysis of neurosis, intrusion of a technique that departs from strict neutrality is thought to be a contaminant if it remains. In *Ego Psychology: Theory and Practice,* we discuss the experience of so many psychotherapists that certain interventions in the treatment of borderline patients cannot be eliminated. In order not to "contaminate" Eissler's definition, we prefer, even in the absence of another term, not to refer to these as parameters.[1] And so, once again awkwardly for the time being, we might refer to them as departures from classical psychoanalytic technique in the less-than-neurotically organized personality. Yet we do not advocate that these departures be made in a less carefully considered way than did Eissler with regard to the self-eliminating parameter in neurosis. In fact, where we are working in the hazy era of subphase inadequacy, so poorly subject to recall, we have to be all the more certain that, whatever the intervention, it be addressed with as much precision as possible to the malformation in organization. We know of no better safeguard against wild psychotherapy than minute knowledge of subphase development.

In that frame of reference, the analyst or therapist does become real to the patient but in a circumscribed way—not really himself, but as a representative of the object world, especially when the patient's connection with the real world is uncertain. Many analysts are finding that they cannot validly sustain the image of nonparticipant observer and interpreter even in the psychoanalysis of neurosis. Although one departs only with great caution from the position of neutrality, no human being can sustain that role in absolute form, nor would it be desirable. Further, processes of internalization that are therapeutically advantageous do take place in the course of an analysis with technique even at its most classical. Ross (1968) makes a most compelling point in this regard about the analyst as bearer of moral values. Observant analysts cannot help noticing that what

[1]*Suggestion* is one of the numerous terms in the vocabulary of psychotherapy and psychoanalysis that, borrowed from the common vocabulary, takes on a more specialized meaning. Hypnotic suggestion virtually eliminates the autonomy of the subject by bypassing the ego and is therefore not conducive to growth promotion. Advice is but one small step away from hypnotic suggestion. Nevertheless, there is a form of suggestion implicit in every therapeutic endeavor. The very act of holding oneself out as a therapist suggests that we profess to know how to help and suggests to patients that they can get better. No longer are the therapist's wishes, value judgments, and commands at issue, for those represent simple suggestion that demands compliance. Now careful evaluation of the patient's growth capacity establishes a therapeutic goal. Loewald referred to this as the therapeutic differential. In itself this differential suggests that patients may strive toward higher levels of organization than they had been able to reach before.

were formerly thought to have been new experiences in the transference are, in fact, new experiences arising out of the real relationship.

It appears necessary to reexamine the technical concept of *working through* in the light of our new theoretical knowledge. When Freud found that cognition alone, that is, interpretation of the id wish, did not suffice to alter the dynamic relationships, he proposed that working through was necessary. He (1914b) says, "we must treat his illness, not as an event of the past, but as a present-day force" (p. 151), and added, "One must allow the patient time to become more conversant with this resistance with which he has now become acquainted, to *work through* it, to overcome it, by continuing, in defiance of it, the analytic work" (p. 155).

The literature on working through is vague about the precise process. Among those who have undertaken to elaborate on Freud's (1914b) introduction of this term into the theory of technique are: Fenichel (1935); Glover (1955); Greenacre (1956); Greenson (1965); Lewin (1950); Novey (1962); Schmale (1966). All or most of the authors regard working through as involved with resistance, particularly resistance from the id. Glover and Greenacre knew that the ego is also somehow involved. Some authors (Fenichel, Lewin, Greenson) liken working through to the process of mourning. Moore and Fine (1967) define it as:

> WORKING THROUGH: A term originally used by Freud to describe the continuing application of analytic work to overcome *resistances* persisting after the initial *interpretation* of repressed instinctual *impulses.* He explained this "id resistance" as a likely occurrence in view of the fact that an instinctual process that has been going along a particular path for decades is suddenly expected to take a new path that has just been made open for it. It is the goal of working through to make insight effective, i.e., to bring about significant and lasting changes in the patient by altering the modes and aims of the *instinctual drives.* This leads eventually to the inclusion of warded-off components in the total personality. Now considered a most important part of the analytic process, working through consists essentially of a repetition, extension, and deepen-

> ing of the analysis of the resistances, which need to be overcome repetitively and progressively [p. 92].

Fenichel (1935) followed Freud in subsuming what might more usefully be regarded as two separate techniques under the single heading *working through*—1) analysis of resistance and 2) uncovering. While it is true that resistance is analyzed for the purpose of uncovering, it is confusing to describe them as the same process or even as two parts of the same process. Defined in that way it consists, on the one hand, of discovery in one place of what one had already found elsewhere; but, on the other hand, it consists of the technical process of undermining resistant positions, especially resistance from the id.

Interesting to our position about affect and drive (chapter 3) is Novey's (1962) observation:

> It becomes increasingly evident that the delay in the development of a satisfactory affect theory in psychoanalysis has been in large part responsible for our failure to understand the process of working through . . . Affect is a prime mover in psychic activity, and affective patterns of experiencing and of response are more resistant to change than cognitive ones. In fact, man's relative lability of response and his capacity to master his environment are closely correlated with his intelligence and ability to use verbal signals and his resultant capacity to alter his automatizations of feeling and behaving. . . .
>
> It is a truism in psychoanalysis that the full affective experiencing of pathogenic conflicts in the transference makes for greater therapeutic effectiveness. However, there has been a tendency to emphasize the genetic interpretative approach to therapy at the expense of the role of the corrective emotional experience [p. 666].

In the light of Novey's inclusion of the affective experience, it appears more desirable now to restrict the definition of working through to discovery and rediscovery, separating it from resistance analysis. Freud, in his discussions of *tact,* was aware that the ability to accept and absorb an interpretation is dependent upon the emotional climate in which it is presented. His paper on *Wild Analysis* (1910) shows in a rather amusing way how futile were the interpretations made by a physician (who was not an analyst) who relied solely upon the patient's cognition without regard for the therapeutic alliance. The nature of the alliance is, after all, a function of the capacity for object relations. This states also that other ego functions come to the aid of cognition.

To eliminate resistance analysis from *working through,* restricting it to discovery and rediscovery within a favorable emotional climate, provides opportunity also to broaden that technical concept by adding that ego functions can be quickened in that climate. We do not agree with Novey that such a technique constitutes a *corrective* emotional experience because to correct implies that an error exists; we prefer to think of it as reparative rather than corrective. Where the patient lived, as a child, in a "climate" that failed to encourage ego apparatuses, the therapist provides or helps the patient provide a more favorable or conducive climate. Then the cognitive and emotional capacities combine to make interpretation usable. Most neurotic patients, being analyzed within a reasonably good therapeutic alliance, already have the capacity to use a correct and well-timed interpretation because interpretation connects with existing cognitive capacities and a high level of object relations. Object relations determine not only the quality of the therapeutic alliance but also transference and even transference neurosis. In most instances, borderline patients cannot be assumed to possess such capacities and so it becomes one of the very purposes of the therapy to promote them.

The case material presented earlier in this chapter illustrates how ego functions may be quickened in the therapeutic endeavor. The "climate," where capacity for self and object relations is deficient, sometimes has to be provided by the patient with considerable help from the therapist in arranging for it. One accomplishes this by helping the patient acquire capacities for self empathy and self soothing. Some of this is transmitted by promotion of selective identification with the therapist's soothing and empathic affects. Often more is needed in the form of actively encouraging the patients to look back at the children that they were and to provide empathy for themselves.

To illustrate that: A young woman, a nurse, comes from her

work and takes from five to fifteen minutes before she can introduce the material of the session. Later, she explains that she must clear her mind of matters that occurred at the hospital before she is able to begin the session. It is superfluous to inform her, as one would in the psychoanalysis of neurosis, that whatever she is thinking belongs in the session. The therapist thinks about her history, known from earlier sessions, and reconstructs from his own knowledge of the maternal inadequacy that this woman's mother had not been emotionally available in provision of experience in making transitions; the patient as an adult struggles with transitions because she has not been offered the opportunity for selective identification in acquisition of transitional mechanisms. Out of the experiences known from the patient's history, the therapist selects one within the patient's memory—coming home from school—observing that those daily moments were probably lonely ones. The patient connects with this. Yes, she had to go immediately to her room after school to do her homework. The therapist comments that transitions are difficult. Patient agrees in a way that implies that she had not thought they could be otherwise. Together, they begin to work on constructing how it might have been had she been able to talk about the day at school before going to her room. The idea of entitlement to the interest of another person in making a transition begins to seep in. The purpose is to promote self empathy about an unfulfilled need that the patient did not even know about. Although it was addressed to a period of life within continuous memory, it had the deeper purpose of addressing a void created by the maternal incapacity for providing transitional experiences throughout this patient's life; this includes the subphase years.

This sort of provision of climate is much different from the simple provision of a benign atmosphere in the therapy itself. It informs the patient that the newness of the benign therapeutic climate is how the object world should have been throughout early life. Here we wish to show how we help patients provide a better vision of themselves in their past life and to empathize with themselves for what was lacking.

Returning now to the theoretical aspects of the technique of working through, we see in a new light that, for the successful impact of discovery and rediscovery, it is necessary that cognition, self and object relations and auxiliary ego functions operate in unison in an appropriate affective climate. The entire process may be described as an emotional experience, but with the new slant that this is more desirably provided by the patients for themselves retroactively. This has the added advantage of preservation of the patient's autonomy, for it is all too easy, with our presumably more competent ego functioning, to force comprehension upon a bewildered patient. This would bind the patient to the therapist as the patient comes to rely more and more upon the therapist's real or presumed competence. Interpretation, in that event, reduces to provision of narcissistic supplies. That is also why we so value intrasystemic over external confrontation (R. Blanck, 1965).

Where the therapist retains the role of catalyst of development, the patient is kept free of interminable need for the therapist as a real object. We do not mean to diminish the importance of the more classical technique of repetition of interpretation from new angles as dreams and associations relating to the same material are produced over and over with the additions and alterations that analysts are trained to listen for each time there is a repetition of "old" material. The new feature within the old always captures our attention precisely because working through requires interpretation now from one angle, now from another. Perhaps Freud would not have included resistance analysis under the aegis of working through had he had the solution to the problem of the "narcissistic neuroses" that psychoanalytic developmental psychology now provides.

We return from this excursion into the problem of working through to the central issue of the role of the analyst as a real object. Every therapeutic situation contains elements which are new and different from other experiences. It is necessary to distinguish between those essential to every therapeutic encounter, such as the benign atmosphere, and those interventions which approach the particular problem at the developmental locus where they are needed to facilitate organization. The role of the therapist or analyst as catalyst of organization in a favorable therapeutic climate is different from a parental role, tempting as it may be to equate them. The real parents, as primary objects, internalized to some degree are, in a manner of speaking, competitors obscuring the interaction between therapist and patient. It is the very internalization of distorted object images that leaves little direct access to the therapist as representative of the object world and that precludes a "corrective emotional experience" in the simplistic sense of better parenting. While distortions exist, the therapist can be experienced neither as real nor as a substitute parent (except transferentially). For the neurotic patient whose object representations are relatively whole, the analyst remains facilitator of interpretation; for the more disturbed patient, the analyst is corrector of distortions and catalyst of organization.

Our position remains as close as possible to the literal meaning of catalyst—a necessary presence, but not a participant in the action. This is a conservative stance which protects patients from well-intentioned contamination of their self and object images. It reserves for the therapist the role of therapist as contrasted with real object even in those pathologies where true transference is not possible. The patient may, for pathological reasons, need to draw the therapist into a real relationship; the therapist nevertheless maintains a therapeutic one. The affective distortions of the object images are exposed by the therapist's nonparticipation in repetition of the damaging object relationship. The therapist uses himself to create optimal circumstances for the patient's latent ego apparatuses to come into play to perform the necessary work of reorganization.

Where, because of low-level organization, the dominant need is still in the experiential realm, the therapist usefully and deliberately allows himself to be experienced as a nontransference object. The more disturbed patient does need a reparative experience. The question remains: when, how, and, in terms of a theory of technique, especially *why* does one use this device. It is reserved for situations where there has been severe symbiotic and subphase inadequacy. It is provided verbally, by *explanation*[2] of the need, with supplementary techniques such as answering questions for the purpose of making the object world more real. In this technical posture the therapist is different from a real object. The interpersonal posture of "being oneself" with the patient is meaningless because we are neither real nor ourselves to the kind of patient we are describing. We can only be a narcissistically perceived aspect of the patient's distorted and poorly differentiated self and object images.

We have described the shift from living experientially (in the interpersonal interaction in the dyad) toward living more within the structure (in the mind) as the fulcrum of development (chapter 5). The technical stance of the therapist is determined by the status of the patient with regard to how successfully shifts have taken place around the fulcrum. This gives the therapist's role a rationale and even makes it possible to propose a rule of thumb: the greater the degree of organization and structuralization, the less effective is provision of experience. In any event, corrective or interpersonal or interactive experience, as these are commonly understood, are most effectively addressed to experiential levels of development. Interventions of this sort are to be carefully considered because they propose to offer a new and better object while the patient longs for repetition of experience with the primary object.

Why not offer the patient a better object nevertheless? Such a question assumes that no object cathexis exists, a matter manifestly impossible even in psychosis. We think it more effective, therefore, to work with the patient to expose the pathological elements in the primary partnership rather than to offer a substitute, even one which we regard as more benign. This emphasizes that an adult comes to treatment with his own primary object experiences, even if he has not been able to proceed very far in creating structure.

What is the technical move then? The therapist of such seriously disturbed patients avoids repetition of the negative experi-

[2]*Explanation,* as a technique, is elaborated upon in chapters 8, 11, and 12.

ences which prevented ego organization from proceeding. With time and encouragement of reality testing, the patient is helped to correct affective distortions of the object world. Autonomy is always maintained by avoiding tying the patient to the therapist as a unique person. Therapists never suggest that they, as themselves, are better, kinder, more attuned and possessed of other such desirable qualities. Patients experience goodness, kindness, attunement and come gradually to realize, not that the therapist is a saint, but that the world offers wider object choices than were available in childhood. The object world expands and the organizing capacity can be expected to take over and build structure with less hostile and distorted self and object images than existed before. We do not intend to encourage undue optimism about prognosis in all such cases. Patients at some borderline levels have had exceedingly damaging early object experiences, have atrophied ego functions because quickening failed, and can be so hostile as to defeat the treatment.

In the middle range of the borderline conditions are those patients who have attained a degree of organization that represents the beginnings of structure. There, too, the therapist is not direct provider of experience, but has better opportunity to promote structure building that has already begun. The subphase inadequacies come more rapidly to the forefront in these cases and the role of the therapist as catalyst of organization remains the appropriate one for that therapeutic purpose. Only with the most poorly organized patients would one attempt belated repair of subphase inadequacy at early levels by providing a limited experience in accord with the growth need. Whenever possible, the therapist maintains the roles of catalyst as well as leader into the object world. These roles do resemble those of a parent in early development, but cannot duplicate or replace them. For one thing, the time is past, and one can no longer treat the adult as though development stopped at a certain point early in life and can now be resumed with the therapist in the role of a more benign parent. It is usually impossible to designate exactly where subphase problems originated. To try to pick up and repair there is equally impossible and is likely to be simplistic. But to guide the patient into the object world as the representative of that world differs from parenting in time even though the task is similar in quality. The therapist's ultimate objective is self elimination to a certain extent. The qualification leaves room for selective identification which is best accomplished when our uniqueness is minimized to reduce the impact of our specific personalities. Identification is with the universal human attributes we possess, perhaps above all, with our growth-promoting philosophy which patients can take with them to continue development as they make that philosophy their own.

CHAPTER 8

Countertransference

Unlike transference, countertransference is not a phenomenon arising out of the patient's history, structure, or developmental and organizational assets and deficits, but of those of the analyst. Often regarded negatively as reflecting flaws in the analyst's personality and, as such, an obstruction to the analytic purpose, it has also been thought to be useful, when, as is true of transference as well, it can be given the right turn. The literature on countertransference has been so competently reviewed by Orr (1954) that it permits our discussion to concentrate on the newer attitudes toward countertransference and on additions to the theory dictated by the discoveries of psychoanalytic developmental psychology. The latter is particularly necessary because, with changing techniques arising out of the relatively recent recognition that certain patients need some sort of therapeutic interaction for structure building, it becomes difficult to sort out what is detrimental activity because of destructive countertransference and what is truly essential to the patient's development.

Since Freud's discovery of its dynamics, transference is unequivocally accepted as an extraordinarily useful therapeutic tool. This cannot be said for countertransference. As Orr indicates, analysts have been uncertain about its value and have different views of what it is and how it may be used. Moore and Fine (1967) define it as:

> the attitudes and feelings, only partly conscious, of the analyst toward the patient. These may reflect the analyst's own unconscious conflicts, and if he is not constantly aware of this, may affect his understanding and therapeutic handling of the patient. In countertransference, the analyst has displaced on to the patient attitudes and feelings derived from earlier situations in his own life; the process is analogous to *transference,* the patient's similar reaction to the analyst, an important instrument in analytic therapy. One of the cardinal purposes of the analyst's own analysis during his training is to make him aware of his own conflicts and their derivatives, so that they do not distort his therapeutic work with patients. The analyst's continuing scrutiny of his countertransference feelings frequently provides correct clues to the meaning of the patient's behavior, feelings, and thoughts, and may facilitate more prompt *perception* of the patient's *unconscious.*

Thus, countertransference is thought of as reflections of blind spots in the analyst out of his own unconscious infantile needs and, in that sense, a potential contaminant of treatment. But it is also regarded as a means of understanding the patient's communications in terms of the analyst's affective reactions to them.

In that period of the history of psychoanalysis when id was synonymous with unconscious and ego with consciousness, the dictum was: where id was there shall ego be. This referred, of course, not to the ego as we know it today but to consciousness. Such excessive valuation of the system conscious was, at that time, a logical consequence of the simplistic theory of neurosis as the deleterious result of repression. And so, for the analyst no less than for the patient, the ideal was to make the unconscious conscious. Then behavior and mentation could be rational, intelligent, reality-based, and was best achieved not only when analysts were in full command of their former unconscious, infantile residuals by virtue of having made them conscious, but also as they adopted a position of neutrality and themselves constituted a "blank screen" or a "mirror" which would reflect only the patient's projections. The patient was thus safeguarded from intrusion of distortions from the analyst's unconscious, leaving the field free for the full elaboration of the patient's transference distortions, misperceptions, and projections. And so the ideal of the "neutral" analyst came to be regarded as offering the best therapeutic opportunity; the analyst could give the patient's associations evenly suspended attention without value judgment and especially was the patient safeguarded against the damaging effect of the analyst's infantile needs.

Some of the most brilliant theorists of technique of the "middle era" of psychoanalytic theory construction were wary of countertransference and were clear in their proposals for dealing with it. Thus Glover, who wrote as early as the 1920s, but whose book on technique was not published until 1955, described countertransference as the counterpart in the analyst of the patient's oedipal, castration, and superego conflicts. He regarded countertransference as negative and destructive in the main, and advised analysts to be alert to their own reactions (irritability, anxiety, overinvolvement) and, in proper British manner, suggested that they look to their own analytic toilet. Sharpe (1930) also thought of countertransference as a flaw in the analyst. She demonstrated how she dealt with it by self-analysis, going so far as to avoid making interpretations in a session following upon her having had a dream about a patient, presumably to insure sufficient time for her to be able to analyze her own dream and thus to make conscious her feelings about the patient. While in one sense this appears today to be an unnecessarily heroic measure, in another it attests to her scrupulous regard for the patient and her profound respect for unconscious processes, whether in the patient or herself. As happens so frequently in the science of human behavior, complexities soon began to overwhelm the comfortable, clear, and sharp conviction that countertransference represents nothing but a flaw in the analyst.

In 1937, when Hartmann presented his lecture, *Ego Psychology and the Problem of Adaptation,*[1] he relieved us of much burden by asserting that the human being cannot and, further, must not be fully rational. While unconscious processes with their distortions do indeed contribute to conflict and pathology, they are also

[1]Published in German in 1939, but not fully translated and published in English until 1958.

adaptive as sources of some of our most cherished ideals—love, including overvaluation of the object, loyalty, and the like. Hartmann asserted that progress does not pursue a straight line, but takes place also by means of detours (dreams and other forms of regression) which contribute indispensably to our human qualities. Patients do arouse feelings in the therapist and analyst. Hartmann's observation that development takes place by means of detours and regressions suggests that the therapist, for technical purpose, be able to traverse the detours and not get dislodged by the bumpiness.

Although Freud advocated analytic purification, surgical coolness, neutrality, absence of value judgment, mirrorlike reflection, how shall we understand his treatment of the Rat Man (1909) "He was hungry and was fed" (p. 303), or of the Wolf Man (1918) whom Freud supported when he lost his fortune? Such behavior by their supervisees would be frowned upon by contemporary analysts, who would most certainly regard them as reflections of overinvolvement with the patient, that is, countertransference. Indeed, Freud's concern was repaid by the Rat Man with complaints about the quality of the lunch served him and, in a less disciplined analyst, might have stirred up negative countertransference. These acts can only be seen as reflecting Freud's human qualities. His advocacy of the cold, surgical stance appears in his writings as so one-sided for emphasis only and is not reflective of his true view of the analyst's role, as is often charged. Surgical coldness, the mirror, the blank screen, are metaphors that Freud found useful for conveying that undisciplined involvement or too much therapeutic zeal contaminate the treatment. It probably did not occur to him (nor do we think he would have cared) that his detractors would seize these figures of speech out of context to mock the psychoanalytic method. They were not meant to connote that the analyst is an uninterested bystander, nor does neutrality mean absence of values. If nothing else, analysts value the organizing process, for structural reorganization has ever been the goal of psychoanalysis. Neutrality means simply that the analyst does not seek to impose his values upon the patient, a far cry from the impossible goal of trying to have no values. Absurdly reductionist questions such as Would you analyze a murderer? reflect some of the unreal challenges to psychoanalysis, as though it is a form of sociology. Ross, in his elaboration of the role of the analyst as the bearer of moral values, adds to Hartmann's presentation of this issue. Especially now, with recognition that identification processes become part of therapeutic interaction, does it seem unreal to maintain the fiction that the analyst has no value system. All of the analyst's inherent humanness and humaneness are necessary to the therapeutic climate. Rather than eliminate them, they are to be put to use. Greenacre (1954) describes a "warming" in the relationship which, while retaining a professional purpose, contributes to the therapeutic work. Analytic neutrality refers to absence of value judgments and is not violated by caring whether the patient gets better, provided that therapeutic discipline is honored.

We are left then with the question, if the analyst is not cold, mirrorlike, a blank screen, unfeeling, surgical, what are the limits of the human responses that may be used to further the treatment? Further, at what point, or with what kinds of responses, do they exceed these limits and become detrimental to the treatment? Such questions cannot be answered simply. There are limits that should not be transcended in any case. But, by and large, diagnostic considerations are important determinants of the form, content, and limits of the analyst's responses. Beginning at the most organized end of the diagnostic spectrum, the standard texts on the technique of psychoanalysis define and discuss countertransference as it concerns the psychoanalysis of the neuroses. There it is assumed that ego organization has proceeded fairly smoothly and that the psychosexual level (phallic with or without regression) and the object-relations level (oedipal) converge. In the ideal neurotic case, analysis is concerned largely with the oedipal conflicts and with the pregenital fixations and regressions. Since the ego is thought to be fully developed and unmodified, the role of the analyst is mainly facilitator of interpretation. It is in the treatment of that form of pathology that countertransference has come to be understood and is thought to be detrimental if it impairs the analyst's neutrality, interferes with his interpretative capacity, and tempts the analyst to violate the abstinence rule.

A strict construction of countertransference seems desirable for many reasons, foremost of which is its use to deter undisciplined interventions. We imply that deviation is valid if embarked upon in a disciplined way, that is to say, when the patient's level of organization rather than the analyst's needs dictate the technique. This resembles Eissler's description of departure from the ideal technique of interpretation, to be made only when the structure (organization) of the ego requires it. We believe that new discoveries will affect the technique of psychoanalysis as we expand our diagnostic purview to include ego organization in addition to psychosexual maturation in our considerations. The degree of convergence of the many developmental lines is a major determinant in organization, no less in the neuroses than in the more severe pathologies. Therefore, techniques formerly held to be inviolate may become modified as knowledge increases.

We are already obliged to reconsider technique in neuroses with subphase inadequacies, that is, neurotic organization containing malformations from the rapprochement, and probably earlier subphases, which affect the form and content of the oedipal organization. This raises certain knotty issues about countertransference such as whether, when, why, and how the analyst accepts the role of a "real" object; whether there is corrective or reparative value in a "here and now" interaction, and if so, how to go about it. We have answered some of this in chapter 7. Confronted with such issues, analysts are forced to go beyond their own training. They have been taught to use the unconscious, to free associate in accompaniment with and in counterpoint to the patient's free associations and fantasies. Through their own analyses, they have acquired recognition signals which indicate adequate emotional involvement, underinvolvement, or overinvolvement. They are not likely, however, to have had a conscious experience in the analysis of subphase inadequacy, although analysands of the more gifted training analysts have surely experienced the analysts' intuitive attunement to these aspects of development. The analysts' experience with abstinence in their own analyses enables them to impose abstinence confidently upon the patient, since they know how it feels and how it can be endured. Similarly, their experience with anxiety constitutes the very instrument with which they become able to gauge the patient's capacity to tolerate it.

It is when we find ourselves obliged to deal with matters such as gross unattunement in the subphases, fear of object loss, incomplete self-object differentiation, and the like that we are on unfamiliar ground, not only because these were not aspects of our analytic experience but because they reflect periods of life which are, by and large, beyond memory. Under such circumstances, potential for deleterious countertransference activity rises, since analysts' use of their own feelings and reactions as therapeutic instruments does not then have the moderating effect of certainty derived from their personal analytic experience. As therapeutic means of dealing with the more severe pathologies evolve, analysts find themselves functioning more in the experiential realm of interaction than in the structured forms of the mind familiar from their training. Under such circumstances the analyst's intuitive reactions offer the possibility of becoming a useful tool for purposes of understanding the patient. Sandler (1976) describes how the patient can establish a situation in the transference which ensnares the analyst into reenacting an unconsciously designated parental role. By self analysis, the analyst discovers how he has been lured into this role and thereby becomes able to interpret the patient's part, that is to say, to reduce it to its genesis.

Countertransference as a useful tool has also been discussed by R. Blanck (1973). An adult enuretic patient described in such engaging and humorous fashion parental attempts to establish urethral discipline that the analyst was almost drawn into sharing the patient's mocking laughter at the failure of their efforts. Only at the last moment did the analyst disengage himself from the wit of this skillful raconteur and, by not joining in the "joke," opened the way toward a useful discussion of the patient's defiance of urinary discipline. Subsequent self-analysis left no doubt that such sympathy for the victims of "parental oppression" has a common root in universal experience with toilet training and the many other frustrations that parents impose.

The useful aspect of the therapist's (unconscious) countertransference derives from the therapist's capacity to interpret his own reaction. This produces the modulating "theory filtered" process which contributes to a therapeutic interchange instead of permitting it to remain a simple interaction. For therapists, therefore, countertransference reactions are subject to self-interpretation.

In cases of "pathological" neurosis, one attends to the phase or subphase inadequacy in order to strengthen organization for the analytic conquest of the oedipal conflict. Here the therapist moves back and forth in the measured steps that we advocate from representative of each of the parents in the triad to that of the dyadic maternal representation only. He has to maintain a freely hovering awareness of these changing roles, which can fluctuate rapidly back and forth between oedipal and subphase parental representations. Appropriate countertransference feelings become somewhat more difficult to control as analysts and psychotherapists find it necessary to leap in unfamiliar directions in their appreciation of the several roles into which they are cast. To illustrate one of the most common difficulties that this presents, a male analyst, experiencing himself as a paternal representation on the oedipal level, must be exceedingly flexible in shifting that self-perception if he is suddenly plied with declarations of love by a male patient. If he leans on the familiar, the first transference role likely to come to mind is that of the negative oedipal position, or homosexuality. But room must be allowed, too, for maternal and paternal representations reflective of subphase levels of object relations.

In addition, since such need-replicating phenomena are, for the more poorly structured, not interpretable because the patient's ego is not up to the task of receiving and utilizing interpretation, the therapist must lend himself as a catalyst to the necessary reparative work.

Negative or hostile transference manifestations also call for countertransference flexibility. As is most obvious, they may very well be expressions of hostility toward the parent of the same sex in the positive oedipal position. But they may also represent aggression in the service of movement away from the maternal object in subphase development. This is intended to illustrate the delicacy of the countertransference role and to show that errors in perception of the representation into which one is cast at a given moment can result, as is already well-known, in erroneous interpretation. But when we consider pathology even more severe than "pathological" neurosis—the lower-level borderline and narcissistic conditions—the countertransference role is even more delicate. There the therapist is confronted with the requirement to take longer steps away from the ideal model of interpretation, to respond to the severely distorted organization with appreciation for the need for reparative object relations. Therefore, perplexing questions about how to go about making these difficult technical decisions to the patient's greatest advantage are bound to arise.

It stretches the concept of countertransference to include under its rubric interventions which, for the psychoanalysis of neurosis, would be altogether contraindicated. Our justification for so doing is that the therapist's affect and self image, especially when treating the more severe pathologies, are the instruments responsive to the therapeutic need of the patient. Not the least difficult of this task is how to distinguish this need from the search for replication of pathogenic object experience. How to use oneself in the patient's behalf is the essence of countertransference in its most positive sense as we become obliged, out of diagnostic considerations, to veer away from interpretation alone toward experiential techniques that serve to aid reorganization. These issues arise because, in descending order of the diagnostic hierarchy, we encounter patients whose primary self-object experiences have impaired the organizing process itself. The therapist is called upon to help the patient repair it by techniques that are in the very process of discovery. We are convinced that adult pathology cannot be repaired by simple interpersonal experience. Prompted by appreciation of the damaging effects of inadequate experiences in the subphases, it becomes tempting to conclude that the adult patient needs better mothering. That, however, contravenes all that we know about the organizing process. Affront at a given phase or subphase does not result in cessation of development. Although fixation and regression may occur in one or several developmental lines, the forward march of the totality of development and organization proceeds nonetheless. Sometimes, with favorable subsequent experience, the sweep of organization carries with it and may even repair the damage of an earlier process by subsuming it favorably. In other instances, development proceeds, now including the distortion, diverting subsequent processes in skewed directions.

We have emphasized that development within the dyadic experience includes the interaction of elements brought to it from both sides of the dyad. How are we to correct, in our adult patients, contributions which emanated from the infant's side, especially if they were comprised of innate givens? And, even if development is conceived one-sidedly in terms of simple maternal relationship, would we not still have to take into account that the concept of organization includes development, structuralization, and internalization and, by its complexity, precludes simplistic therapeutic endeavors?

Sometimes the more severe disruptions of competent ego organization are to be attributed not to belated but to precocious ego development. This is often a feature of innate endowment and not necessarily of external overstimulation, although that, too, can obtain. In either event, the child, so to speak, gets ahead of itself. For example, "too good" endowment may lead to detection of parental flaws at a developmental time when belief in parental omnipotence is still needed for optimal development. This results in abrupt disillusionment and object loss and can be the etiology of a form of narcissism that is described in chapter 11, where the self-object negotiations proceed in distorted form because they move outside of continuing contact with the real object. When it is parental ambition that promotes premature development ("Be a big boy," or "a smart girl"), pride in the child's "independence" tempts the parent to abandon protective roles when these are still needed. One most frequently encountered form of premature overstimulation is the sexual sphere. Kernberg shows how parental seduction imposes upon phase-specific earlier developmental need, resulting in distorted organization with condensation of genital and pregenital features. We would expand this description to include features of ego development in the phases and subphases. In chapter 6 we described how an oedipal wish can be infiltrated by persistence of symbiotic longing. This double-layered pathology is familiar in psychoanalytic thought. Greenacre (1953a) had already described how castration anxiety at the phallic level can, in some instances, be burdened by unabated faulty body image persisting into the phallic phase from an earlier time. There, interpretation of the anxiety at the higher level alone is of little avail. It has to be dealt with on both levels so that the patient's ego can come to comprehend how distortions from one period of life have resonated with the other.

Patients bring to all encounters, including the therapeutic one, the organized end product of early interpersonal experiences—of the interaction of their innate endowment with the maternal environment. Since the therapeutic situation, too, is dyadic, the primary experience is revived, but embedded now in distortions and condensations of later levels of experience and development. Revival, then, is in a final, organized form, not really as the experience took place in infancy. As it presents itself in the therapy, it hardly resembles a revival. Although the therapist does indeed become a partner in a dyad, the therapist resembles the primary partner from the patient's misperception only, because of need for object replication, and even then after the organizing process has come to the relative rest it attains in adulthood. "Relative" takes into account that development continues throughout life, but at a slower pace than it does in early childhood and with the ego that was first organized in early life.

Despite all of these qualifications, there is left for us to consider that the therapist has a role in the dyad in whatever form it revives in the treatment situation. He takes on more of an interpersonal role than was understood when countertransference, defined in its strictest sense, applied to neurosis only. Whether phase and subphase inadequacies are to be treated because such treatment constitutes a prelude to strengthening organization at the oedipal position to bring about its resolution, or whether the pathology is such that therapeutic goals must be limited to improved organization at whichever level is possible, there is an experiential feature in the therapeutic relationship that has only recently begun to be appreciated. The relevant work of Sandler and Joffe and others is well summed up by Lichtenberg's description of psychological structuring as a process in which the child develops the capacity to live a little less in the body and a little more in the mind. Since here we are discussing problems which arise from subphase inadequacy, patients at such lesser levels of organization cannot be expected to have made as much progress toward structuralization as the neurotic; therefore they still live more in the immediacy of experience than in the mind. All the more, therefore, does this call for careful evaluation of the therapist's own feelings and responses in the therapeutic dyad.

The strict and narrow definition of countertransference may now be expanded to include appropriate response from the therapist's knowledge of subphase levels of experience, if we prefer to think of countertransference in its positive sense as a useful therapeutic tool. In its negative sense, it would involve reflections of the therapist's subphase inadequacies and needs. Especially now that we understand that the therapeutic need for reorganization of the patient's subphase inadequacies calls for some sort of experiential interaction with the therapist, must the therapist be in communication with his own phase and subphase adequacies and inadequacies. Patients with severe, and sometimes even moderate inadequacy approach the therapist in search for narcissistic supplies in attempt at replication. To put this in terms of differentiation, the search is for a partner who will participate in interaction that will perpetuate or even exacerbate the pathology. The therapist is called upon to respond to the invitation to join the dyad, but must do so in growth-promoting ways. This does not diminish but, rather, increases the intensity of the involvement. Hence, clarity about the therapist's own needs and responses, extended to phase and subphase levels of development, is essential if "countertransference" is to be used to catalyze reorganization in a growth-promoting direction.

In this endeavor, the therapist does not have the advantages that the primary object brought to bear on development. Principally, the primary object was indispensable, while the therapist can be dismissed. Dismissal need not result from the therapist's errors, but from the repetition compulsion which can power behavior such as acting on rejection or acting on the aggressive thrust away from the object. If it is the latter, however, a good grasp of the subphase-specific use of aggression in that growth-promoting way can help the therapist give it a favorable turn. If successful, one can avert premature termination of treatment, that which Glover regarded as the crassest resistance of them all, for it is often something other than resistance. In many instances it is a form of acting on the positive thrust in development when the drives, operating in concert, take the patient away from the therapist temporarily. The therapist can accept the purpose without supporting the act. This can be accomplished by helping the patient understand the purpose, separating it in his mind from the means he chooses to accomplish it. Such technique is but another form of promoting ego functioning—judgment, anticipation and delay in this instance—to enable the patient to decide whether the action best serves his purpose. Then he becomes free to understand his need, to act on it or to refrain from action, or to decide upon a more appropriate course of action. The purpose is to bring the need and its behavioral manifestation into the verbal realm, that is, under control of the ego. This may avert action and promote higher levels of internalization, although there is no assurance that every patient will be responsive to such effort. The therapist must realize that ambitendency propels resumption of closeness—the use of libido to move toward the object. If the thrust away has been permitted in action, it forecloses the second phase of this concerted developmental movement. The very awareness of this diphasic aspect of drive deployment already distinguishes the therapist from the primary object who may have contributed to phase and subphase inadequate development because she could not attune herself to the ambitendent movements toward and away from. The maternal object who could not tolerate closeness would have rejected the libidinal movement, while the one who needed too much closeness would have felt affronted by the aggressive separating thrust. The therapist may not usefully repeat these failures of attunement. But avoidance of repetition does not, in and of itself, correct past affront. For reorganization of skewed development at such early, preverbal levels, we rely much on explanation as a technical precursor of interpretation. We search out, with as much precision as is possible within the current state of our knowledge, where and how in the phases and subphases, development veered too far off optimal course. Then, very likely, the patient will test us out. Here is the point in treatment where reorganization can be aided if the therapist understands his role well, for here it is a crucial one. Not only is the therapist required to be more attuned than was the primary object to the movements toward and away from, and to "roll" with them, but he must have the right "feel" for how much permissiveness is optimal, how much constitutes overindulgence, and, on the other side of the same coin, how much abstinence is best and how much is too harsh and depriving.

A young man of twenty-three begins treatment by describing symptoms associated with the borderline condition—vague feelings of emptiness, rootlessness, inability to sustain relationships, no direction in life. Having recently returned to the city where his mother lives with her fourth husband, he became intrigued with the vocational opportunities inherent in his new job, and in the employer as well. "I want to make this opportunity work, to stick with it," he says, after describing the ease and facility with which he tends to change jobs, partners, cities. "I just hop on my motorcycle and take off." Discussing frequency, he can manage once a week, although he would prefer twice a month.

The therapist's association, at this moment, is to Freud's patient, a woman who could spend six weeks in Vienna while he was to cure her of her twenty-three-year-old affliction. Freud

(1913) wrote that it was akin to asking a man to pick up a heavy table with two fingers. In this case, the negative counterreaction to the demand for the impossible confronted the therapist, who thereupon surrendered the highly intellectualized, pseudo-professional thought process in favor of thinking (to himself, of course), "This kid wants a magician." The thought drew the therapist's attention to the subphases, the need for magical omnipotence, how well the patient's meticulous appearance, history, and symptoms fit the grandiose expectations. Still unanswered is why the therapist's reactions took this detour and why he could not have appreciated more directly the diagnostic implications. This, too, had to be thought out, the reason to be sought in the therapist's own history. Out of these considerations, the therapist was able to address himself in a more attuned fashion to the present—that, while he could appreciate the problems involved, financial and the like, it would not be in the patient's best interest to make therapeutic arrangements that would replicate the very problem for which he seeks treatment.

The therapist here admits the patient's wish for primary object replication into the interaction, but avoids the sought-for repetition of overpermissiveness by insisting upon appropriate frequency of sessions. The patient's response confirms one aspect of the diagnosis—he is favorably impressed by the therapist's conviction; this resembles the senior toddler's profound respect for and admiration of strength.

After the patient "accepts" such beginning, the difficult process of involving him in an object relationship ensues. Test after test is arranged or occurs fortuitously. His admired employer needs him to go on a week's business trip that may be combined with a vacation, and so he must cancel appointments. That he would have to pay for the missed sessions is another rude shock; this is tempered by the observation that he had not even thought of attempting to reschedule them. Why! This is best taken by the therapist as an opportunity to "roll" with the aggressive (individuating) thrust. It is suggested that he can take a vacation to coincide with the therapist's vacation. Surprised by the therapist's cooperation, the patient accuses him of deciding such issues only on the basis of his own need. Here, the therapist must try to avoid defending himself. The patient has introduced a projection. The therapist's needs are used by the patient to confirm the narcissistic view of "everyman for himself." Missed sessions for which the patient does not wish to pay are particularly delicate, technically, where the patient's level of object relations cannot encompass the therapist's separate needs. A useful intervention, when the patient resents that he will be paying for the therapist's "free" time is, "I would prefer that we be together so that we can go on working."

Because of revival of subphase experiences and inadequacies, the therapist is cast into the role of primary object for purpose of object replication; therefore it is necessary to emphasize that he retains the role of therapist, sustaining his difference from the primary object by understanding, explaining, illuminating matters which the patient, as a child, could not have understood. To demand compliance and behavioral change threatens to repeat the experiences of the past. That would constitute countertransference in its most negative sense, for there the therapist would be taking the patient as his own object from whom he seeks gratification of his zeal, perhaps determined by his own subphase needs.

Were it not that some non-Freudians use conscious countertransference responses in the interaction, it would be superfluous to say here that we are obliged to spare patients the conclusions of our self-analysis of countertransference. The belief that it is useful to share one's feelings with the patient fails to appreciate the nuances of the patient's developmental needs. It demands too much of patients to impose our neurotic reactions and even our analyzed conclusions upon them. A somewhat more compelling argument for "sharing" is presented by those who value interaction between patient and therapist, believing that behavior can be altered if the patient is confronted with its effect upon others. That may be. But behavioral change is not structural change and compliance is not adaptation. We (1968) distinguished confrontation from without from intrasystemic confrontation. The latter comes about when patients are able to look at themselves, their past, their own functioning, as the observing ego confronts the behaving self. It effects change when the patient is ready for it, and not at the therapist's behest. It eliminates the danger of incurring compliance to a demand from an external source.

Schur (1955) explains that ventilation of affect, usually negative, toward the analyst in the present cannot alter problems originating in the past. Ventilation of affect, catharsis in general, can provide a temporary discharge of accumulated tension but cannot of itself prevent a reaccumulation, as Freud discovered at the turn of the century when he abandoned the cathartic method. Conceptual clarity may now be added to Schur's observation. Ventilation does not support cognitive distinction of present object from past experience; it adds to the obfuscation. The therapist who encourages ventilation for its own sake is involved in establishing himself as a better parent in a countertransference that fails to contribute to expansion of the impeded ego function responsible for the accumulation of tension in the first instance.

This is not to say that nothing takes place between the two partners in the therapeutic endeavor. Indeed, it is our very purpose to show that interaction can be used and should be used for the patient's purposes; it has a different quality from simple interpersonal interaction, a different purpose from behavioral change, and a therapeutic effect different from both of those. Interaction is restricted to the areas of the diagnostic spectrum where the organization process is malformed. Responses which might be subsumed under the broad heading of countertransference are used under appropriate safeguards. Since therapeutic effectiveness rests upon aiding the capacity for organization, the therapist avoids intrusion upon ego autonomy by remaining in the role of a catalyst to the degree that the level of organization permits. If, out of subphase inadequacy that militates toward adult pathology, the therapeutic need is for repair of self-object distortion, the therapist must in some way constitute more of a real object than was traditionally regarded as necessary and useful. He begins his work by creation of the therapeutic climate, important to the treatment of all pathology as Dewald pointed out. But climate alone only provides the milieu for cure; it cannot constitute cure per se. To this must be added the essential aspects of therapy. If the therapeutic need is for a better object experience, then the therapist becomes, quite deliberately, the representative of the better object world. In this role the therapist resembles the careful surgeon who does not hack away wildly in the hope of finding the diseased appendix, let us say. He diagnoses the pathology, determines its site, makes the incision, and repairs only the minimum that is diseased. The healing process is a factor of the patient's capacities.

As knowledge about early levels of organization deepens with refinement of research data, the theory of technique for the more disturbed patient will become more secure and possible to conceptualize. Probably then, and as therapists experience their own subphase inadequacies in training analyses, there will be less need to lean upon countertransference affective response. Treatment techniques for the more disturbed patient population will become systematized and might even approach reliability similar to the techniques for treating neurosis. Meanwhile, we use the instruments that we are with discipline and caution.

CHAPTER 9

Resistance Revisited

When we speak of resistance (the use of defense in the analytic situation) we assume the existence of a level of organization that includes capacity to employ defense and defense mechanisms. Customarily, we tend to think of the defense mechanisms on a hierarchy of efficiency, with denial, projection, and introjection on the lower order; isolation, reaction-formation, undoing, and the like in a middle range; and repression as the most effective and most sophisticated of mechanisms. As negotiation of the fulcrum of development proceeds toward structuralization, higher degrees of internalization are simultaneously attained. Thus, with fusion, for example, the smoothly separating toddler (Mahler, Pine and Bergman, 1975) is able to accept that the "good" and "bad" object images are those of one person. Whole self and object representations are now more rather than less internalized. This facilitates structuralization and capacity to tolerate conflict "in the mind." Signal anxiety is attained and the higher order of defense mechanisms becomes available to a now structured ego. Environmental interactions will be superseded more and more by inner processes.

We are left with the question of how to understand and classify those processes that take place before psychic organization and structure sufficient to mediate transactional events exist. This leads to still another question: What is the nature of those processes, traditionally categorized as defense mechanisms, as they operate on not-yet-structured levels of organization? Basing our position on data provided by Jacobson and Loewald, we suggest that denial, projection, and introjection belong in a category separate from the higher-level defense mechanisms.

1. Jacobson describes projection and introjection as processes that occur at a time of life when boundaries between self and object representations are still obscure.

2. Loewald describes the maternal functions as gathering together the as-yet-undifferentiated urges of the infant, enabling that infant to organize them into a frame of reference provided by the maternal environment. Thus, the infant introjects the mother's responses as organizing references for recognizable stimuli, such as hunger and discomfort, to replace the global response of organismic distress.

3. Brazelton et al. (1975) demonstrate, in films, that the infant at about ten weeks of age vocalizes responsively, which suggests that the cooing sounds proffered by the external object are introjected and then projected, creating a brief moment of dual unity. Projection and introjection, viewed in this light, are evidences of libidinal activity, the binding together and creation of ever greater unities (Nunberg, 1931; Freud, 1940). In this manner the self-object unity is created. With increasing degrees of differentiation the capacity to distinguish self representations from object representations eventuates. These earlier connecting processes may be regarded as the precursors of selective identification.

In reconsidering splitting we have seen it as a feature of the developmental phase before the attainment of the ability to tolerate that good and bad object images refer to the same whole person. The fact that this phenomenon may persist beyond the age-appropriate level does not of itself convert it into a defense mechanism. Persistence of splitting may very well represent lingering with the good object longer because it is needed for developmental purposes, just as Mahler found that some children prolong the symbiotic phase when it has been too meager in order to make up quantitatively for qualitative inadequacies.

Such persistence, while necessary in one sense, distorts the overall organization as it pivots around the fulcrum. Thereby, a child who does not yet have whole self and object representations is retarded in structuralization, identity formation, and in shifting from experiential to intrapsychic negotiations. This leaves less than fertile ground for time-appropriate acquisition of higher level capacity for defense.

Anna Freud (1936) presents a lucid description of denial in fantasy in the structured personality. This is consonant with developmental theory, for any individual whether neurotic, borderline, or even psychotic can *regress* to levels where denial, projection, or introjection are operative. In neurotic or near-neurotic borderline structures there can be regression (dedifferentiation) under the stress of anxiety. With reduction of anxiety, more coherent organization is retrieved, enabling the well-structured individual to resume a more differentiated level of functioning. Considering the nature of developmental processes and their profound dependency upon the process of separation-individuation, it is little wonder that the human being is prone to regress to the "safety" of oneness. Significantly, it is the very potential for regression that is so important in differential diagnosis in the less than neurotic structures. There, one searches for the regressive "floor," the level of which determines how competent is the capacity to recover.[1] When the "floor" is too low, progressive leaps are too difficult; therefore, regression is relatively more difficult to reverse. The defense per se is regression to a less differentiated state where cognitive capacities are laid aside temporarily. The extent or depth of regression and whether it is reversible in the service of the ego reflects whether the fulcrum of development has been transpassed, partially negotiated, or barely reached.

Defense and, therefore, resistance are intrapsychic phenomena dependent upon the existence of structure. Resistance-like behavior is often viewed erroneously. Fenichel (1941b) writes of

[1]Kris (1956b) wondered how control of regression develops out of the conflictual constellations of early childhood, especially since "The control of regression forms one of the nuclear parts of the integrative functions of the ego" (p. 450).

the defensive ego as "our enemy" (p. 37). Greenson (1967) says, "Resistance means opposition . . . operating against the progress of the analysis, the analyst, and the analyst's procedures and processes" (pp. 59–60). Menninger (1958) regards resistance as aggressive, self-destructive and in opposition to treatment. It is true that Freud thought, very early, of resistance as a bar to recovery, but by 1917, long before Anna Freud gave us her clarifying insight into the defensive function of the ego, Freud had shifted his philosophy about resistance to that which he had already adopted with regard to transference. One uses it to give the treatment a favorable turn.

Freud's changing attitudes toward resistance constitute a model of scientific development. He was able to abandon hypnosis when he found that it bypassed the ego (and therefore the resistance). In reporting on Elisabeth von R., he (1895) notes that his attempt to put her under deep hypnosis failed. It occurred to him to try applying pressure to the patient's head to "extract" (his term) new material. "In the course of this difficult work I began to attach a deeper significance to the resistance offered by the patient in the reproduction of her memories and to make a careful collection of the occasions on which it was particularly marked" (p. 154). Even after he discovered that the patient was fending off an incompatible idea, love for her brother-in-law, and after he revealed it to the patient, "It was a long time before these consolations of mine (attesting to her moral character) made any impression on her" (p. 270). The task then became one of overcoming, by "psychical work this resistance to association" (p. 270).

In 1912, Freud established the technical precept that we regard as the model for therapist as catalyst. He disclaimed omnipotence by comparing himself with the surgeon, Ambroise Paré, who described himself as a dresser of wounds, but not the curative force. Interestingly, Freud said about such technique that it "is the only one suited to my individuality" (p. 111). He cautioned against selection of material, stressing evenly suspended attention, for if the analyst follows his expectations he will discover nothing new, and if he follows his inclinations "he will certainly falsify what he may perceive" (p. 112).

While Freud was struggling toward accepting the patient's resistances as useful to the treatment, some of his writings betray the difficulties inherent in working through this monumental task of countertransference. In the lecture on *Resistance and Repression* (1916–17), he describes resistance in contradictory fashion. He calls a patient "to account for having broken the sacred rule" (p. 288); he views resistance with "pained astonishment" (p. 288); he uses metaphors about criminals and sanctuary; the resistance "is successfully defying us" (p. 289); he laments the fact that when "we succeed in extorting a certain amount of obedience to the fundamental technical rule from the resistance—[it] thereupon jumps over to another sphere" (p. 289). On the other hand, he says also that resistances should not be condemned; they provide the best support for analysis; there is dissatisfaction with the work if resistances are not forthcoming because working through the resistances is the essential function of psychoanalysis. "Resistance of neurotics to the removal of their symptoms became the basis of our dynamic view of the neuroses" (p. 292). While one cannot really measure the many difficulties in learning and development, surely one of the most arduous ones is the task of learning to respect the patient's resistances.

Whether we are dealing with neurosis or with more severe pathologies, the rule of interpretation—defense (and therefore resistance) before content—still applies. The problem is a clinical one: how to distinguish between defense against an id impulse that has become involved in intersystemic conflict, and the situation that obtains where there is insufficient organization (structuralization) for that to be possible. This reintroduces the issue already raised about transference. Now we ask, at what stage of development is the capacity for resistance attained? This is merely another facet of the success or failure of negotiation of the fulcrum. And, analogous to the capacity of the less-structured patient to engage in forms of relationship with the analyst that have not reached the status of the transferential capacity of the neurotic, resistance-like behavior in the borderline conditions may also be mistaken for the kinds of resistance possible in neurotic structures only. Clinical phenomena that appear similar can reflect problems arising from different developmental levels.

Let us illustrate first the use of psychoanalytic developmental psychology as it influences technique in the treatment of the better-structured personalities. We (1974) show that the familiar character manifestations thought to be derived from the anal phase may represent progressive developmental activity rather than regressive pathology—that the defenses established at the anal level may be used in the service of resistance, but that they are also victories for the ego in the sense that important skills are attained. The physical capabilities of the toddler increase dramatically simultaneous with the anal phase. Therefore, if we prefer to use the single term *anality,* we must now include within it psychic and physical maturation; conquest of bowel control; capacity to say No as a consequence of identification with the aggressor (Spitz); a level of object relations that allows for volition so that Yes will be said soon after No; a marked thrust into the practicing and rapprochement subphases; sound secondary narcissistic bodily cathexis; accelerated sense of separateness of self from object images; shift in the entire developmental fulcrum. Especially pertinent to discussion of anality is acquisition of the capacity to use defense mechanisms such as repression, reaction-formation, undoing.

In treating adult patients who have regressed to this level of development in the service of defense (resistance), we are dealing with a complex set of phenomena calling for sorting out the adaptive features that can be freed to promote development from the truly defensive and maladaptive ones. While we will also want to free the patient from the latter because they, too, are growth-encumbering, the technical issue is which to approach first and how to go about it. We (1974) propose an addendum to the analytic rule of defense before content—support of the developmental thrust before interpretation of conflict-bound resistances. Thus, in the treatment of neurosis proper—in our present example the anal character, anal regression, and obsessional neurosis—one would consider the developmental features as well as the defensive and treat each differently.

For these reasons, the technical decisions to be made when dealing with manifestations of oppositionalism, negativism, stubbornness, withholding, defiance, and the like are more complex than was heretofore thought. When withholding or refusal, for example, is partly in the service of growth and partly directed against the object as a hostile act, we have to support the one and interpret the other separately (G. Blanck, 1966), to acknowledge the developmental and adaptive aspects, the thrust toward growth, so that these will reinforce the therapeutic alliance by their very functioning.

The matter is even more complex when dealing with conflict such as in obsessional neurosis where, because the struggle is intersystemic, the object of hostility is the ego, as superego and id combine to punish it. Classical technique teaches us to wait it out, that the analyst will become the object of reproach when projection of the superego onto the analyst makes it appear as though he is the cruel superego. We think these prolonged, repetitious reproaches and the tedious waiting can be shortened if the matter is first approached from the developmental angle. We wonder whether the length of time involved in analysis of obsessional neurosis could be curtailed if the first approach to this matter is the adaptive one. Might we thus separate the growth aspects from the conflictual ones by acknowledging the function of the former in development, and could this militate toward attenuation of the harsh superego? We have known patients to be vastly relieved of guilt when we do not side with the superego by taking a pejorative view of stubborness, stinginess, negativism, and the like. We do not mean this as a corrective experience with a more benign parent figure; the degree of internalization in obsessional neurosis would preclude that. What we intend is to make the patient aware that his capacity to oppose is an exercise of volition, necessary for the child to employ and enjoy as part of his burgeoning sense of identity. This helps patients appreciate why they needed it then; to decide with their reasonable egos whether they still need the exercise to that extent now; it removes connotation of guilt from behavior that was once adaptive but has become maladaptive; it relieves the superego of those internalizations that are distorted because they were acquired prematurely and all too harshly. The conflict loses power and intensity, liberating the id aspects to be interpreted at the phallic-oedipal level sooner than heretofore as the analysis is relieved of some of the anxieties of the earlier psychosexual phase to which the patient has regressed.

The many movements toward and away from the analyst in the transference and transference neurosis as well as in the relationship formed by the less-structured patient have already been described. Much can be elaborated as we consider which are growth-promoting and which are truly hostile, negative, or otherwise object directed. We take first the basic rule. Is every breach of the rule a resistance? The neurotic patient, no less than the borderline, may have adaptive reasons for withholding associations. "I don't want to tell you about that now," may, in neurosis, represent an assertion of independence and not necessarily a blatant violation of the rule. One respects this by waiting. Some of the "rules" were promulgated before the discoveries of ego psychology; they hark back to the early days of analysis when Freud thought that the authority of the physician could carry the treatment. Even then, Freud did not insist upon immediate compliance. Although he made it clear (to the Rat Man, for example) that he could not abrogate the rule, he was forebearing about the timing. Tact in interpretation may be likened to patience about compliance with rules. The ego is freed to volunteer information without having its autonomy violated. This appears to state the obvious. Yet, the simple device of awaiting the patient's readiness, thus avoiding even the semblance of a challenge to autonomy, appears to some as a failure to deal with resistance. We recall here Freud's (1916–1917) own observation that resistance should not be condemned, his (1913) admonition against "express" interpretations, and Sharpe's (1950) impressive illustration of forebearance. Sharpe was an intuitive ego psychologist. She dealt patiently with the famous red handkerchief. Her patient brought the handkerchief to his session and, with elaborate ceremony, tied it around his head. Sharpe asked only, "Is the headache helped that way?" (p. 58). She then waited four weeks for the reason for this puzzling symbolic behavior to emerge. Her patience was rewarded when she learned that the red handkerchief was related to his wife's menstrual period. Because Sharpe had not pounced, the patient revealed his secret identification with his wife in his own good time, which was when it troubled him, not the analyst.

This connects with another proposition—that resistance and like phenomena, especially in borderline and narcissistic pathologies, more usually represent unsuccessful attempts at separation-individuation than opposition to the treatment. For example, a clinically sophisticated social worker already engaged in private practice seeks therapy, but is adamant about coming no more than twice a week. She says, 'A number of my friends have been 'analyzed' to their detriment, ending up, in my opinion, worse off than they were before." The obvious question arises. Why did she come to a therapist known to be an analyst? This has to remain unasked in order not to challenge, to buy time to diagnose differentially whether this move represents symbolic fear of engulfment or whether it is resistance derived from a later period of development. Even if it proves to be the latter, nothing is lost by avoiding a head-on confrontation; rather, much is gained by such attunement to the patient's communications.

We do not regard autonomy as synonymous with allowing patients to do anything they please. As defined by Hartmann (1950a), autonomy represents the relative freedom of the ego to function outside the area of conflict. A conflict-bound ego is incapable of rational decision, and we do the patient no favor if we are overpermissive about behavior that is likely to lead to real danger. This restricts acting out and impulse discharge.

To illustrate how we do use the concept of autonomy: A patient who bides his time before telling something to the analyst may have had an intrusive parent; the patient's behavior reflects fear of interference with processes of separation-individuation. In such instance, the patient needs the analyst to wait in order not to repeat the growth-retarding experience. Then volition is invoked to tell the analyst that which will contribute to cure. The not-too-severely impaired ego of the neurotic can expand if the peripheral (that is, other than transferential and interpretive) techniques of analysis take into account the vicissitudes of the subphases. While that is not the main subject of a chapter on resistance, it has its place here because it refers to resistance-like behavior that reflects moderate subphase inadequacy. Those not-too-impeding interferences with the requirements of the subphases correct themselves in analysis, just as they do developmentally, if the subsequent subphases have been adequate enough to bring them along in the long pull. We think again of the analyst as adopting, not a parental role but, rather, a catalytic one, that is, one which provides optimal opportunity for growth.

A rather common violation of the "rules" of analysis by the patient is "leaking" material outside of the session. In such instances, specific reasons for this behavior may consist simultaneously of a resistance, an acting out, a developmental thrust and a hostile defiance of the analytic rules, if not of the analyst. We think here of Freud's magnificent metaphor, although he used it in a different context—each rope holding the ship to the pier has to be untied one by one, but the journey does not get under way until the last rope is untied. Each aspect of the specific behavior has to be understood in its unique meaning and may not bring therapeutic gain until all are understood (see also chapter 7 on working through). To subsume all under the rubric of resistance is to underestimate the complexity of human behavior and is likely to be therapeutically ineffective. Candidates sometimes think that a correct interpretation before the fact can avert acting out. Some acting out is to be expected in the course of an analysis. Also, interpretation needs to be complete as well as correct (Glover, 1955). One pronouncement cannot encompass all the facets of behavior which appear in condensed form as a single resistance. As to the order of interpretation, it is worthwhile to repeat that the adaptive aspect is the one likely to gain the patient's self appreciation of his developmental thrust and is usually the most effective first intervention.

The following illustrates the uncovering of a resistance within a resistance:

The patient, familiar with the rules of analysis, told his wife a dream before arriving for his session. He gave the analyst the benefit of his wife's interpretation and the analyst asked whether he was pleased with it. This opened up a tirade against his wife; he had not told her the dream to solicit her interpretation; he had only wanted to use this method of fixing it in his mind so that he could remember it; she went too far and interfered with his analysis; she should have known better. Since he was not defending the "interpretation," the analyst could use the opportunity to explore the anxiety about forgetting the dream. Was it the usual one of attempting to overcome a resistance to the dream thoughts? But the patient went on, "If I don't bring a dream I have nothing to say." And so, by refraining from invoking the rule against telling another person one's dreams, a deeper layer of resistance was uncovered—namely, the attempt to use the dream as a resistance. Having waited, the analyst has arranged for the patient's self-confrontation, always more effective than confrontation from without. This case illustration also extends Freud's argument that resistances are the best supports of an analysis. While the earlier philosophy that resistances must be overcome is on the wane, it is not always clear that resistance is best resolved when the analyst does not oppose it; as Sharpe (1950) put it, we "go with the patient" (p. 32).

Resistance in neurosis is competently described in the literature and the techniques for dealing with it are carefully spelled out. We shall not cover that same ground again. We turn, rather, to resistance-like phenomena in the less-structured personalities. Since ego organization, in those patients, is not at the level where signal anxiety, defense mechanisms and countercathexis are in "working order," we look to how defenses are employed and especially to the clinical manifestations as they represent sometimes resistance and sometimes developmental thrust that can be mistaken for resistance.

Fusion of good and bad self and object images leads to consolidation of a higher level of self-object relations, and, as the organizing process proceeds past the fulcrum, capacity to use signal anxiety and higher level defense mechanisms also ensues along with the many other aspects of structuralization. In the borderline states, the individual does not possess these capacities and so less competent defensive maneuvers must be employed, especially regression (dedifferentiation) and withdrawal. As it appears clinically, withdrawal resembles the cold aloofness, sometimes termed *schizoid,* of the narcissistic arrangement whereby a pseudo self-sufficient self-object unit excludes other persons (see chapter 11). Similar in clinical appearance, but different in content, is the distancing of the patient who defends against the wish for symbiotic merger; attendant fear of loss of identity causes such patients to appear to be aloof. More morbid are those situations where quick attachments are made; there, defense is inoperative, and the person tries to merge with any potential need-gratifying object. In those circumstances, the layman tends to think of such persons as "outgoing," "sociable," and the like. Therapists know that such social behavior can be indicative of thin ego boundaries and almost limitless regression.

We offer a few clinical illustrations involving use of the telephone and other devices, hardly ever employed in the treatment of neurosis proper except where an appointment has to be changed and like "business" arrangements are conducted. Many borderline patients never think of telephoning the therapist, no matter how bad they feel. There are shadings, each one reflective of a different object relations flaw. In one instance, the object images may be lost as soon as the patient leaves the treatment room. We describe this kind of forgetting in chapter 2. In another case, object image obliteration may be a more active process powered by excessive hostility toward those images. In yet another variation, there might have been severe premature or abrupt disillusionment in the object, militating toward object loss (Jacobson). In cases where there is fear of loss of identity, the organizing process has gone astray earlier; then symbiotic need outweighs the gratification of separateness and independent functioning; defenses are minimal, as it would be logical for us to expect of patients whose levels of organization are lesser. Where there are prominent narcissistic features one has patiently to build sufficient trust so that "chinks" in the narcissistic armor begin to appear. The analyst must be alert to these and insinuate himself into them in order to become a part of the narcissistic unit (see also chapter 11).

A patient proudly presented herself as belonging to a large family. She was the eldest of three children of her father's first marriage, had grown up also with three children of her father's second wife, and with two half-siblings who were the product of this second marriage. In the name of strict discipline, the children were permitted no autonomy. The patient had made few decisions in life that were truly her own and had severe identity problems. Her real mother, who was overtly psychotic, was hospitalized after the birth of the second child. The patient was two years old when she experienced the birth of the sibling and the first of her mother's many hospitalizations. These hospitalizations were intermittent thereafter throughout our patient's childhood. She does not remember a distinct person who took care of the children, just unnamed babysitters. Mother returned home for a few years, during which time another sibling was born. Shortly after the patient's fifth birthday, the parents divorced, with the father acquiring custody of the children. She hardly ever saw her mother again. The mother died when the patient was seventeen. She attended the funeral and thus began some contact with the maternal grandmother who, representing the longed-for mother, seemed engulfing.

Between the ages of five and the time of presentation for treatment, she was charged with the care of the younger siblings and with household duties that seem beyond the capacity of a child. By age twelve she also helped in her father's business. Her education was entirely directed by him, the objective being that she would not marry but would be forever available to take care of the younger children as an adjunct to the stepmother.

Treatment began with to and fro movements which could be mistakenly characterized as ambivalent or resistant; our assessment of the organizing process is that it had not yet led to such capabilities. The patient wanted treatment but did not want to attend more than twice a week. We regard this, not as resistance, but as indicative of a lower-level defense. Many months later she verbalized her fear of "becoming dependent," a fear rather frequently expressed by patients for varying reasons. This patient had a narcissistic-like self-sufficiency in union with her father's omnipotence. The therapist never challenged her utter obedience to him in order not to deprive her of object connection and also to avoid creating a conflict of loyalities too early in treatment. For a while the father remained a god while the patient struggled against her growing need and attraction to the therapist's softness. Rather familiar to most therapists is the fact that such patients, while protesting against dependency, are quite dependent nevertheless. As treatment progressed beyond this point, the fear was expressed that the therapist would disappear just as her mother had. Bridges were built, especially around vacation times, using the telephone and "pieces of paper." She was told that she had not been able to talk with her mother while she was away in the hospital but she could talk with the therapist. (We do not advocate substituting a colleague in our absence because we see the main thrust of treatment as building solid self and object images with one consistent person.) She never telephoned, but cherished the slips of paper with the phone numbers as transitional objects. She said she felt secure just having them in her pocket.

Another device is the postcard, which we use sparingly with neurotic patients, but have found to be invaluable in cases such as these. On a two-week winter vacation, an innocuously worded card was sent after one week. Upon resuming treatment, the patient told the therapist how important the postcard had been. Just as she was reaching a point of despair and depression, the card arrived and buoyed her up. The object image was reestablished. A most valuable feature of a postcard is that it is postmarked with a place on the map that the patient can connect with in her mind. The therapist still exists, and there is a locus that helps expand the object image to include a geographic area that is real. In these ways the therapist establishes continuity of self and object images and begins to enter into the formerly "closed shop" of the narcissistic unit as a consistent, reliable, dependable catalyst for development.

Suddenly, the patient began arriving late for her sessions. To have regarded this as resistance as it is traditionally defined would have been damaging. The therapist took it as a stepping away. The patient grinned as it was acknowledged as such—her first unopposed expression of independence. It was a triumph of the therapeutic relationship that she became confident enough to venture into behavior that resembled a belated practicing subphase.

More traditionally, lateness is regarded as resistance, including negativism, withholding, obsessional ambivalence, hostility, destructive opposition, and the like. Clinical experience also discloses that latecoming can represent a struggle between libidinal and aggressive needs as we are using those terms to connote union and independence. One patient habitually arrived late even if there were only five or ten minutes left to the session. Often enough, this was because of faulty reality testing, in that the wish to have the session overrode the reality of how long it would take to get there. However, as he said, it was so good for him to touch home base that he didn't mind making the effort even if that left him with only a few minutes of the therapist's time. Another patient described how his ego was not in control of his behavior. "I was thinking about the hour and looking forward to it while my feet carried me onto the wrong train." Exploration of the theme of lateness was discontinued by the therapist. Surprisingly, the patient began to initiate discussion of lateness when he no longer felt it to be the therapist's concern. The therapist's purpose was to maintain libidinal ties; by avoiding harassing the patient about his tardiness, not only was his need for independence affirmed but the patient was relieved of fruitless and puzzling discussion which could only evoke feelings of failure, since the patient did not have the capacity to deal with that issue. M. Ross (1976) quotes a psychotic patient who tells us an important truth, "Why is it that you psychiatrists always think that what is important to you is important to the patient?" (p. 316).

In another case the patient became sufficiently curious about latecoming herself and even asked for an additional hour per week in order to have more time to consider what she now experienced as her own problem. One young man found it possible to arrive closer to the appointed time and one day remarked appreciatively how much more we were able to accomplish with more time. The analyst recognized this as selective identification, since he had used the same phraseology much earlier in suggesting that more could be accomplished with more time. It did not seen desirable to remind the patient that he was echoing the analyst, but merely to welcome the aggressive thrust by which the patient claimed the thought as his own.

The importance of distinguishing affect from drive (chapter 2) is illustrated by the following: A patient thought to have had experienced a barely adequate symbiotic phase began treatment largely in silence frequently punctuated by angry outbursts. To view such outbursts and silences as manifestations of hostile aggression and resistance overlooks the fact that libidinal needs brought this patient to treatment. When regarded as affective reactions, the residues of ungratified libidinal phase and subphase needs, there is opportunity to respond to those needs, not necessarily in the form in which the patient demands, but certainly in acknowledgment of their existence and pressure upon him.

The following experience with the silence of a patient illustrates how complex these issues are and how necessary it is to view silences from many standpoints. At first the patient's silences were caused by rage reactions typical of her impulsiveness; indeed, it was the failure of impulse control that brought this woman to treatment. Aware of how tenuous was the therapeutic alliance, the therapist helped the patient to begin the hour, breaking the silence himself. The therapist cannot know the reason for the silence and does not venture assumptions that will be experienced as wild guesses, although he may feel the pressure of the patient's silent wish that he guess what is on her mind. He helps her in steps which serve increasingly to "zero in" on precisely why she does not speak. First, "Shall I help you start?" This was welcomed by the patient and that informed the therapist that she needed outside support to mobilize her organizing capacities. After some sessions the question became, "Do you still need my help?" This begins to turn over the task of organization to the patient by implying that she may be able to take on that task. As the patient responded more favorably to the expectation that she could do it, the intervention became, "Now you try." The autonomous organizing capacity has been promoted and will continue to operate more effectively as treatment proceeds.

As the therapist continued with carefully considered interventions designed to lead, gradually, to increasing the patient's capacity to take over and to stretch her frustration tolerance as well, the balance shifted; ultimately the task of beginning the treatment session devolved upon the patient. Her intellectual acceptance of the appropriateness of the goal did not deter her from testing the therapist's readiness to hold to it, and this culminated in a totally silent hour, after which the struggle ended. Later, the silences took on a different quality. She liked a moment to think, to savor an interchange, to experience some symbiotic oneness; at other times she was silent without knowing why. Ultimately, these issues were dealt with by means of a formula worked out between patient and therapist. "Are you stuck, do you need my help, or do you just need more time?" These invoked the patient's participation in working on what the silence was about.

We (1974) described the silent patient and reviewed the classical literature that classifies silence as a form of resistance, and so we repeat only briefly here that reasons for silence, such as the need to be together without words, have little to do with the kind of silence traditionally thought to represent repression or suppression of hostile thoughts toward the analyst. Thus, psychoanalytic developmental psychology forces reconsideration of the concept of resistance to exclude those behavioral manifestations classically regarded as such, but which really present opportunity to use the drives and affects for structure building and for strengthening self and object images by means of promoting selective identification. Under many such circumstances, compliance with the fundamental rule may represent simple obedience rather than volition or the exercise of autonomy. Engaging the patient in the therapeutic task may be viewed, in and of itself, as promoting the identification process. An observing ego is born as the patient begins to grasp that the analyst is not the primary ungratifying object. The reality of the nonhostile analyst serves ego dominance over hostile affect by establishing that there can be gratifying experience; this tends to weaken the barrier of hostility that had hindered developmental progress, and it frees both drives to begin the upward spiral.

After a period of positive affective reactions from such patients, one may again expect renewed hostile responses. These, however, couched within the framework of an ongoing libidinal relationship, resemble the negative tinge which Kris (1956b) describes as heralding the "good hour." Aggression in the form of attenuated negativism serves separation needs. These are actually aggressively tinged movements designed to undo connections on one level in order to form more internalized connections on the next. Therefore, the therapist encourages the forward thrust. An ever-spiralling effort is promoted as selective identifications replace the external object in ever greater degree. The patient begins to live more in the structure and can, in the most prognostically hopeful situations, acquire signal anxiety and, with it, capacity for defense and resistance. For the less structured patient, the therapeutic alliance constitutes a relationship in which the major technical task is to illuminate the affective distortions caused by subphase inadequacies arising from the relationship with the primary object. Since the interactive experience itself plays a more important part in the therapuetic process where organization is deficient, the therapist uses himself within the therapeutic alliance.

Moore and Fine (1967) define the therapeutic alliance as: "A positive basic relationship between analyst and patient [that] has to be maintained to safeguard the analytic situation if a successful resolution of the *transference neurosis* is to be achieved" (p. 15).

We would extend that definition to include a relationship of positive affective valence for the patient within a context of the therapist's awareness of the subphase inadequacies and consequent developmental distortions. This equips the therapist to avoid replication in the treatment relationship of damaging object relations from the past. In this way the therapeutic alliance becomes the very tool to work with the patient's "resistances." Instead of working against them, or even of interpreting them, the desirable technique is to demonstrate that they were appropriate, that is adaptive, in the past. This will clarify their present inappropriateness. Part of the therapeutic experience consists of the therapist's interaction with the patient in finding the maladaptations. This is to be distinguished from interpretation of transference resistance in the more structured patient. As long ago as 1916, Freud counted it as a great success when the patient could be induced to take the analyst's view and to reckon with the existence of resistance. In this, he did not, of course, distinguish between resistance and the lower-level defensive behavior we are here describing, but he did indeed understand the therapeutic alliance.

These considerations have the purpose of suggesting that resistance-like transference and other behavioral manifestations in the therapeutic situation are best understood within the context of psychoanalytic developmental psychology if we are to find their specific rationale. We need the patient's participation to accomplish this. In classical psychoanalysis, the patient's participation is assured by the analytic compact whereby the patient accepts the fundamental rule. Assumed there is the existence of an unmodified ego and ability truly to accept the method, as distinguished from compliance. In the more severe pathologies, autonomous participation cannot be expected. The therapy cannot rely upon structuralized identifications and relatively differentiated, evenly cathected whole self and object representations because these do not yet exist but constitute the very areas where ego building is required. The therapist is thrust into a replicating role powered possibly not by the repetition compulsion so much as by ungratified or overly gratified and certainly distorted needs that have their pathogenic origins in the subphases. As in the transference neuroses, the therapist avoids gratifying inappropriate needs. Different, however, is that appropriate reparative work, not needed by neurotic patients, can be accomplished with the borderline patient. Essential to that goal is that resistance-like behavior be distinguished from resistance proper and that different techniques be employed to deal with each.

CHAPTER 10

Dreams: The Royal Road to Preverbal Life

When Freud (1900) discovered that dreams include something from the present (day residue) and something from the past (infantile life), his interest lay in retrieving memory of that part of infantile life that hovers around the oedipal period. Yet, in his analysis of the Wolf Man he recovered a memory from the second year of life through a dream that occurred at age four. For the most part, however, preverbal life is blanketed by amnesia. Mahler (1975) quotes A. Frank who refers to preverbal life as "the unrememberable and the unforgettable" (p. 197). The concept of an organizing process clarifies that well-known fact. Only with time and development do memory traces gradually become organized and attain continuity. Further, in order to be able to tell the analyst or therapist even a remembered experience, some capacity for symbolization and a level of object relations including semantic communication would have to obtain for experience to be cathected to words. That is different from the psychotic use of words as things without cathexis to experience or to objects.

Freud thought that the very purpose of analysis is to bring infantile amnesia out of repression. But he meant, not the amnesia of preverbal life, but of the oedipal verbal period. Although psychoanalysis has become far more than uncovering alone, analysts are adept at the techniques required for that process. That they may be less so in dealing with the amnesia of early life is because the process itself is more difficult and often impossible. Early experience is not forgotten, nor is it repressed. It has not been processed through an organized structure and, therefore, is not retrievable in the same way as is later experience. Freud's work with the Wolf Man had the thrust of finding the single event, in that instance the primal scene, but the recovery of that event was by means of reconstruction, not anticathexis to lift memory from repression.

Now it seems more logical, in the light of what we know about the organizing process, to focus our efforts not on real occurrences, for the most part, but rather on the resultants of the interaction in the dyad. These are more likely to appear clinically in the form of character, impaired structuralization, behavior, replication or transference and, of course, in dreams, as has always been implied in dream theory. That is not to overlook that there may have been outstanding events that, in themselves, have affected the organizing process—birth of a sibling, prolonged absence, illness or death of a parent, and other trauma.

We reserve for chapter 12 the techniques for seeking out the effects of preverbal experiences as they appear in these other clinical manifestations in order to focus here on preverbal life in dreams. The psychoanalytic truism that nothing is ever lost applies not only to the repressed, but to every aspect of life, even the earliest. It only remains for us to develop techniques for seeking them out. There, more than in any other area of technique, we are at the bare beginning.

We are most familiar, out of our own memories and dreams and those of the more intact patients, with disparate memories from the preverbal period that are often condensations of experience or screen memories. Persons with coherent structure usually report dreams as dreams; they know where the dream begins and ends and can distinguish clearly between dreaming and the waking state. The borderline patient whose development hovers around the fulcrum sometimes knows and sometimes does not know where sleep ceases and waking life begins. Where distinction is hazy, it is preferable not to attempt to work on the dream, but on supporting the organizing process to enable the ego to retrieve and retain its foothold in the higher levels of its organization. This will bring the patient to the position where his dreams more resemble the dreams of the neurotic patient. Then they are analyzable in the manner that has long been familiar.

The principal purpose of ego-building therapy is to further structuralization and organization. When these reach higher levels, interpretation becomes the therapeutic tool of choice, as it has always been in neurosis, and for the same reason—there is a competent ego that can include the interpretation within its organization. In working with the borderline patient many dreams often presented over a long period of time have to go by the board. Forbearance is usually rewarded. One works on structuralization (ego building) in many ways simultaneously, depending almost entirely on the material that the patient brings—one day a dream, another day an event in the present, still another day a demand for replication. Ego-building technique seizes whatever material comes to hand, with the degree to which the fulcrum has been negotiated always in mind. Interpretation is in order when the fulcrum is balanced in the direction of neurosis, while the technique that we, in chapter 12, define and describe as *explanation* is more appropriate when the balance is toward less structuralization. In many borderline situations, especially at the outset, one "sacrifices" the incoherent dream in favor of first building the ego. This is not really a sacrifice to those who do not overvalue dreams. As we pointed out in 1974, the Via Reggia is not the only road. That does not except the road to preverbal life. There are other avenues to preverbal experience. To stay within the metaphor, we make many trips to Rome in the treatment of all structures, sometimes by one route and sometimes by another. Yet, with respect to very early experience, no less than to the repressed, dreams remain the royal road. Let us begin with a broad example:

A patient dreams that he wants to get somewhere in a hurry. He feels unsteady on his feet, falls, crawls, stands upright again. Try as he might, he cannot proceed to his destination as fast as he would like, while others around him pass by at a rapid pace.

We deliberately omit explication of this specific case because we wish to use this dream for generalization. Probably it would be an oversimplification in any adult case to take the dream as referring only to the time of life when locomotion was uncertain. There are three major themes—frustration, incompetence, and a goal that cannot be reached. Every dream is, by definition, a regression. On high levels of organization, such a dream would be used defensively, employing symbolization and condensation. Unquestionably, the patient was at a stage of unsteady locomotion at one time in his life and felt frustrated then. By condensation and regression, later frustrations are anchored to that early one. We use this dream here because it shows so clearly how preverbal life may be depicted in a dream. We are left only to ponder why this patient used an unrememberable time of life as the manifest content of his dream. To answer that, we would have to know the patient and to work with his associations to the dream. On an oedipal level it would perhaps represent feelings of incompetence in comparison with rivals who perform better; in the transference it might refer to the analyst or therapist as more able; as a resistance it might express, by reversal, reluctance to speed the treatment; knowing the patient, one might refer it to phallic, anal or even oral psychosexual levels. Whatever the appropriate interpretation, factors of organization, structure, therapeutic goal, transference versus object replication, resistance versus lesser capacity, and the like are involved in the preverbal experience that appears in the dream. It cannot be taken simplistically as an expression of that experience per se, but as condensed with later frustrations and other factors. This illustrates and describes the very essence of the concept of ego as organization. Some of the first feelings of incompetence, frustration and competition work their way into later levels of experience and appear in dreams as organized with later elaborations of similar themes. Lipton argues that it is unnecessary to uncover the precise initial experience. With that we can agree, but probably on different ground. Usually it is not possible to "uncover" a preverbal experience as an event. Even in the rare instances where it might be possible, the information would be of little therapeutic value because what actually happened matters less than the outcome of the event as it combined with the environmental feature to become organized in the psyche. We need to know at what level of organization the event occurred; how it was influenced by previous organization and how it, in turn, has invaded next higher levels of organization.

The next dream illustrates the uncertainty between sleeping and waking states in the third year of treatment of a patient who had lifelong night terrors. She begins better to be able to distinguish night from day as she tells the dream in the presence of the therapist who has worked on repair of the unfavorable balance between negative and positive cathexis. The patient's mother was rigid, unfeeling, unempathic. She had left the patient alone as a child to put herself to bed as soon as she had the physical competence to go to her room, undress herself, and get into bed. She used to lie awake for hours and, when she slept, had nightmares. She tells a current dream:

Patient: I had two dreams last night. You were in one. The only thing I remember about that one is that it was the end of a session. I'm not sure now whether I dreamt this. Did we shake hands at the end of the session yesterday?

Therapist: Let's defer answering that until we understand your dream. (They had not shaken hands, nor is that the usual procedure unless before and after a long vacation or other special circumstance.)

Patient: It was a dream. (The therapist does not take on the task of sharpening reality testing because, having worked toward this with the patient for so long, the timing seems ripe to allow the patient to try to clear this up for herself now. She is able to do so easily when the therapist holds off, not in utter silence, but by deferring an answer in order to give the patient a chance to work it out, and yet also extending hope that there would be help if the patient could not do it alone.)

Patient: In the dream you kissed me on the cheek, as though to say goodnight. Then I became frightened because maybe it meant that the treatment was ending. In the second dream a hideous looking monster appeared. It looked at me and said, "Don't be afraid, I'm not going to hurt you."

Therapist: Let's listen to what occurs to you about the dream. (The therapist puts it in the singular to convey that the two dreams are one without explaining dream theory.)

Patient: This is the first time a monster was friendly in the dream. Makes me feel good.

Therapist: So now you have a good monster and that makes *you* good too. (The design is to stress that both object and self images are becoming more benign.)

Patient: But then I worry that the treatment will end. (A common fear of borderline patients who are improving. As the aggressive drive powers the progressive thrust of the separation-individuation process, separation anxiety ensues.)

Therapist: Why would it end just when you find a good monster?

Patient: Oh, gee, the monster must be you.

Therapist: I think you're right. Why do I appear as any kind of monster though?

Patient: You also kiss me goodnight. My mother never did that.

Therapist: You're afraid you'll feel good about yourself and me but it won't last?

Patient: Yeah. That's it. (Reassurance would not be helpful here. The patient has to endure her separation anxiety in the context of the ongoing treatment that remains constant.)

Therapist: We still have not solved why I'm a monster.

Patient: It doesn't sound flattering.

Therapist: Oh, but I'm a kind monster. Try to imagine how a baby feels looking up at a giant of an adult.

Patient: Oh, yeah.

Therapist: And when she doesn't make you feel good she's a bad monster.

Patient: Yeah, yes, um.

Therapist: But she must have made you feel good once in a while or

> you wouldn't be able to dream about it. She may even have said some nice things to you.

The therapist ventures this because he leans on dream theory. The spoken word in a dream has been heard before; the therapist connects that in his own mind with the thought that infants in the latter part of the first year often understand speech even though they cannot yet speak. Also, the patient is far from psychotic. The assumption is that symbiotic and some subphase experience was adequate. The therapist wants to firm up the good self-object experiences in the dyad. This may be done only when there is considerable certainty, lest we give the patient a false biography.

Another patient dreams that she has a pain in her mouth. She says, spontaneously, that it must have felt that way when the breast was taken away. It is better to take this with some skepticism and with close self-examination lest the therapist's interest in preverbal experience has been somehow conveyed to a compliant patient. But the association is to be taken seriously nevertheless.

A homosexual man dreams that his legs are being sawed off by a woman.[1] He associates to a woman he knows who, in reality, uses a saw in her work. The therapist, a woman, has to think about transference or object replication. She asks the patient about the affect during the dream or after it. There was none. It seems unlikely that a man at the phallic level would not feel anxious if this were, as appears from the manifest content, truly a castration dream. The affect in the dream might well refer to another matter, but patients usually report something like, "I had a terrible dream," which are the feelings that occur upon wakening.

Therapist: Both legs?
Patient: Yes, why do you ask?
Therapist: What would happen to you if you had no legs?
Patient: I wouldn't be able to walk.

[1]Dream contributed by Jane Hall.

Therapist: Why is a woman doing that to you?
Patient: You know, my mother never let me do anything. She was so afraid I'd get hurt. I have always been afraid of any kind of physical activity. I never had a bike or played ball. Gym classes were hell to get through.
Therapist: Do you think you dream that your legs are sawed off so that you won't have to do these things?
Patient: That's an idea.
Therapist: A woman is doing it. Is she a carpenter? (The therapist has to determine whether the dream figure is a man disguised by the dream work as a woman, that is, whether the castrating father is concealed, or whether the object relationship is preponderantly dyadic.)
Patient: No. She's a window dresser really.
Therapist: What does she look like?
Patient: She has short cropped hair and wears jeans all the time.
Therapist: I have short hair.
Patient: Yes, it might be you.
Therapist: What am I doing to you?
Patient: Protecting me. I just thought cropped hair, cropped legs, making me resemble you. Oh, and that woman is a dyke. (Self-images are not well distinguished from object images of an omnipotent phallic mother who is, paradoxically, also castrated.)
Therapist: What am I protecting you from?
Patient: I'd never leave you. I wouldn't be able to walk out of here.
Therapist: Would that be all good?
Patient: I'd probably get to hate you.

Thus, working with the dream has arrived at the etiology and level of homosexuality. One does not interpret as a fact that, very likely, the malformation in organization results from the mother-child interaction in the practicing subphase. One can only reconstruct in one's own mind, to await further evidence, that this man's mother, already in his practicing subphase, interfered with the main purpose of that subphase. The interacton resulted in compliance, absorption into his self images of her anxiety, and intense rage. Since blurred self and object images still exist, normally, at that developmental phase, distinction of gender identity became too difficult. The relationship with the therapist has the quality of object replication, not transference, as shown by the wish to repeat the experience of being merged with the object. It is interesting to note that the therapist elicited the affect, rage, in order to capture, in the replication, that forgotten aspect of the interaction. It will serve the therapy well to have that fact in the open henceforth for it explains the compliance, passivity and homosexuality in terms of the impact on organization of thwarted developmental thrust. Castration anxiety, also, is symbolized by the sawed-off legs, but therapeutic intervention on that level is best postponed until more work with the malformation in organization revealed by this dream helps the patient reach higher levels. There is hope, in the very long run, of treating the homosexuality directly, or that it may be subsumed in the developmental thrust.

A young woman whose pathology appears also to be derived from inability to negotiate the fulcrum successfully, dreams that she is in the living room of her parent's home:

> I was sitting in a chair. A little girl maybe two or three years old was holding me. My mother was standing in the middle of the room with her back to me. The little girl suddenly turned away from me and walked over to my mother. She pulled at her dress to get her attention, but my mother just looked at her indifferently. After a while the little girl turned away from my mother, came back to me and put her head in my lap. Then I found myself in a bathroom flushing the toilet and was afraid that I'd be flushed down too.[2]

The patient identifies both little girls as herself. She attempts to function in a maternal, comforting role towards herself but does not succeed. The manifest dream, including the action and the age of the child, suggests rapprochement disappointment. The patient said that she had been told that she was an unresponsive

[2]Dream contributed by Rena Shadmi.

child. The manifest dream can lead only to an hypothesis that is useful for the therapist to have in mind. It is not interpretable yet, but perhaps can be used in an interpretation of object replication as opportunity presents itself in the therapeutic relationship. When it does, the therapist will be alert to it and will be able to use it to help the patient encompass the rapprochement disappointment in a new way. Because we are on uncertain ground here, the therapist should not proceed hastily. Not only do we need more evidence; also to be encompassed is the reported childhood unresponsiveness. Was it a flaw in the inborn capacity to extract? Possibly, although that usually so impairs the symbiotic experience that psychosis is the outcome. Had the child become unresponsive because of maternal aloofness? Was it the mother's projection and rationalization for her own coldness? This cannot be answered yet; it will have to await developments in the therapy.

The following is a story told by a psychotic adolescent. Because his thinking is largely in the primary process, it has the status of a dream. It illustrates how early, preverbal life can be reconstructed. It is especially useful because we find in it information that neither the patient nor the mother would have been able to provide from memory.

> There was a spider who spun a large web and caught a fly. The fly was about to be eaten. Someone came along and smashed the web, spider, fly and all.[3]

The mother is identified as the spider and the father as the fly. The mother is known to function in the symbiotic mode even in her current relationship with son and husband. Her parasitic symbiotic needs are in very large measure responsible for the boy's psychosis. The passive father is content with the marital relationship because it fulfills his own symbiotic needs.

The story reveals that the father failed in his function of rescuer of the toddler from the symbiotic unit. Normally, this should have taken place somewhere in the second year of life.

[3]Material provided by Dr. Carolyn Saari at a case presentation to the senior faculty at the Smith College School for Social Work.

The patient does not know this theoretically, of course, but explains it with dramatic clarity in his story. Also evident is his unmitigated rage and wish to destroy both primary objects because they have failed him in his aborted developmental thrust.

Finally, we present a dream that illustrates how the phallic-oedipal position is barely reached by an organization that is not equal to the tasks of that phase. In this case, the phallic-oedipal material, including dreams, resonates with residues from the subphases that impaired oedipal resolution. The patient is a man, thirty-four years old, single. He would like to marry but is fearful of sex. He comes from an intact family. The father was neither very encouraging of masculine identification and strivings, nor did he impede them too severely. The mother was a haven whenever there was the slightest disappointment, frustration, anxiety. The therapist pictures her in her mind as a mother hen with her wings always open, always available for her son, not leaving opportunity for him to work out coping mechanisms for life's small hurts. There were no major trauma such as separations, illnesses, nor even much negative affective experiences. Typical of the blandness is that, when the son came home from the Korean War, the parents had theater tickets and so they went on with their business as usual while he spent his first evening at home alone. The therapist is a woman.

The session begins in a desultory way. "I have nothing to say." The therapist waits a short while.

Patient: Now I remember a dream. It's vague. Something about a piece of furniture. I'm holding onto it. I think I should save it in case there's a fire.

Associations: When I think of holding onto something I think of my genitals. (Pause.) Last week I was ready to give them up in order to be like you.

Therapist: The problem is how to be close to me and retain your masculinity. (Because of tendency to merge self and object images.)

Patient: The danger of fire comes in. If I get close I'll get

	aroused, too hot. It's dangerous. I don't know what the danger would be.
Therapist:	Whatever your associations tell you.
Patient:	I'd get stuck in you.
Therapist:	Why?
Patient:	I guess the wish to be close.
Therapist:	How's that?
Patient:	I wouldn't want to let go. (Here we see the double layer of holding onto genitals at the phallic level and to maternal object at a more regressed level.) Part of me would want to stay there and I wouldn't be able to get away.
Therapist:	(To emphasize the progressive wish.) But you'd also want to get away.
Patient:	You and I would be stuck together. Then I'd want to get out. Then I'll want to be back again. It's circular.
Therapist:	Can you get yourself out of that cycle? (Mother did not let him struggle alone.)
Patient:	Once I get in I can't get out. That's what's happening right now. I can't think of a way out. I feel like leaving. (Session is far from over.)
Therapist:	Maybe there's another way.
Patient:	If I stay I'll get unbearably anxious.
Therapist:	Try. It may not be as unbearable as you expect, and we might learn something.

The patient found he could endure more anxiety than he thought. Hopefully, this will lessen the need for maternal protection and help him find his own resources. Later, it will serve him to cope with castration anxiety proper.

In this case preverbal experience was not retrieved directly. The therapist worked with the entirety of subphase interaction, repairing those aspects that impeded growth, particularly the mother's provision of a defensive haven that failed to equip him for dealing with conflict.

While dreams constitute but one of several pathways to recovery of preverbal experience, with increasing skill in this relatively unexplored use of dreams they may well become the most important pathway. Dreams are analyzed daily in terms of recovery of postverbal memories and of the spoken word; it takes but one small step to apply that which we know about dream theory to preverbal life. Loewald (1977) describes the meaning of the analyst's verbal communications to the patient as follows:

> verbal interpretation itself, the mainstay of psychoanalytic intervention, takes on connotations and aspects of meaningfulness—of which we as analysts need to be aware—that derive from or hark back more directly to that "magical" power and significance of words which play a predominant role in the preverbal and early verbal period of life and in the resonance and responses of the young child to parental verbal material.[4]

There is but a short period of life when the child, still in the dozing, coenesthetic state, protected by the stimulus barrier, is unresponsive to words. Even though the child cannot repeat them yet, he hears words spoken around and to him. Thus preverbal life is short indeed, for it only precedes the infant's first verbal auditory experiences. It is in that sense that Loewald refers to verbal experience as first emanating from the parents' communications to the child. It explains why patients tend to place so much emphasis upon the "magic" of interpretation. So far as dreams are concerned, it does not require revision of dream theory to search for preverbal experience, only for revision of our thinking about when verbal life begins. Beyond that, it calls for a searching therapeutic ear attuned to reflections of early life as they appear in dreams as well as in other material.

[4]Unpublished paper presented at the Margaret S. Mahler Symposium, Philadelphia.

CHAPTER 11

Pathological Narcissism and the Borderline Conditions

Pathological narcissism reflects deficiencies in the simultaneous and mutually enhancing elaboration of self and object esteem. The specific form of the pathology is the outcome of the manner in which the organizing process proceeds as it is forced now to include within it the consequences of affront to development at particular levels. Therefore the secret of narcissism and the borderline conditions is not to be sought in behavioral manifestations, but only in developmental vicissitudes. It follows, then, that neither the borderline conditions nor pathological narcissism are, in themselves, diagnostic entities, nor is narcissism merely a diagnostic feature but, rather, a developmental one.

Pathological Narcissism

Narcissism has been considered in its normal developmental aspects. Now we search out its pathogenicity which we continue to suggest is best understood when studied within the developmental frame of reference. It does not yield its secret readily, as Freud's struggles with it testify. His repeated attempts at understanding led him to think of narcissism in many ways—to link narcissism with libido theory, to separate sexual libido from ego libido, to see narcissism as reflected in the narcissistic neuroses (psychoses), in megalomania, in homosexuality. Libido theory alone sheds very dim light indeed. Nor did it help matters greatly when the dual drive theory was added. The mystery of narcissism is broader than drive theory alone. It reflects vicissitudes of drive maturation, of affect development, structuralization, and internalization as a whole. It is an intimate and inseparable aspect of the organizing process itself.

In normal development, repeated experiences of tension reduction form clusters of undifferentiated self-object images cathected with positive affect. Already in the symbiotic phase there is pathogenic potential if symbiosis is not sufficiently gratifying to evoke such positive cathexis. Deficiency may be the consequence of mismatching because of inadequacy on either or both sides of the dyad. These vicissitudes arise from the incapacity of the infant to enter the symbiotic unit, from an imbalance in the differentiating drive configuration, from inadequacy stemming from the maternal contribution to the dyad, or from combinations of all of these. Such incapacities make for failure in the fitting-together that Hartmann (validated by Mahler) regarded as so essential that it even takes precedence over the process of adaptation. An optimally gratifying union with the primary object promotes a gradual shift of cathexis to the exterior in anticipation of tension reduction and pleasurable experiences emanating from the object world. The smiling response has been used repeatedly to exemplify this dramatic turn to the outside. We may designate such nodal points as embryonic self-object love, differentiation of self and object images having not yet begun. The still-merged self and object images benefit from positive affective reactions and, in pathogenic circumstances, suffer from insufficiency of them. As differentiation proceeds to next higher levels, a balance of libido and aggression is necessary to maintain continuous libidinal connection, while aggressive thrusts toward separation propel the individual ever forward toward psychological birth. The capacity to deal with normal separation anxiety is best developed when there is an even balance between the drives. Then "bite-sized" (Tolpin, 1971) movement toward independence and mastery becomes tolerable, especially because accompanied by self-soothing mechanisms acquired by means of selective identifications.

As development is continuous, so is pathogenic threat. An arbitrary pause to describe pathogenicity is analogous to the moment when a movie projector brings the motion picture to a still for close inspection. These "stills" at certain developmental levels within the continuous motion help to clarify how pathological narcissism looks at its inception at different levels of organization. This states also that we do not regard such pathology as stable but rather the result of malformations that can ensue anywhere along the growth continuum. Development proceeds nonetheless but now includes in its progress distorted effects in organization. This position leaves open the possibility that distortion may accompany other developmental failures, may be overshadowed by them, or may be pulled into a state of remission by later developmental successes. Our view of the configurations that are called *narcissistic personality disturbance* (Kohut, 1971) and *borderline personality organization* (Kernberg, 1975) rests upon the understanding that development is so complex, multifaceted, and subject to influence, both positively and negatively, by so many factors, that diagnostic categories tend to obscure our understanding of the pathological development and how to treat it. To see pathology as the result of organizational malformations asserts that stability is a consequence of the organizing process. Viewed in this light, pathologically narcissistic configurations and borderline conditions can be regarded as uneasy attempts at adaptation. Narcissistic disorders appear in protean form. Jacobson (1966) describes the cold, narcissistic grandiosity in schizophrenia. Grandiosity is also descriptive of the practicing subphase toddler, to designate only one developmental phase where such narcissism is normal in childhood.

In a developmental scheme, no single phase or subphase can

be designated as the seat of narcissistic pathogenicity. Mahler correlates specific forms of narcissistic and borderline vulnerability with inadequate development within the several subphases of separation-individuation. She regards each subphase as making its particular contribution to normal or pathological narcissism. Bodily libidinal supplies are especially necessary during the symbiotic phase and the differentiation and practicing subphases. At the practicing subphase, self-love, primitive valuation of accomplishment and omnipotence contribute to narcissistic formation and are normal and necessary to further development. They are vulnerable to subphase inadequacy. The rapprochement subphase has been described as even more delicate. There is continuing reliance upon "subphase adequate mothering" if narcissism is to develop normally.

Narcissism takes pathological forms not only when there is affront to its phase-specific developmental formations but also if it fails to proceed as it should in equal balance with its partner, object love. If one side of this dual unit of ongoing development should outpace the other, the organizing process will henceforth proceed in pathological directions. Self esteem, if sacrificed in favor of excessive valuation of the object, will remain fixated in primitive form while organization, now skewed, will proceed nonetheless toward disturbances in identity formation. If the imbalance is in the other direction, narcissism will grow in exaggerated form at the expense of capacity to love and will reflect, in adulthood, its infantile distortions.

Narcissism has been so baffling to investigators, even to one with Freud's clinical acuity and keen theoretical mind, for two reasons: 1) The very nature of the pathological narcissistic arrangement is such that it has been all but impervious to attempts at therapeutic intervention, and 2) It has its beginnings in early, preverbal life and therefore yields its secrets in language which we were, until recently, unable to comprehend. Now that we are in a better position, clinically, to understand reflections of preverbal experience as they appear in the therapeutic situation, we can begin to think about the early origins of pathological narcissistic formations.

The following is an attempt to correlate the origin of pathological narcissistic formations with levels of affront to ego organization.

Within the borderline range, the most virulent form of pathological narcissism has its origin in the symbiotic phase as the result of a too-meager gratification of symbiotic need. Usually, in such cases, there may have been enough gratifying symbiosis to avert psychosis but barely enough to propel the infant "with both feet" into the separation-individuation phase. The opposite circumstance may also lead to pathological narcissism and to other borderline conditions. What Mahler terms *parasitic symbiosis,* the result of overly prolonged and overly gratifying symbiosis because of a pathological need on the maternal side of the dyad, prevents "hatching" from the symbiotic membrane. In such pathogenic circumstances, development along many lines is blunted. As every need is anticipated, as the child's mind appears to her or him to be read obviating the necessity to verbalize, as the object is ever available—even too close physically—ego boundaries remain blurred and ego skills develop poorly. In such instances, realistic self-evaluation is obscured. Entry into the subphases is retarded.

Jacobson describes the need, at some midway point in the process of self-object differentiation, to maintain a temporary, developmentally normal illusion of parental omnipotence. With normal development, this illusion gradually yields to reality testing if the situation is conducive to exposure to reality in small and therefore tolerable doses. Then one can bear the fact that the parents are not all good and omnipotent. We cited Mahler's data in this same regard to show how the child, at this stage, splits the object images into all positive and all negative because it serves development to maintain good object images separate from bad for the purpose of buying developmental time. If the life circumstance permits formation of solidly established positive object cathexes, these provide the cushion which absorbs gradual doses of negative object experiences. In such fortunate circumstances, the child can afford, so to speak, to permit and tolerate inclusion of the negative object images into the representation of a single person. Simultaneous with such fusion of the good and bad object images the self images also cohere.

In less than such optimal situations, splitting, which had begun as a normal developmental phenomenon, tends to persist and development tends to become fixated at this level because the good object images have to be preserved. This is because, if there is developmental affront somewhere midway along the ascending scale of differentiation of self from object images, it touches upon a particular vulnerability by creating too early or too abrupt disillusionment, leading to precocious differentiation. This is where pathological narcissism can be created in the form of a distorted self-object unit, consisting of self images which participate in the illusory omnipotence of overidealized object images. In that event, the self is deprived of opportunity to participate in continuing negotiations with the object-in-reality, creating, instead, an omnipotent object-in-fantasy. In some other circumstances, such as unusual endowment, pathological narcissistic formations are created because of premature disillusionment with the object; ego functions such as cognition and reality testing enable the gifted infant to discern parental flaws too soon, that is, while omnipotence is still necessary to development. Lichtenberg (1975) describes how self-reliance, which we believe to be a feature of sound secondary narcissism, may be impaired:

> The identifications that do occur often have the aim of defensive merging, or a protective massive incorporation of the object; self-images . . . shaped in this way . . . retain the quality of primitive fantasies of pathologic union. . . . It is most difficult to integrate such identifications into a cohesive self, distinct from the object and well-linked to reality [p.464].

The clinical illustrations that follow illuminate the specificity of pathological narcissism and will direct our thinking toward techniques for treatment. We do not intend to present yet another competing theory, but only to demonstrate that existing theory explains the puzzle of narcissism quite adequately.

A patient was twenty-eight years old when she started treatment. She could not verbalize clearly what brought her to seek help, just a vague sense of missing something in life. She was in a graduate program where her friends and colleagues thought of her as a tower of strength because she was doing extremely well. She herself had uncertain and wavering feelings about her competence and value. When in a relationship with a man she admired she felt at her best. As such relationships ended, feelings of emptiness would ensue, accompanied by self-devaluation. According to Kernberg (1975), paucity of libidinal investment produces such feelings of emptiness.

Her mode of "falling in love" is interesting. One time, she had needed a one-day hospitalization for a biopsy which, fortunately, turned out well. A man she barely knew was good enough to volunteer to escort her home from the hospital. She fell in love with him immediately, out of a need to endow him with great power at a time when she herself felt weak and helpless. This is a reflection of uneven distribution of cathexis between self and object images. At early phases of development we expect that there will be fluctuation and imbalance between self and object valuation. Only with psychological birth is some stability approached. The familiar mechanisms of projection and introjection are in this picture. It can of course be said, looking at one side of the balance scale, that this patient was projecting omnipotent self images onto the object. The obverse side of narcissism is patent when the self images become imbued with omnipotently perceived object images. Jacobson has already discussed this. Integrating her theory with that of Mahler on subphase inadequacy, one can say about this patient that at the practicing subphase something was already amiss, specifically reflected in excessive regard for the omnipotent object images, excessive even when compared with the temporary, phase-appropriate period in childhood. There is too much projection of magical omnipotence onto the object as compared with normal practicing subphase imbalance where the shift is in the direction of temporary, phase-specific self overvaluation. Here it is justifiable to suppose that the elation of the practicing subphase was largely missed. Mahler (personal communication) thinks that inadequacy in that subphase, as it affects narcissistic development, is attributable to paucity of maternal interest in the child's body and to her inability to share some of the elation that the child experiences. We might think that, for practicing toddlers, because of relative nonindividuation from the object, the elation will not be carried forward into the rapprochement subphase unless shared and affirmed by the maternal object.

The salient features of the patient's history are presented. The parents lost a child two years before she was born. When she was six months old her maternal grandmother died. When she was eighteen months old her mother had an operation which necessitated three weeks of hospitalization. Two examples of the interaction with mother in latency will illustrate the quality of maternal attunement, which we assume to have been a part of the mother's character and, therefore, to have existed in similar form in the patient's infancy. When she was about six years old she took a ten-dollar bill from her mother's purse and bought a doll from a toy store about five blocks away from home. She made all the crossings unaided, including a ten-lane major artery with two islands. Her mother's response was to praise her for being "such a big girl." Thus she affirmed and even supported the child's sense of omnipotence and promoted premature separation. Also to be noted is that she overlooked not only the danger but the stealing. We may expect that this might affect superego formation and ability to deal with oedipal pressures competently.

When she was about ten years old she darted into the street after a ball and was pushed over by a car just as it was brought to a stop by an extremely vigilant driver. Her mother, in the apartment upstairs, hearing the screech of brakes, looked out, saw that it was her child and asked if she was all right. The child said she was fine, so mother returned to her housework. The patient remembered this incident as a turning point in her life. She felt that she no longer had a mother. As we see it, this memory condenses many mother-child experiences and informs us that she had abandoned object negotiations long before the single incident which encapsulates her disillusionment. The necessary balance between autonomy and object dependency was missed.

As we understand this patient's presenting behavior, it seems that declarations of love and adoration could be made only to persons with whom possibility of real connection was minimal. Her choice of lovers was always popular and attractive men who presented a fly-by-night quality in their capacities for object relations. Thus, real object love was precluded. Rather, she used these relationships when she needed to bolster her wavering self-sufficiency. It seemed as though the presence and power of these men provided fuel when her own self-esteem threatened to flicker out. They could not attain the status of constant object representations because she had not reached this level in her development. They could only serve as temporary sources of reassurance when she felt empty.

Treatment began with opposition to attending sessions more than twice a week, a defended, pseudo-self-sufficient arrangement. It is this rather familiar clinical feature of narcissism that has made the problem so difficult to approach theoretically and to acquire sufficient clinical data to flesh out our hypotheses. We refer to the apparent self-sufficiency as an arrangement, for the time being, and plan to illuminate its nature. Those who have dealt with such arrangements clinically are well aware that, although they are shaky, they are far more complex and thorough-going than a mere façade. The patient was given ample time to enter treatment at her own pace. The prospect of intensive involvement with the therapist threatened dissolution of her narcissistic solution to the traumatically impaired early steps in object relations. One has to reduce that kind of anxiety gradually by demonstrating over and over again that the desire for merger emanates from the patient alone. This is best accomplished by appearing not too eager to lure the patient into intensive treatment too soon.

The patient was a student in the mental health field and thus an accidental event in the therapist's life served her need to merge with his "omnipotence." She discovered a book he had written and used it to participate in her exaggerated view of his greatness. For a while she referred to him as "the great Dr. X." Her sensitivity and alertness to flaws was ever-present, however, as she searched for appearances of fatigue, for a thoughtful look that was construed as a frown, for a slight clearing of the throat that, to her, suggested that the therapist suffered a major illness. The question arises, why do we not regard these concerns as indications of hostility, a thought which automatically comes to mind when a patient is so overly concerned with the well-being of the therapist? For the patients whose pathology is attributable to so early an affront to development, it is a moot matter to attempt to deal with hostility, anger, and rage while the need for union with the omnipotent object is dominant. Although these affects do indeed exist, to elicit them too soon would serve only to sever connection, thus reinforcing the precocious differentiation which was the very affront that led to the pathology. There is a time in treatment for expression of negative affect. That time is when a sufficient reservoir of positive object cathexis has been established so that rage can be tolerated without fear of object loss. As libidinal connection is maintained, the patient will include the analyst in the formerly "closed shop" of the omnipotent unit. This revival in the therapeutic relationship is analogous to transference neurosis in the structured personality and is welcomed similarly because the therapist can use it to build positive cathexis and to point out the distortions. When the ego corrects them, orderly, ascending progression in the developmental line of self-object relations can be promoted.

To be more explicit about this. It goes without saying that we never create an artificial situation. Had the therapist not written a book, this patient would have found other evidence of his "greatness." Every therapist is familiar with "accidents" which arise because they are needed and knows how to give them a good therapeutic turn. In this case, without protesting his real importance which, of course, is considerably less than the patient's overidealization would have it, the therapist nevertheless accepted the invitation proffered to make himself part of the omnipotent unit. The particular technical measure of "joining-in" meets the need of certain narcissistic and borderline patients to "linger" with the good object. This resembles Kohut's technique, in part, but is derived from a different theoretical conviction. We regard the purpose as structure building and consider this to conform with a developmental frame of reference which suggests that the patient be helped to progress from pathological narcissism to normal self esteem as the process of organization proceeds.

If, in the life experience, symbiosis has been parasitically overly gratified, preventing smooth development into the separation-individuation phase, then we would not employ the technique of joining the omnipotent unit. Here, one must interpret the need but not gratify it—a form of abstinence. Our technical approach is dictated by the purpose of repairing developmental malformations and distortions, and so we find it appropriate to that purpose to "join-in" only in situations where the etiology of narcissism is deprivation of closeness at the phase-appropriate developmental time. But we have already indicated that this is one of several possible places where affront to development results in pathological narcissism. And so we would apply our technique with great caution and with careful consideration of the exact developmental causes of the pathology as we can detect them. Most of the time, because the information we seek is preverbal, we have to look to the behavior in the therapeutic situation for clues which lead to reconstruction of the traumatic situation. Similar to revival in the transference neuroses, the preverbal experiences of narcissistic and borderline patients are replicated in the therapeutic relationship. A well-attuned ear is required to hear the echoes of early object negotiation and its distortions. But as we learn to listen in that way, we learn to designate the point in development where affront took place and pathology ensued.

We are not wholly dependent upon a good ear. There is always some history which contributes its own data for us to form diagnostic hypotheses to test out as we treat. In the case presented, clues in the history that the patient was able to provide allow us to make certain assumptions. We adduce from the facts that an infant died before the patient was born and that the maternal grandmother died shortly after the patient's birth, that the patient's mother had not yet decathected her own lost objects, that is, had not completed mourning. While we cannot guess precisely what kind of affective connection she was able to make with the patient, we can be sure that it was considerably less than optimal, so we feel justified in hypothesizing that symbiosis was deprived either in duration or in quality. It has also been demonstrated that the mother encouraged premature individuation and that there was inadequacy in the subphases. The mother's relative unattunement is shown in incidents of childhood and latency that the patient can remember. Clinically, her need to regard the therapist as "great" completes the picture of pathological narcissism.

The therapist encouraged the patient to resume object negotiations at the only place where she could, that is, where the need for an omnipotent self-object unit existed. Seen in this light, "joining-in" is circumscribed not only by developmental need but it is time-limited as well. The precise moment in therapy when the corner has been turned is difficult to recognize. It can be sensed by a developmentally oriented therapist who is ever-alert to the phase-specific nature of the patient's needs. The omnipotent unit is joined for the purpose of leading the patient toward less skewed development. When the corner is turned, it is timely to curtail one's narcissistic availability, or, to put this in another way, to provide the optimal frustration that promotes growth. The patient is thus invited to venture out of the narcissistic unit and to join the world of reality. Connections are never severed in this process; rather, the therapist who joined the patient in omnipotent union when that was indicated now makes himself available for resumption of object negotiation.

This case illustrates how a situation appears clinically when normal development of object relations is hindered by too early individuation and precocious differentiation from primary object images resulting in failure in the normal progression of increasing cathexis of the self images with value because continuing negotiation with the object in reality has ceased. Instead, the resources of the good inborn endowment are deployed toward creation of an omnipotent self-object unit to ease the pain of disillusion and separateness. Regression is to a less differentiated position, but now union is with a fantasied good object. Development does not cease; it proceeds henceforth in a distorted direction. Especially does it become organized into pathological forms as psychosexual maturation proceeds. Spitz' (1965) concept of cumulation is applicable here. The qualities of the experiences of earlier phases are carried forward in some form into later life. In pathological narcissism, the quality is determined by cessation of object negotiation; further development is severely distorted by its absence. Normal propulsion into the rapprochement subphase, so dependent upon separation anxiety and resurgence of need for the libidinal object, is precluded by the abandonment of object negotiation. This is how inadequacies in one subphase affect the form and quality of later subphases of separation-individuation.

Overvaluation of the now impervious self-object unit, however, does not connote a psychotic arrangement. Reality testing is lost only with reference to self-object relations but remains intact in other respects. Our proposition is, therefore, that *the central organizational failure in pathological narcissism is an impairment in the developing capacity for reality testing in the circumscribed area of self-object relations.* It comes about because of inadequacy which can occur at any phase or subphase, but it is the specific site of the injury that gives it its particular form and coloration.

With narcissistic arrangements of a higher level of development there is a qualitative difference even though the clinical manifestation, aloofness, makes it appear similar. Here, it is not identity that is threatened by merger, but the intactness of an arrangement that is now used as a defense against object negotiation.

A man, thirty-seven years old, comes for treatment because he had been told by friends who are therapists that he needs it. He does have discomforts that motivate him. Especially is he troubled by the inability to establish a stable relationship with a woman. He would like to marry and to have children. He fears that he has let too much time go by and that he may never have a family. He is attractive and women seek him out, but he does not ever make the first approach. There is more than simple passivity that is the deterrent here; as he puts it, he would be so severely hurt if the woman were to refuse him that he would be depressed for weeks. Self esteem is at a low level. He bolsters it by careful attention to grooming and to exercise which is pursued without pleasure, but rather grimly, to improve his body.

He was the middle of three sons in a family that kept rather aloof one from the other. His father was mildly alcoholic, but this did not interfere with success in his profession; it did, however, keep him in a bad temper at home. He had no patience for his children and offered them little companionship. He tended to be tyrannical toward them and toward his wife in their presence. The children lived in fear of him, while their mother meekly and masochistically appeased him.

She had little to offer our patient in his childhood beyond the physical necessities of life. Transitions such as going to school and rather too soon to camp were not supported. The father did not lend his participation. The mother expected the child to be able to accomplish these separations without troubling her with his feelings. His brothers, having been treated similarly, had no comfort to share. It was a family living under a common roof with no emotional warmth. Materially they were comfortable.

The patient thinks he spoke late. We hypothesize that he was not much spoken to, nor did it appear that he was particularly regarded as in any way different from his brothers. The picture was of a cold, dutiful mother who provided physical care in an emotionally detached way. The boys were not individualized. They were fed in a group of three, sent off to school, left with relatives when the parents went on vacation, hardly at all distinguished according to age and ability, nor even addressed by name very often; they were "the boys."

The patient's memory of his childhood is a blur of loneliness and much anxiety. Anxiety persisted throughout life and entered the treatment situation, of course. Its first form was in his relationship with women in two phases. One phase, as described, was the initial approach. The second came about when the relationship became intensified to the point where the woman wanted some permanence. Although the patient consciously wanted to marry, he reached a level of panic whenever a woman he had been seeing for several months expected that he would have developed some love for her. Not only was he unable to love but he terminated one relationship after another when deep commitment was demanded of him.

After four years of treatment, this same phenomenon, akin to a transference neurosis, entered the treatment situation. It was marked by resistance-like behavior in the form of withholding conscious thoughts out of fear of becoming too involved with the therapist. Yet, he was involved. He attended sessions regularly and valued the therapy while fearing that it would become too much a part of his life. Then he wished to withdraw on the ground that his men friends saw no reason for him to spend money that way. To them he appeared to be living the ideal bachelor life that they envied. They did not know of his intense anxiety and low self esteem.

The treatment reached a crisis when the patient said, "I have been anxious and afraid all my life. I'm used to it. I know what it's like. I can live with it. I'm not sure I can live with beginning to care about you." This case is described at the critical point where the relatively intact self-object unit—the narcissistic formation—begins to yield. The therapist acquires some value, threatening the self-sufficiency of the narcissistic arrangement. Before that point was reached in the treatment, the patient spoke of his anxiety as less desirable. Sometimes he railed against the therapist for not relieving him of it. He begins to know that he will have to resume object negotiations in order to get well, and he is understandably fearful of taking that giant step into a relationship with another person where he will feel vulnerable to repetition of narcissistic injury. The therapist knows that this must not be repeated. The patient will have to test the water by entering one toe at a time.

Diagnostically, it was thought that the dyadic experience was adequate in the symbiotic phase, but that the patient had to extract from a reluctant mother in the subphases of the separation-individuation phase. He described the many ways in which he became prematurely self sufficient. He was closed off from continuing object negotiation early in the subphases and missed also the opportunity for continuous affirmation of his physical and intellectual accomplishments throughout the subphases. It is hypothesized that the narcissistic unit was formed somewhere around the practicing subphase when the mother withdrew physically, perhaps because it was a blow to her own narcissism that the child became so apparently independent of her. Therefore, she was unable to respond to him in good enough measure beyond that level of development, and he tried to provide self affirmation through pseudo-independence. Such attempts are bound to fail to secure sufficient narcissistic supplies to build healthy self esteem.

In some of his verbalizations, this patient confirmed the well-known kinship between narcissism and homosexuality. He was not an overt homosexual, but fantasied what it would be like. In the context of his many complaints about women, mainly their physical (genital) flaws, he accepted the interpretation that he would perhaps find it easier to love someone more like himself.

Figure 3 depicts formation of narcissistic units at different subphase levels and shows how these foreclose ongoing object negotiation at the point where the narcissistic affront is experienced and the self-self unit is formed in lieu of the self-object unit.

At any level of narcissistic formation, one has to be moderate about urging more intense contact than can be tolerated. It does not take too long for such patients to realize that, despite desperate struggle against feared dependency, they are nevertheless quite dependent. By this time, however, the therapist has built up a nonintrusive climate of trust, and the patient has no choice but to acknowledge the need and to engage in a therapeutic alliance. Such alliance becomes first one of participation in the therapist's omnipotence. At such times the therapist's realistic self-evaluation is required to avoid what Greenacre (1959) terms a *narcissistic alliance,* that is, one which feeds the analyst's narciss-

FIGURE 3.

Levels of Pathological Narcissistic Formation

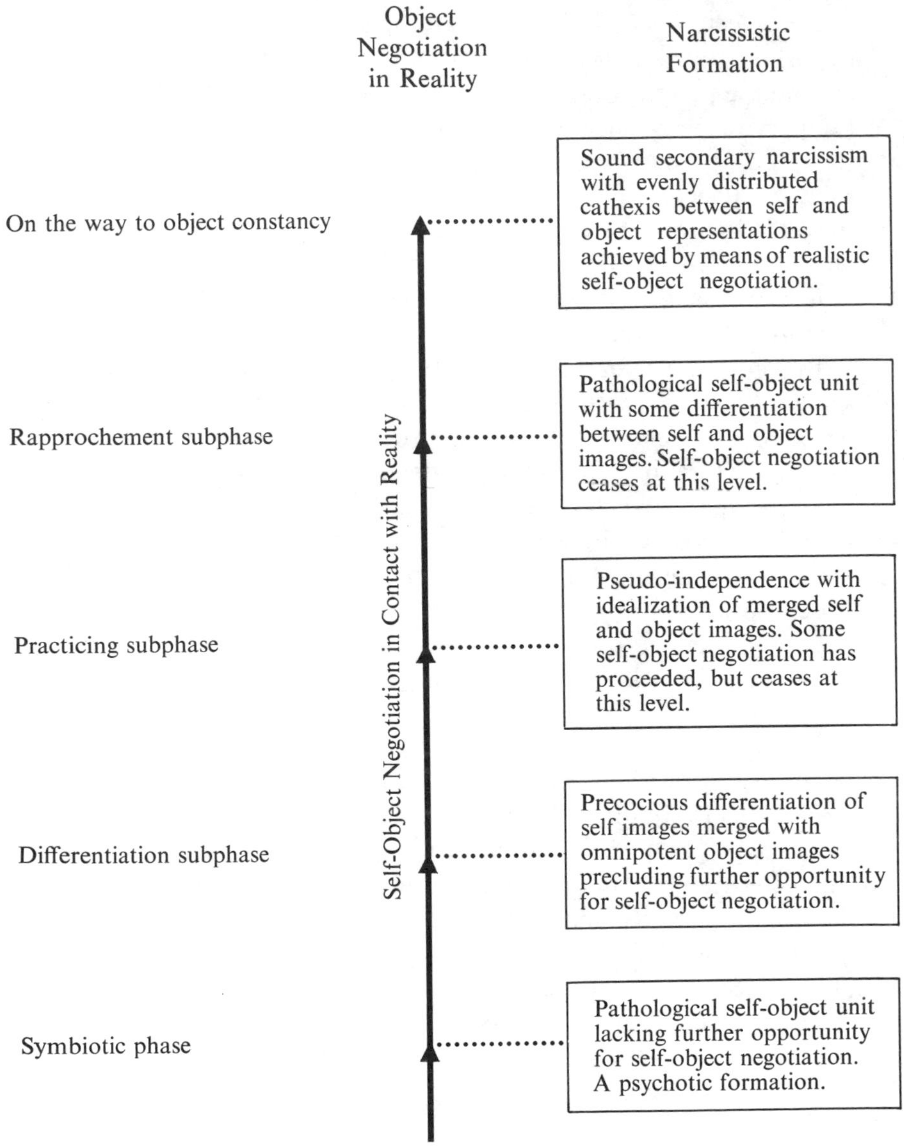
Object Negotiation in Reality
Narcissistic Formation
On the way to object constancy
Sound secondary narcissism with evenly distributed cathexis between self and object representations achieved by means of realistic self-object negotiation.
Rapprochement subphase
Pathological self-object unit with some differentiation between self and object images. Self-object negotiation ceases at this level.
Practicing subphase
Pseudo-independence with idealization of merged self and object images. Some self-object negotiation has proceeded, but ceases at this level.
Differentiation subphase
Precocious differentiation of self images merged with omnipotent object images precluding further opportunity for self-object negotiation.
Symbiotic phase
Pathological self-object unit lacking further opportunity for self-object negotiation. A psychotic formation.
Self-Object Negotiation in Contact with Reality

ism by way of eager acceptance of the patient's overvaluation and overidealization. Yet, it is necessary to accept the patient's temporary need for union in the only manner that is possible for the patient.

Ego psychology, as Freud predicted, provides the theoretical solution to the problem of narcissism and this all-encompassing theory of human development, we believe, serves to explain narcissism, both normal and pathological, as it explains so many other aspects of normality and pathology. There is promise that, as this theory is refined, much that is still unknown to us will become clear.

The Borderline Conditions

Much has been written about the rather hazy diagnostic category, the borderline state, or condition, or organization. The designation, *borderline,* is a geographical metaphor used to define a broad area bounded on the one side by neurosis and on the other by psychosis; hence, there are two borders and two lines defining them. In general use, however, the entire area is designated as borderline, and so we remain bound to that use in order to communicate in the same terms as the literature. It is worthwhile, however, to review the history of the evolution of the concept.

Freud divided pathology into the analyzable transference neuroses and the unanalyzable narcissistic neuroses. The latter term, no longer in use, referred to those pathologies that one would now designate as the borderline conditions, pathological narcissism (a feature of borderline phenomena), and the psychoses.

In the struggle to understand the varied clinical phenomena that the borderline conditions present, this extensive area of psychopathology became subcategorized in a proliferating diagnostic terminology such as severe neurosis, character disorder, ambulatory schizophrenia, pseudo-psychotic neurosis, prepsychotic condition, schizoid personality, as-if personality, among others. There are not clear evidences of psychosis in these cases—no delusions, hallucinations, gross failure in reality testing. Terminology alone served only to clarify that there was confusion. Rangell (1955), reporter of the panel discussion on *The Borderline Case* held at the St. Louis meetings of the American Psychoanalytic Association, reports Zilboorg as saying, "we seem to seek we know not quite yet clearly what" (p. 285).

A particular asset of the psychoanalytic method is the open-ended attunement to the patient's productions, so well conceptualized by the phrase, evenly suspended attention. As a result, analysts could not but notice that classical techniques were found to be ineffective for an ever-increasing number of patients. Close attention disclosed that free association was not helpful in such cases; often it precipitated unexpected and undesirable results. Regression could not be restricted to psychosexual levels and, as a body of experience accumulated, serious reconsideration of the method as well as of the problems was necessitated. Thus, many panels, symposia, and discussions were held, perhaps the most notable of which was consideration of the widening scope of indications for psychoanalysis (see chapter 6). There the borderline conditions, or borderline conditions with neurotic features, were discussed as perhaps extending the rubric of analyzability. In that discussion, however, the distinction between psychoanalysis as a therapy and psychoanalysis as a group of metapsychological propositions became blurred, for the usefulness of psychoanalytic conceptualization, now an ever-broadening general psychology of human development, far transcends its more limited status as a treatment for neurosis.

The era of ego psychology precipitated a breakthrough in the attempt to understand borderline phenomena. In 1971, Mahler suggested that its etiology lay in failure of completion of the tasks of separation-individuation—in our terms, a failure in the organizing process. Later, she refined more precisely the nature of these tasks in each subphase of separation-individuation. The continuity of development as it affects pathology is described by Ritvo (1974a):

> Our greater appreciation of the wide variations and fluctuations within the normal range over the course of individual development affects our concepts concerning diagnosis and technique in borderline conditions and neuroses. We are less likely to be doctrinaire in regarding imprecise clinical entities such as the borderline conditions as being completely distinct from the neuroses [pp. 164–65].

The borderline conditions are now recognized to exist, not as one borderline, but as a wide range of pathology within two borders. Recently, much attention has been paid to the pathology lying near or even crossing over, in some of its features, the neurotic border. The fulcrum of development (see Figure 1) defines the precise tasks involved in negotiating that border. The usefulness of this approach is that, without the support of statistical data, one may suppose, nevertheless, that the average clinician sees a preponderance of such cases, regardless of whether he classifies them as neurotic with borderline features or borderline with neurotic features. These are the cases that reach their organizing crises more in the rapprochement subphase than in the full-fledged oedipal phase. Loewald (1974), in accord with Ritvo, states:

> the sharp distinction between the classical neuroses and borderline conditions or narcissistic disorders, from a clinical standpoint, is not justified. One might say that neurosis and developmental deficiencies of ego are intermingled, with a preponderance of neurotic conflict in the neuroses, and a preponderance of developmental deficiencies in the narcissistic disorders [p. 187].

Kernberg (1975) deals with pathology on the psychotic border and in the middle range as well as on the neurotic border. To him, the descriptive diagnostic features of the entity that he designates as "borderline personality organization" are condensed or telescoped levels of faulty development, low frustration tolerance, low anxiety tolerance (the nonspecific ego weaknesses), employment of primitive forms of defense such as projective identification,[1] and the like. His technical model is the psychoanalysis of neurosis where the dominant defenses are sought out. To Kernberg, the major defense in borderline personality organization is splitting; the technical purpose follows logically—interpretation of the defenses and of the primitive transference paradigms in a process of modified psychoanalytic psychotherapy which, in some instances, may become psychoanalysis proper.

Our elaboration of the nature of borderline phenomena revolves around the position that it is the organizing process that orchestrates differentiation and integration throughout development but, most importantly, in the subphases. Malformations that may occur there are incorporated into the ongoing sweep of organization, in some instances seriously distorting that process, in others becoming swept along by it. The ingredients brought to the dyad by both partners and the quality of the interaction determine how successfully the organizing process will proceed through the oedipal conflict, latency, adolescence, adulthood, and on through the life cycle.

Considering now the technical implications and also how the patient deals with the therapist in the therapeutic situation, these depend very much upon whether development has proceeded without regression below our imaginary line. If fixation or regression is to levels of ego organization before the third or fourth subphase, object negotiations are likely to appear clinically as a search for replication of the less than fulfilled requirements of the primary dyadic experience. Such a patient is still living, so to speak, in the immediacy of the dyadic relationship. The causality is explained by Mahler's careful delineation of subphase needs and her description of the minimal essential interaction in the dyad that is required to avert psychosis, to acquire sound secondary narcissism, to promote internalization,

[1]The term *projective identification* connotes that there is a failure in differentiation of self from object images. We think it more precise to refer to that phenomenon as self images experienced as object images. To the followers of Melanie Klein, the term implies a degree of differentiation which developmentalists believe to be impossible at the primitive levels of organization where that phenomenon is assumed to occur.

and to build structure. Patients who seek such replication have not succeeded in approach to object constancy, that is, they lack structure and internalized whole self and object representations. Therefore, they need to live in the immediacy of interaction, or to put it in clinical terms, they search for replication of primary object experience.

Where object replication is sought, special techniques not applicable to the more structured personality must be created. Attunement to subphase inadequacy is essential in order to be able to decide upon therapeutic procedure. Our methodology focuses upon the therapeutic alliance in which searches for object replication appear. Attuned understanding is used to diminish the preponderance of hostile affect towards self and objects. *Explanation* for developmental lesions is sought, and this technique rather than confrontation or interpretation dominates, especially in the early phases of treatment. Uncovering, interpretation, and especially eliciting anger while the need is for positive affective connection are contraindicated early in the treatment. We reserve them for later phases when, with our help, the patient has more successfully negotiated the fulcrum.

The important aspects of treatment are quickening of poorly functioning ego apparatuses (see chapters 2 and 7); gradual reworking of replication of infantile object experiences as specific subphase inadequacies are illuminated in the therapeutic situation; catalyzing developmental processes in order to enhance the patient's organizing capacity.

In emphasizing attunement as a basic technical tool, we are careful to remember that for separation-individuation to proceed there must be optimal frustration as well as positive connection. Because skewed developmental processes have resulted in malformation of organization, the need for connection requires special emphasis. The therapeutic alliance offers both. The nonjudgmental, interested, noncritical therapist offers the positive connection; the normal limits of the therapeutic arrangement usually provide sufficient frustration. When appropriate to increasing levels of tolerance, the abstinence rule may be invoked, as some of our case material illustrates. It also becomes appropriate, after positive cathexis of objects begins to overthrow the hostile imbalance, to deal with angry affect. As for defenses, they are the props of organization, whatever the malformation. Therefore, it is not desirable to challenge them. Working with the totality of the organizing process and addressing interventions that deal with the specific malformations wherever it is possible to find them will propel organization in the direction of the fulcrum. Then, a stronger ego attains capacity for signal anxiety and an adequate defensive function is acquired, as are other higher level functions. Meanwhile, the adaptive purpose of whatever primitive defenses preexist is the more important focus of ego-building endeavor and must remain unchallenged until better organization is attained.

A patient who had come to better terms with his parents in the course of treatment visited them and found it possible to enjoy them more. The therapist, perhaps overly eager to capitalize on what appeared to be a better balance of positive over hostile affect, used the opportunity to illuminate those therapeutic encounters where object replication still persisted, where the patient misread the therapist's activity as hostile. The patient said, justifiably, "You don't understand. I never told you that my parents' way of making me obey was to threaten to send me to the 'hill' (the local orphanage). I'm only beginning to grasp how frightened and angry I was." And so peace with his objects remained an uneasy one until this deeper layer of rage could be worked through. Meanwhile, the therapist may expect that there will be rage in the therapeutic situation and will have to ride through the storms until the patient experiences, by much repetition of finding one thing after another to be angry about, that the therapist is not provoking that affect. Treatment in this middle phase is not quick, easy, nor even rewarding to the therapist. These patients have been more damaged than neurotics, have less capacity to test reality and to maintain true ambivalence, and so they lose sight for longer periods of time of the difference between therapist and negatively cathected primary object.

Another patient marries against the wishes of her parents. Against the wishes of her husband, she puts herself through professional school. She accepts positions in firms forced to open their doors to ethnic minorities and to women, and she achieves outstanding success. There is no elation because narcissistic self regard is almost entirely absent, with the possible exception of her mode of dress. Here too, however, although she takes pains about it, the emphasis is much more on conveying a discretely appropriate image to others and not at all for self adornment. "When I'm at home, I don't even think about what I'm wearing; probably I look like an utter slob!" In her work life she is an expensively tailored executive partner in a prominent firm, but her professional self disappears almost instantly with anxiety. She has two children, but does not enjoy them because narcissistic affirmation of self, extended to children, is lacking. So she copes with the responsibility without pleasure.

Here the treatment issue is how to build positive cathexis of the self images. The mother's admiration of the practicing infant's exploits appears to have been missing. According to the history, the patient was raised by her poorly functioning, psychotic father who was at home, while her mother worked and supported the family. The intertwining of various levels of development is always a factor. In this instance, the problems of the psychotic father seriously burdened the patient's development and led to severe malformations but obviously did not stop organization from proceeding. The next step in the process will be to promote higher organizational forms (structuralization).

The goal is always in the direction of the fulcrum and, desirably, past it. This procedure requires detection of where development toward the fulcrum lags and of where promotion is most likely of success. The latter is important because, since one aspect of development hinges upon another, more than one feature of the fulcrum can be aided at the same time. Promotion of affect differentiation illustrates this. The patient who can be helped in that area acquires higher level object relations in the process. Functions formerly bound up in failure of the totality of development are freed to pursue autonomous goals. It becomes noticeable when affective cathexes toward self and object images become more positive. Patients do not necessarily announce progress in so many words. While sometimes they do, more often we recognize it in the quality of the therapeutic alliance as ego functioning, self-object relations, diminished hostility, all become incorporated into higher forms of organization.

The following case illustrates the precise nature of attunement to subphase need:

A forty-year-old man began treatment because he was depressed over the termination of his marriage. He found himself almost unable to function or to make decisions in his work. He needed marijuana to bolster both his mood and his anxious sexual performance with various women who had not much meaning to him. Although these women disappointed him in some vague way, he feared being alone. Therefore, he saw many women, but would leave one for another who seemed more promising. In treatment, he both wanted more time with the therapist and also threatened to leave treatment when she displeased him. The movement toward leaving was prominent in every disappointing exchange, that is, when he felt that the therapist did not understand him. Then he would become angry and disappointed and distant. It took a long time before he began to realize that he was reacting to the realization that the therapist was not perfect. He needed to retrieve the ego state of narcissistic omnipotent union of the practicing and early rapprochement subphases which had been interrupted when his mother became pregnant. A brother was born when the patient was two years old.

Approaching the end of three years of treatment, he went through many moods, behaviors, and exchanges with his therapist over a succession of treatment hours. He began awkwardly and hesitantly to express curiosity about the therapist, always a sign of improving object relations.

Patient: I think about you a lot, especially when I'm not here—on weekends. I shouldn't do that.

Therapist: Why "shouldn't"?

Patient: It's wrong. I have no right to want to know about you.

Therapist: What is wrong about that?
Patient: I don't belong with you all the time.
Therapist: There are some good wishes there.
Patient: Well, I do wish I could know what you do when I'm not here. I'd feel closer.

In another session:

Patient: I don't feel well today.
Therapist: I'm sorry. What's the matter?
Patient: I don't know, but I remember that I thought you didn't feel well last session.
Therapist: And so we feel the same?
Patient: (Becoming anxious about the closeness.) I don't know. Maybe it's because you'd like it that way. Then you'd like me. I'd be a good patient.
Therapist: Maybe that's your way of being with me more. You're afraid of those wishes.
Patient: I'd become too dependent on you.
Therapist: That does frighten you.
Patient: Yes. I might even have sexual feelings. (He blushes but continues.) I do feel very fond of you. It surprises me. You probably enjoy this. Maybe you need to hear how much I care about you.
Therapist: It's not clear to you whether your feelings are for me or for you. Really, what you need most is to be yourself, to know what you feel, whether it be the same or different from what I feel.
Patient: (Excitedly.) Oh. That is something! I always feel I have to show people that I feel the same as they.
Therapist: If you have to do that, it means that you are clear about what you feel.
Patient: Yes, but it scares me, so I pretend to feel like them.
Therapist: Is that how you get close?

The therapist's vacation was approaching.

Patient: I feel more removed from you today.
Therapist: Do you know why?

Patient: Not really. I know that I do it.
Therapist: You distance yourself?
Patient: Yes. I get my independence back that way.
Therapist: Our objective is to help you become truly independent. Is this it?
Patient: I wish it were. I'm afraid it's because your vacation is coming.
Therapist: So you move away. Will that make it easier?
Patient: It has always worked that way. I see you as a crutch.
Therapist: Crutches have a useful purpose, you know. They help people walk until they can walk without them.
Patient: Will I ever walk on my own two feet? You never tell me what to do, yet I feel so lost without you.

The patient then began to sniffle and said that he had a cold. He wondered if the therapist also had one and if, over the weekend, she wasn't in bed ill. In exploring this it was learned that, as a child, he used to see his mother lying in bed with his baby brother cuddled next to her. He remembered attempting to enter the room and being pulled away by the nurse. He felt angry and lost as he wandered about the house with a stranger-caretaker by his side. He remembered wanting to make his mother understand his needs. He now wants women to understand him perfectly. When they don't, there must be something wrong with them.

The wish to be with his mother may be seen as condensation of oedipal and subphase levels of organization. In order to aid reorganization, the therapist chose first to deal with the subphase underpinnings. The need for marijuana as a bolster for sexual functioning combined with the feeling that women are flawed suggests fetishism. A new dimension appears as we understand the wish for closeness and the consequent belief that both self and object are flawed because the separation feels like physical severing. (We omit discussion of the phallic implications in order to focus on the subphase aspect.)

Also illustrated are the aggressive thrusts away from the object, sometimes in anger, but more often expressive of the separating and individuating thrust, and the search for identity despite the subphase inadequacy (deprivation) that fixates the wish for closeness. The therapist follows each movement, toward and away from, "tracking" the patient in attunement to each movement. Thus, whether he is close or distant, she is with him throughout.[2]

The following case illustrates how subphase inadequacy can impair self-esteem regulation:

A thirty-five-year-old woman characteristically demonstrated an inability to take pleasure in her accomplishments and to enjoy praise from others. She took her achievements for granted, and only the problems she had not yet solved, or the words she had not thought to say at the right time, held any meaning. The values in goals she sought disappeared once the goal was met. As the patient began to recognize this pattern, she drew the analogy of the carrot at the end of the stick; she never reaches her objective. The patient's self esteem was chronically low and was untouched by external accomplishments which she could not integrate into her self representation. Early in the therapeutic relationship, she seemed hungrily to seek approval, but with much suspicion. She did not believe the sincerity of the therapist's affirmation of her adaptive functioning and feared humiliation if she allowed herself any feeling of self pride. With time, she began to think of abandoning this self-deprecating stance but feared that the therapist would humiliate her. The patient vividly recalled repeated instances of humiliation by her mother at any demonstration of mastery and accompanying self esteem. Her negative stance was seen, therefore, as an adaptation to that humiliation, a defensive position whereby the patient had identified with the negative response she received from the object and turned it upon herself to protect against object loss. This kind of interpretation rang true for her, but was incomplete and therefore only minimally usable to modify existing internalizations.

We assume that this patient's difficulties began with entry into separation-individuation. It seemed that her mother had been

[2]This case was contributed by Toni Tompson.

able to take little delight in her new abilities. As an adult, she seemed, by herself, to be able to extract whatever pleasure she could from the physical sensations of upright locomotion. She joined a jogging club and ran in the Central Park races. These appear to be adult replays of those earlier feelings. With the inadequacies of the practicing subphase in mind, her adult behavior now appears to be much more than a defensive reaction to maternal humiliation. It is a demonstration in adulthood, modified by later development to be sure, of failure to experience a sense of elation during practicing within the still partially merged self-object. In more desirable interaction, that would have led to positively cathected self and object representations as separation-individuation proceeded, forming the core of self esteem.

The reflection in the treatment situation was her fear and mistrust of positive responses which she experienced as seduction into regressive merger with the object. In her words, "I can't let myself feel good about what you said. Then I'd be tempted to hang on your every word and I'd get completely tied to you."

This case illustrates that the flaws in self esteem arise during the subphases and must be understood to reflect inadequacies in early organization of that function of the superego components that regulate self esteem, which are different from regulation of behavior. Therefore, for intervention to have therapeutic value and effect, the address is to something different from cohesive superego.[3]

Freud (1923) defines the superego as a differentiated grade within the ego and heir to the Oedipus complex. Placing that definition within the context of psychoanalytic developmental psychology, superego proper represents a feature of a high degree of organization. Hartmann and Loewenstein (1962) elaborate that superego *components* constitute the ingredients of which superego will ultimately be constructed but are not, in and of themselves, discrete superego. Identification with the parents and their disciplinary functions perforce become component parts of superego formation, but much depends upon whether

[3]This case was contributed by Susan Schneider.

such identification is the result of the gradual process of selective identification or whether it is the pathological process of merging self and object representations, the defensive identification described by Freud in *Mourning and Melancholia.*

We are left with some question about why these cases take so long. The described tasks themselves provide an answer. To be added is a particular phenomenon in the middle phase of long-term treatment of the borderline patient. When the anger is attenuated as it becomes balanced by positive cathexis in the atmosphere of the therapist's consistently positive mood, these cases reach a lull. The patient finds comfort in the benign climate after anxiety about separation from the hostilely perceived primary object diminishes. This may be one of those places that laymen describe as "dependency" or "a crutch." We think of it, rather, as analogous to the need of the subphase toddler to "buy" developmental time by lingering in the experience with the good object. The therapeutic situation appears to be at a standstill, but important progress is being made. Patients at this phase of treatment begin to fear termination even though the therapist does not raise this issue prematurely. It is unfamiliar to their experience that they can be wanted while feeling good. Analysts long ago knew the hazards of undertaking treatment to cure symptoms. Freud (1912) thought that the patient would leave treatment prematurely upon simple symptom alleviation, losing opportunity for structural change. We are finding that the less-than-neurotically structured patients linger. But the comfortable niche of the treatment situation is to be accepted as a developmental need that will pass. We have not known patients to become "addicted" to treatment if the therapist remains continuously aware of his role of catalyst of development and respectful of the patient's autonomy.

Another impediment to rapid cure is that these patients have not, in their first round of development, encompassed some of the experiences of the more neurotically structured patients. The latter may regress, to be sure, but they have been there and they will be able to find their way back by means of analysis of the defensive regression. One of the major developmental pathways untrod or trod in distorted form at best by the borderline patient is triadic object relations that begin early and proceed to a secure oedipal level. Just as the mother has her role in promoting development, so does the father (Abelin, 1971). He provides the child with experiences different from the maternal ones and becomes, first, the person who so intrigues the child, boy or girl, that he or she is "lured" out of the exclusive dyadic relationship (Greenacre, 1966). His second major task is to be a figure for selective identification and internalization. Only later does he become the oedipal father in the child's representation. But for the child's development to proceed smoothly, the second and third roles depend more than is usually considered upon the first. Obviously, if the father is absent altogether, he cannot fulfill any of these roles. Especially important is that the father introduce the child gradually into the wider object world. We wonder, here, how many phobic patients have missed experiences in childhood that would have heightened the "love affair with the world" (Greenacre, 1957). Coinciding, as does exploration and interest in the triadic object relationship, with the practicing subphase, the mystery of the wider world captivates the child if his curiosity is quickened. Such missed experience may be a contributory factor to the complex matter of phobic formation. The agoraphobic might not fear venturing out if there had been a gradual, object-related introduction to adventure early in life, when to venture into the outside world with an admired and admiring adult acquires a pleasurable affective cathexis. Self and object esteem are nourished, and venturesomeness beomes a quality in the total organization of character. It may be thought of as analogous to the acquisition of signal anxiety by way of first having been soothed and thereby becoming capable of internalizing self-soothing mechanisms.

Where aspects of development have been missed, does the therapist make up for them? Does the therapist adopt the role of mother in the dyad and father in the triad? These are important technical questions that are being answered differently in different quarters. We have stressed that the organization of the adult patient is not the same as that of the developing child and that, therefore, "parenting" as a technique is simplistic. Nevertheless, many if not most borderline patients need a reparative experience. We would address it as precisely as possible to the place where organization began to become malformed; we would provide experiences that have been missed, such as the triadic one, verbally, by explanation and self-empathy as already described. Only with great caution would we enter into a true "real" relationship, for exceptionally cogent reason. The following dialogue illustrates how to do reparative work without acting in reality.

A patient whose father had left the home when the patient was an infant fantasies with the therapist's active encouragement and participation:

Patient: I'm going to play ball with my office team. I wish you'd come.
Therapist: I'd like to be there. How would it feel?
Patient: It's okay if we just talk about it. It would be scary if you were really there.
Therapist: Okay. Let's talk about it.

The patient continues to fantasy about the game, what they would do afterward, and so on. Such fantasies can be pursued over many sessions and have a reparative effect.

In another case, that of a woman who has missed some important aspects of subphase mothering:

Patient: I saw a beautiful house I'd like to buy. (It was far beyond her means, of which she was aware.) I have it all planned out. There's this large, sunlit room that you can have. It has bookshelves, a desk, a fireplace.
Therapist: What would I do there?
Patient: You can sit there and write.
Therapist: Would I ever go out?
Patient: Only when I let you.
Therapist: When would that be?
Patient: While I'm out. But you'd have to be back when I get there.

Therapist: Would I eat?
Patient: Oh, yes. We'll have a cook who will bring you a tray while you're writing. Sometimes you'd bring me tea and toast, though.
Therapist: When would that be?
Patient: When I need it. That's why I want you there. I'd call on you now and then. But I wouldn't want you on my neck all the time. Only when I need you.

Thus the patient describes repairing the unattunement of subphase needs by "owning" the therapist and dictating the rhythm of contact. Noteworthy is that the fantasied relationship is exclusively dyadic. The therapist, perceived as the mother of very early childhood, has no other interests, objects, or needs. The only concession to reality is that the therapist has to be occupied. Since the patient knows that she writes, she is accorded the comfortable room from which she will certainly not want to stray to gratify other needs. These kinds of fantasies are only useful where reality testing is intact, and the therapist is certain that a so-called "transference psychosis" will not ensue.

For a long time psychoanalytic theory held to the position that psychic structure could not be altered by a relationship in the present. But two issues alter that contention. One is that we now deal more with patients in whom structuralization is not complete. The other is that development continues throughout life. As Loewald has shown, even relatively well-structured patients are not impervious to new experience. In the borderline conditions, especially at lower levels, the experience carries the treatment. We describe and illustrate the nature of the reparative experience as one quite different from a real one. The willingness of the therapist to elaborate on the fantasy becomes the identificatory feature that helps the patient experience gratification of subphase need. The expectation is that, by means of selective identification, the self images will acquire a more positive cathexis.

In essence, developmental theory accords no special place to the "borderline" category. Kernberg's designation, borderline personality organization, is felicitously chosen to emphasize that the pathology consists of a malformation of the organizing process. We are deterred, however, from considering it to be a diagnostic entity. Many such patients demonstrate that high-level functioning exists side by side with low-level processes, a clinical expression of the multifaceted complexities of development. Fundamentally, it is the organizational malformation, as we have stressed repeatedly, that requires therapeutic address, regardless of the diagnostic categories that we find necessary to use at times for purposes of communication among therapists. It is interesting to look back to the Panel Discussion of the American Psychoanalytic Association of 1955 (Rangell, Reporter). There Zilboorg advocated return to the "Golden age of psychological curiosity" (p. 286) to look, not at the nosology, but at the inner structure of the psychic apparatus in the given individual. Psychoanalytic developmental psychology, as it has evolved so many years after the Panel, affirms Zilboorg's position by providing theoretical support that had not been available to him then.

CHAPTER 12

Ego-Building Techniques

Reduced to its fundamentals, ego building consists of a number of technical procedures based upon the level of the patient's organization and designed to advance the organizing process. Determination of the level of organization is guided by the fulcrum of development described in chapter 5. One may think, roughly, of three levels—the poorly structured individuals; those whose level hovers around the fulcrum, who constitute the bulk of out-patient borderline cases; those whose psychic organization has proceeded beyond the fulcrum and are preponderantly neurotic. The treatment tools in the analyst's or therapists's repertory range from the more classically psychoanalytic in the intact structures to a number of interventions that we have elaborated for borderline levels of organization. These proposed interventions include repair of malformations in organization that derive from subphase experience and may be detected through the degree of success or failure in negotiation of the fulcrum of development.

Theoretical Determinants of Technical Intervention

The following are technical guidelines:

1. Ego-building techniques are elaborated out of the totality of

psychoanalytic developmental psychology, especially of the organizing principles that we have derived from Freud's definition of ego, Hartmann's redefinition, Spitz' concept of the organizers of the psyche, and Mahler's enunciation of a new organizing principle. To these we add our own proposal that ego is organizing process. Taken together, they dictate that the therapists design their interventions to promote that process.

2. Malformed organization in the adult patient is not reflected directly, but in the form of distorted, telescoped, and condensed variants which appear clinically in fluctuating stages of exacerbation and remission. It does not precisely replicate the malformations as they have occurred in the first round of development. Spitz' discovery that organization is continuous from birth, as the indicators of organization have informed him, is exceedingly useful here. When this is conjoined with Mahler's delineation of the subphases of the separation-individuation phase, it is indeed a temptation to think that one might construct developmental indices that could be used for diagnostic demarcation of malformations in organization. For a while, that was our hope. In one of the cases already described we refer to the absence of elation, the hallmark of the practicing subphase. Can that be regarded as indicative of a malformation originating in the practicing subphase? Probably so, but that tells us too little about the organizing process as it has proceeded beyond that subphase. The patient, so efficient in many areas of life, arrived at adulthood with considerably more than simply a flaw in the practicing subphase. Mahler notes that, even in infants, the developmental process had become so complex and so unique in each individual by about 20 months of age that her research team could no longer group the data into general formulations. Spitz, too, observes a similar complexity. He writes (1965):

> It is difficult, if not impossible, to find a formula to express the multiform, silent ebb and flow, the mute invisible tides, powerful and at the same time subtle, which pervade these relations. It can never be sufficiently stressed, nor too often repeated, that object relations take place as a constant interaction between two very unequal partners . . . that each provokes the responses of the

> other; that this interpersonal relation creates a field of constantly shifting forces [pp. 204–5].

He also describes an action-reaction-action cycle which, in a certain sense, constitutes the very basis of developmental diagnosis and of ego-building techniques. It clarifies that development cannot be thought of as a progression that goes from 1 to 10 in which, if there are malformations, the progression would be 1–2–3–6–7–8–10 because 4, 5, and 9 are flawed. Rather, each action and reaction produces a new action which is greater than the sum of the parts of the initial action and reaction. This, in turn, introduces an even more complex element that enters the process and becomes the action factor in the next action-reaction-action cycle. That exponential effect of malformations in organization has long been apparent from the clinical vantage point. Kris (1956a) describes events in the life of a child and speculates how these would appear in considerably mutated form in the analysis of that same person in adulthood. Memory of childhood events, Kris thought, is patterned as the result of distortion, condensation, by telescoping later events with the earlier ones, and by inclusion of fantasies as well. Unraveling those is one of the many tasks for which we need the patient's continuing participation in the therapeutic endeavor to sort out with the therapist the many elements that go into a "memory." Kris refers to this task of the analytic process as restoring to the patient his true biography. It does not imply that the cumulative effect of the organizing process is a phenomenon of pathology, but simply of that process itself. And so analogy to childhood developmental process has to be given strict construction, to be taken as analogy only, lest there be misapplication of the theory by simplistic transposition to the treatment of adult patients. Development in the subphases as reflected in adult behavior serves as a guide to understanding the effects of the interaction in the dyadic encounter as it has affected the organizing process and as it appears in later organizational forms. It can hardly appear in adult normality or pathology as a simple replica. To be considered also is that, as development advances, favorable circumstances may serve to correct earlier potentially pathological formations. Thus, we have to take into account the vicissitudes of the first round of separation-individuation, of post-infantile development in latency, puberty, adolescence, and adulthood, and to include the life circumstances as well, for all of these may add further mutations to already existing distortions in the organizing process, or may contribute to their correction.

3. Each individual is the unique product of the interaction of his innate endowment with the maternal influence in the dyadic experience. This restates Mahler's organizing principle and stresses that no two individuals are alike.

Historically, the infant's endowment has been viewed differently at different times. Before Kraepelin, "morbid taints" (Mendelson, 1974) were postulated to explain behavior for which true explanation was not known. Heredity has ever been the fallback position for the unknown. When, in the progression of theory construction, the importance of maternal psychological nurturing was discovered, the mother became accountable for pathology in the child. Even Spitz thought that there are psychotoxic disturbances, the effect of maternal anxiety conveyed to the infant who, as a psychophysiological being, reacts with psychosomatic symptoms. He was undoubtedly correct, but considering the infant's endowment as it contributes to such an encounter, we might think the stimulus barrier, inborn and varying from infant to infant, fails to shield some from the impact of the environment; that there are also variations in intelligence and adaptive capacity. The poorly endowed child, as Mahler has discovered, may not be able to engage in the symbiotic experience and thereby is prone to psychosis; or the endowment may be good enough and yet constitute a poor match for a given mother. A mother who needs a responsive child may not be able to reach out to a quiet one; a child's level of intelligence good enough for one family may not meet the demands of another; the overendowed child is prone to the hazards of premature development. Potential mismatching may occur in numerous combinations.

Freud (1937) refers to the possibility that there are inborn qualities in each individual. This is emphasized by Hartmann

(1958). It is from that that Hartmann arrives at his own proposition regarding the innate endowment, later to be confirmed by Mahler's observational studies. These showed not only that there are individual differences in the innate endowment but that the normally endowed infant at birth and for some time after is at a peak of adaptive capacity. Without resort to "morbid taints," then, current theoretical assumptions include the infant's adaptive potential as a prime factor in the organizational forms that will develop out of the dyadic experience. Now one considers the balance between the mother's receptivity and the infant's "sending power" (Mahler, Pine, and Bergman, 1975, p. 202). These matters are difficult enough to discern in an experimental setting where the mother-child interaction is under continuous scrutiny by skilled observers. At this stage of our knowledge, they are close to impossible to sort out in the adult patient in a clinical setting. Nevertheless, we venture some beginning steps toward such determination in the section on assessment of organizing capacity. By and large, however, one can only provide broad guidelines rather than clear demarcation of differences in organization among normal, neurotic, borderline neurotic, borderline proper, borderline psychotic, and psychotic personalities.

It is difficult to forsake the certainty that neat categorization provides for the less secure ground of searching out organizational strengths and malformations; evaluating the degree to which each individual has negotiated the fulcrum; discriminating between conflict-free and conflict-bound functioning, between regression and fixation and, probably most difficult of all, to follow the fluctuations in the middle-range borderline situations where material is presented now in structured form, now in experiential, as movement shifts forward and back around the fulcrum. Yet clinicians rediscover daily that, despite the category into which the patient has been cast, they have to grope for the unique features in the individual patient; borderline patient *A* resembles only in the broadest terms borderline patient *B*. A form of certainty is provided by the concepts of psychoanalytic developmental psychology, not in how-to-do-it procedures to be followed by rote, but by the security of a theory that helps us know where to address the patient in his unique struggle with the life task of organization, where he has succeeded and needs affirmation, and where he has failed and needs therapeutic repair of the malformations. Beyond that, there is the daily excitement of knowing as precisely as present knowledge allows what is going on in the patient, what we are doing, and why.

4. We now redescribe the role of the adult partner in the dyad, the environment in Hartmann's sense, while keeping constantly in mind that the lion's share of adaptation rests with the infant, with the endowment that she or he brings to the encounter. Therefore, in the discussion to follow, much technical emphasis is placed upon enabling patients to participate in the therapeutic endeavor to correct their distortions and to advance their levels of organization. Were adult pathology derived simply from the maternal side of the dyad or from the wider environment how much easier our task would be. But psychoanalytic developmental psychology is not a one-sided object relations theory, but a theory of interaction.

Optimally the mother of symbiosis is sufficiently attuned and flexible so that she can become the mother of separation as the aggressive drive of the infant begins to achieve phase dominance over the libidinal drive that has maintained the symbiotic connection. Ability to regress in the service of the ego (Kris, 1952) in her mothering role and to progress, that is, to move flexibly within it, are usually factors of the mother's development. In practical form, she cooperates with the child's aggressive thrust out of the symbiotic membrane (Mahler) aiding and even nudging the child into separation serving activity. Similar gentle nudging by the therapist is illustrated in some of the dialogue in chapter 10. The mother of separation recognizes and abets the infant's first attempts to do for itself that which she had been doing for the infant. Let us take two easily recognizable examples, feeding and language.

Infants grab at the feeding spoon quite early, using aggressive drive energy to wrest it away from mother in the mutually reinforcing processes of selective identification and development that we have described elsewhere (1977). The mother yields the spoon and can live comfortably with the temporary messiness attendant upon surrendering it to the still imprecise fine muscle control of the infant. Similarly with regard to language, recognition of the child's attempt to communicate fosters development; the child acquires the capacity for symbolization and moves toward the higher level of object relations involved in semantic communication so well described by Spitz. Growth-retarding are criticism, mockery, infantilizing imitation of the "cute" words. Optimal, tolerable frustration provides the opportunity to develop conflict-solving capacities. With frustration, there will be hostility, anger, even rage, unless it is dosed and provided within the context of optimal gratification as well. Where frustration is excessive, the ego does not have the gradual opportunity to bring affective reactions under control, that is to say, to incorporate them comfortably within the organizing process.

5. Ego functioning is highly valued. Basic to our reformulation of developmental theory is the proposal that the ego *is* the process of organization, defined by its functioning. This reflects a conceptual hierarchy that values functioning, a sine qua non of mental health. Here we follow Rapaport's definition of activity as ego functioning, something quite different from simple motor action which may pursue passive aims or reflect simple motor discharge. Any therapeutic intervention that promotes ego functioning, therefore, constitutes ego building by extending the capabilities of the ego. One clinical observation that led us to the formulation that ego is organizing process is that improved psychic life is reflected in better functioning. The process of enabling patients to further their levels of organization by helping them employ latent ego capacities strengthens the ego.

Our proposal regarding drive development (chapter 3) includes the suggestion that an ever-widening, ever-ascending spiral of differentiation and integration proceeds as identification (libidinal object retention) facilitates also an ever-widening scope of individuating activity (aggressive drive dominated separation). The organizing principle as enunciated by Mahler involves aspects of ego organizational drive differentiation and affect organization. To achieve this technically, we stress the importance of maintainance of a positive affective climate in the therapeutic situation. This replicates the necessary positive affective balance of experience with the primary object so essential for structuring. Involved is a complex process in which two elements are intricately intertwined:

a) Evenly distributed cathexis between self and object representations (Jacobson) attained by the time of psychological birth. This captures precisely the essence of the necessity for a favorable balance of positive affective investment in self and object representations.

b) For that to eventuate, separation processes require optimal fueling—enough frustration and absenting of mother to nudge the infant on, not so much that the positive balance is overthrown. If it is overthrown, self esteem is impaired, as is object esteem. These are developmental achievements that are promoted within the dyadic experience if all goes well. The growth-promoting task of the therapist as catalyst of development, although modelled along lines similar in affective quality to the primary experience, is not a duplication of parenting, as we have stressed.

Reality, of course, can be quite different from the ideal developmental situation, that of the well-enough endowed infant in interaction with the attuned mother. The potential patient population, especially the borderline population, consists of persons who have endured growth-impeding life experiences—absent mothers or fathers, broken marriages, psychotic or alcoholic or abusive parents, unmarried mothers who are themselves children, parents who are seriously ill, who die. The child itself may have had unfortunate illnesses, accidents, physical handicaps; may have suffered an unusual traumatic experience, disaster, displacement, or even war. Some conditions tax the parent's ability to provide an "average expectable environment" (Hartmann) and the child's capacity to adapt and to proceed with the organizing process.

The ego apparatuses require quickening for functions such as perception, memory, anticipation, and the effects derived from them to become of use to the individual in involving him in interaction, sorting out inside from outside, psyche from soma, self images from object images—the totality of differentiation and integration—the organizing process itself. With time, functions such as reality testing, the senses such as smell and hearing, the motor apparatus (especially locomotion) aid this process. Hartmann notes that any listing of ego functions is intrinsically incomplete. We have not attempted to present an exhaustive list, only an illustrative one. Our main purpose is to emphasize that functioning is highly valued. In the succeeding sections on technique, we allude to additional functions.

6. The therapeutic interaction in the less adequate structures will be marked by search for repetition of experiences with split object images whereas, in secure structures, transference is prominent. Where malformations have occurred early in the organizing process, hindering adequate negotiation past the fulcrum of development, the therapeutic situation itself is likely to become the milieu through which narcissistic supplies are sought. As indicated in chapter 8, these situations are delicate for the therapist. They call for attunement to the patients' needs, to their lowered capacity to distance themselves and to distinguish past from present, and for simultaneous attunement in the therapist to his own conscious and unconscious responses where these sometimes constitute the only signals about the patient. While this holds true for the structured patient as well, the demands upon the therapist are less in those cases, and the therapist can even rely on the better structured patient to correct the therapeutic errors. Narcissistic injury in the lesser structures is less likely to be forgiven.

7. The extent to which the fulcrum is negotiated determines which areas of organization call for ego building and, in an overall way, determines not only the form of the treatment but the role of the therapist, that is, whether the therapist is to be principally catalyst or interpreter. The many tasks of the fulcrum are negotiated gradually, progressively, and regressively, with detours (as Hartmann put it) and are interrelated. Of special importance alongside of quickening of functions is that affects differentiate and acquire shadings—elation, joy, pleasure, sad-

ness, sorrow, depression, gratitude, love, envy—shadings which become involved with the ego in mood regulation. We take a special view of hostile affect as an element of affect differentiation that comes under the control of the ego as the fulcrum is negotiated. Technically, we regard hostility, when it appears clinically, as an integral feature of differentiation and organization. We deal with it as we would any other aspect of development even though it can tend to take over the treatment itself. This is less likely to occur if we do not give it star billing in the patient's performance. As we observe the results of such technique, we are rewarded not only by our own excitement and pleasure but by the even greater one of seeing the patients get better and, often enough, hearing their own wonderment and pleasure expressed.

Identification of Malformations in the Organizing Process

As the clinical companion to chapter 10 on diagnosis, this section illustrates how the therapist "tunes in" to malformations in organization. The entire thrust of psychoanalytic developmental psychology prepares us, when we meet the patient, to keep the whole person in focus as we place the magnifying glass of our theoretical knowledge on the problems to be identified. In that way, we see not only the pathology but the adaptive features, and how both intertwine with a third feature, larger than these two alone, the total organization. The first gambit is, of course, the prerogative of the patient, sometimes clearly taken in the presenting request. More often, the presenting request is a façade behind which we have to seek the real problem. In either event, the therapist is called upon to respond in some way. The therapist gears his responses to serve the dual purpose of opening pathways that will lead to more and more information and, simultaneously, to begin to establish the therapeutic alliance. The ensuing engagement carries the process forward.

Freud (1913) used a trial analysis as the only way he knew to ascertain whether the structure could tolerate psychoanalytic procedure. This is a paradigm of diagnostic exploration of ego organization. While we would not subject the patient to analysis at the outset, we retain the philosophy of exploration. Freud's decision, after the trial analysis, was either to continue the analysis or to dismiss the patient. That was before the large repertory of psychoanalytically oriented psychotherapy had been elaborated. Now we have a number of treatment procedures at our disposal and we can be versatile about choosing the one best suited to the patient's organization. Therefore, we suggest meeting with the patient for a number of sessions for the purpose of evaluation, deferring decision about the form of treatment to be undertaken until the form of organization is determined. In such diagnostic evaluation, we assess not only organization and its malformations but also adaptation and capacity for change. We reserve for the therapist alone determination of the form of treatment to be recommended. Many patients "prescribe" the treatment, usually in the form of frequency. Because of the current prevalence of fads, some ask for a particular form of therapy that they have heard about. We do not recommend involving oneself in discussion about the pros and cons of the various forms, and especially do we not argue about the fads. But we do consider that the therapy is not to be Procrustean, and so we recommend versatility on the part of the therapist. So far as the patient is concerned, we use whatever technique, in our judgment, best serves him.

A young married woman with two preschool age children is referred by another patient who is happy about her own progress in a classical analysis. The referring patient's friend is having serious marital problems and she wants to direct her towards the kind of treatment that has been so helpful to her. The potential patient arrives with her mother because, as the therapist learned not long after, she is afraid to travel (by taxi) alone. The children are totally cared for by a nurse because the patient is unable to function as a mother. She is asked, after the appropriate polite introductions and handshaking, whether she would like to come into the consultation room alone, while her mother remains in the waiting room. This attempt is always to be made, whether with a marital couple or parent and adult child, as in the case under discussion. The response tells us immediately whether separation can be tolerated by either or both persons. Here, both the patient and mother agreed rather readily but, the therapist sensed, not easily. It appeared more as though they felt so desperate and helpless that compliance to the authority of the therapist dominated their decision.

In the consulting room, the patient "talked freely," but in a frantic, rapid torrent of words that had little focus. The therapist did learn some facts about the life history, the primary family, the marital relationship, several suicide attempts. The diagnostic picture is that of a level of organization that is failing to retain much grip on the secondary process and has already failed in whatever defensive arrangement might have been organized before (decompensation). The patient wanted analysis like her friend so that she could remain at home, maintain her marriage, and continue life as usual. The therapist decided that appropriate treatment could best be carried out on an inpatient basis and made the necessary arrangements.

This rather simple example is especially useful for beginning therapists; we use our own judgment and do not get swept up by how the patient would like to arrange the treatment. But we have inserted it here, also, to show that, where psychotic organization is patent, we have the least difficulty in decision-making. The diagnosis in terms of organization is not so clear-cut in the many borderline situations that we encounter. Therefore, it is desirable to see the patient as many times as necessary, usually between one and six, by which time there is likely to be a fair grasp of the level of organization, whether a preponderance of development has passed the fulcrum, whether it hovers around the fulcrum, or whether those developmental tasks have not been well-negotiated. Putting it in other terms, we wish to know how much patients are living in the immediacy of the experiential interaction, how much in the structure, and, in the in-between cases, how they move back and forth from time to time. Rarely can this be determined in a single session, but its rough outlines will be revealed in the course of a few sessions in which the therapist seeks out the following:

1. Is the presenting request specific or vague? That is, are there identifiable problems, symptoms, logically thought-out reasons why treatment is sought—indications that secondary process thought may be in operation. This is not wholly reliable, but serves only as a guide. A patient whose development pivots back and forth around the fulcrum can pull his thoughts together for presentation, while the regressive trends may reveal themselves later. Overly anxious patients may appear to be more regressed than their usual level. If there is a vague feeling that life is not as good as it might be, that too is only the roughest of guides. It may be because the patient is not at a level of organization that makes it possible for the patient to formulate his problems clearly for presentation, but vagueness may also be a characteristic of a relatively symptom-free character neurosis in which secondary process thought is intact.

2. How does the level of anxiety appear and, especially, how does it fluctuate? It is not likely that any prospective patient comes to a first consultation without anxiety. In many instances, because the therapist has met the patient with kindly interest and because the unknowns about the therapist, the arrangements, the fee, and the like, even what the therapist looks like, are no longer a mystery, the anxiety abates towards the end of the session or is noticeably less in the second meeting. Psychiatrists in certain situations where they can see the patient only once, for diagnosis and assignment or disposition, test the anxiety tolerance to the limit. This is contraindicated if the same therapist is to continue treatment. We are relatively unfamiliar with the administrative needs of a large institution and so we might concede, reluctantly, that it may be necessary to challenge in some situations. If it is, it is a necessary evil, possibly more dictated by pressure of time, bulk of patient load, and other considerations having little to do with the needs of the patient, for it is difficult to imagine any

situation in which it would be useful for the patient to be challenged and traumatized.

3. How does the patient handle anxiety? Although every patient is anxious, some tolerate it better than others and even use it as a stimulus that calls forth the best ego functioning. Thus, there are many persons, probably but not exclusively, with a high level of organization who show themselves in the best light under stress. This capacity comes to their aid, for example, in job interviews, in crises, when taking examinations, speaking in public, and the like. We can know from this whether ego functions are conflict free or conflict bound. Patients who are unable to function in the stress of anxiety are not necessarily less-structured; it may be that certain ego functions are bound up in conflict. To speak publicly, for example, as is traditionally known, may be so enmeshed with exhibitionistic wishes that there is an inhibition of function. One could go on with such examples, but a long listing would hardly be better than reading *Inhibitions, Symptoms and Anxiety* (Freud, 1926).

The patient whose anxiety does not abate, who cannot employ competent defenses nor tolerate the small doses of anxiety that we all live with, who is in terror most of the time, who does not have self-soothing mechanisms but needs to be soothed, or the one who cannot even accept soothing, is living with levels of anxiety that have not diminished to a signal.

4. What is the affective repertory range? Beyond anxiety, are there other affects? Is there not even anxiety? Is there too much overt hostility, or its opposite, too much compliance? Is the affect appropriate to the material, to the life situation, to the immediacy of the therapeutic encounter? What are the mood swings, how wide, and in which direction? Is affect preponderantly depressive? If so, does depression ever abate? Under what circumstances? Is there optimism, if not in the present, about the future? Can the patient love? What is the level of self esteem?

5. How are frustration and disappointment handled? With excessive rage? With withdrawal? Is there paranoid ideation?

6. Is regression reversible, that is, under the control of the ego? Along what lines does regression take place—psychosex-

ually, in ego functioning, object relations? Is it in the service of the ego (Kris), that is, for pleasure or creativity, or does the organization crumble with it? What is the history of accomplishment or failure? The capacity for work and leisure?

7. What is the motivation for treatment, unconscious as well as consciously stated? We do not take seriously conscious opposition or statements such as "My wife wanted me to come." We navigate with the wind and tide, making the best use of these to carry the patient a small distance beyond where he is. So we deal with the fact that the patient is here in our consultation room to tell us, "I don't really believe in therapy." Hardly anyone would think it useful to pay a fee to say that. Therefore, we look behind that to where the favorable wind blows. What really brought the patient there? We try to connect with that. "Even though your wife sent you and you don't believe in therapy, let's use the time, as long as you are here, to talk more about your situation." To be assiduously avoided is debate about the value of therapy. What we search for is where to capture, if even for a moment, the spot where the "unmotivated" patient feels troubled, for that is what really brought the patient to our door.

8. First cousin to the question of motivation is resistance. Does the level of organization include capacity to defend? On what level? With an intact ego in response to signal anxiety? Without adequate defense and with fear of annihilation? With some vacillation between those two poles because the fulcrum is not fully negotiated? What defenses are used? How completely? Have they become rigid and maladaptive? Is the patient aware of that? Are the defenses organized within the structure? Are they on a lesser level? Does the patient defend against unconsciously wished-for-merger? In terms of resistance, does the patient fear the immediacy of the relationship or conflict with id or superego?

9. How does the patient enter the therapeutic alliance as it is proferred? Is the patient easy to engage? Too easy? Does he meet the therapist half way? Does the therapist have to reach out three-fourths of the way? Nearly all the way? What are the reasons? Passivity, dependency, lack of functioning, poor endow-

ment (intelligence), withdrawal, hostility, fear of engulfment, pathological narcissistic self sufficiency?

10. What is the nature of the therapeutic relationship that the patient is able to form? Is it transference proper or object replication? What are the patient's object relationships outside of the therapeutic situation?

11. Does the patient have a clear and firm sense of gender identity? This should have been acquired in the second year of life. Who were the major primary identificatory figures? Was there opportunity for and movement toward triadic relationships with the father, siblings, and others? What was the patient's ordinal position? How soon after the next older sibling and before the next younger was the patient born? What were the sexes of the other siblings? What is the picture of the adult relationships with parents and siblings? If a parent has died, was she or he mourned appropriately according to the age level of the child? Does the patient experience himself as a progenitor?

12. What is the patient's childhood and adult sexual history? What is the nature of the patient's present sexual functioning? This is not usually possible, nor perhaps even desirable to ascertain too early. If the patient is completely defended, the details will emerge slowly in the course of treatment. In any event, whatever is told at the outset is often vague or even unconsciously distorted. In the case described in chapter 4 where fellatio was, not uncommonly, the preferred form of sex, the patient did not reveal that for two years, glossing over the details of his sexual activity until then. Women often feel reluctant to acknowledge frigidity before the therapeutic alliance is firm. It used to be thought that patients who reveal their sex practices too soon are undefended. In the light of today's greater freedom and openness about sex, we may have to revise that as a secure diagnostic sign. In our teaching experience we find that beginning therapists, especially if unanalyzed, are more reluctant to ask about sex practices than their patients are to tell them. In any event, the caution not to pounce upon, force, or challenge the patient applies in this regard as well as elsewhere in the evaluation and treatment.

13. How far have self and object images differentiated? Have the separate images coalesced into distinct representations or is splitting of the self and object images a feature of the clinical picture? To what degree is there an evenly distributed positive cathexis between self and object representations if these exist? Is there fluctuation in degrees of differentiation?

14. How far has internalization and superego formation proceeded? To cohesive superego or disparate superego components? Again, who are the major identificatory figures? If superego is formed, is it too severe? Does the patient experience guilt, fear of loss of love, fear of object loss? Again, is there fluctuation in levels?

15. Has the Oedipus complex proper been reached? With or without subphase flaws? Has there been regression? Along what developmental lines? Is the oedipal organization too burdened by subphase need for competent resolution?

16. Are there any major or unusual illnesses in the life history?

It is not possible for the therapist to keep all these questions in mind, nor to find the answers to more than a small fraction of them in the first few meetings with the patient. More will be answered in the course of treatment. Not all will be answered even by termination but, by then, much will have been changed by the treatment. The questions can help us to listen, to know what to listen for and what kinds of questions to ask. It is not desirable to ask questions of the patient in the form presented here. Much will come spontaneously in many cases. It is the therapist's task, as he listens, to formulate hypotheses, revise these as further material emerges, discard them for new hypotheses if the information leads in other directions.

Some cases are presented to illustrate how the beginning sessions appear clinically:

The first case illustrates the presenting request as a façade, and, at the same time, shows important determinants of whether and how successfully the fulcrum of development has been negotiated; it also delineates the long-term therapeutic tasks. A thirty-two-year-old professional woman is referred by her husband's former analyst. The husband has completed treatment. She presents her problem as excessive anxiety, especially in her work. This turns out to be the very tip of the iceberg. As the exploration goes forward, a slightly deeper reason for her wanting treatment is revealed obliquely. Her husband, having been analyzed, has something good. A bit of resentment is mixed with the more overtly expressed pleasure at his vast improvement. Her treatment is to be the equalizer. The therapist thinks, of course, about phallic envy. That soon turns out to be the least of the matter. The therapist takes his time. A barrage of questions might elicit information more quickly, but that is uncertain and would be at the expense of the therapeutic alliance which provides the climate within which information is volunteered more trustingly. So we offer a kindly interest; the therapist waits, listens, and formulates hypotheses, asking occasional questions to test them out. The patient discloses gradually that the anxiety is not confined to her professional functioning; it is pervasive. She describes events that make her paralyzingly frightened. She had gone to lunch with a colleague at a restaurant frequented by many persons she knew. Nevertheless, when a friend greeted her unexpectedly from another table, she was thrown off balance and became exceedingly anxious, as though the ego function of anticipation had not been competent enough to have prepared her for such an encounter. This suggests not only failure to anticipate, but also that signal anxiety fails or possibly has not even been attained.

In another session, shortly after, having felt the therapist's empathy for her distress, she ventured to reveal also that she is a "compulsive" handwasher because she is panicked by dirt. Thus, the façade of sophistication gradually disappears, revealing a terrified woman behind it. The revised hypothesis now becomes that there is borderline organization far below the fulcrum, and is borne out as regression to primary process thinking appears too quickly, without the gradual loosening of cathexis characteristic of higher levels of organization. The therapist begins to look for where, in the subphases, something might have impaired the organizing process. As has been indicated, there are many places where one might search—the life history, dreams, and elsewhere, depending upon the material presented. Here, transference-like manifestations come to hand and so the therapist explores whether these represent true transference in the sense of distinction between self and object representations, or object replication where subphase longing propels search for narcissistic supplies. The therapist searches for clues that will tell him whether there is a distinction between past and present, self and object images, whether the images have become representations of whole persons, and for the affective charge, features of the organizing process that will inform about the level attained.

By this time in the evaluation process, treatment will inevitably have begun, for we cannot separate diagnosis from the treatment process. Sometimes we try, if we are going to refer the patient. Then, we content ourselves with a more general impression of the level of organization. Often enough, despite effort to minimize our impact, transference is formed. If the patient is at the object replication level, the wrench of referral is usually even more painful because the immediacy of the need is so great. An apparent exception is the narcissistic patient, sometimes referred to as "schizoid" because of the clinical picture of aloofness. This is deceptive. The patient may appear to be impervious to hurt, but is easily wounded.

The patient we are discussing begins to bring every panic situation to the therapist. When her child becomes ill, she telephones the therapist before the pediatrician, a presumptive sign of object replication where need obscures judgment. The patient's panic takes precedence over the child's illness. More simply stated, the therapist has become the need-gratifying object, the omnipotent maternal figure to whom the patient turns as would a young child, as the immediate source of comfort and wisdom. This, indeed, does suggest that the present is confused with the past and that the patient is still living in the immediacy of the dyadic experience. That hypothesis is borne out as more information is obtained about the maternal anxious overprotection. An anxious mother is a poor soother and cannot be identified with for self soothing. Certainly, then, attainment of signal anxiety is precluded.

Anxious overprotection is a global description of the maternal climate. We still have to search for the specifics of subphase impairment, the collision point so to speak, where maternal anxiety collided with appropriate subphase need—the point where flawed organization had its inception. That search will proceed, perhaps over the entire course of treatment. And so once again we have demonstrated, this time in an ongoing case, that the presenting request for psychoanalysis is the patient's prescription only. Diagnosis is based on careful identification of the malformations in organization which cue the therapist into the best treatment modality as well as help the therapist determine the specific locus where growth promotion is to be addressed.

Another case, presented more briefly, illustrates in a more circumscribed way how failure in the capacity to distinguish adequately between self and object images is sometimes seen clinically. A forty-year-old divorced businessman is in treatment for almost a year. The therapist has had a brief winter vacation in February and now the patient wishes to have an Easter vacation to spend with his young daughter who lives the year round with her mother. He asks whether he will have to pay for the missed sessions. He has been in treatment with other therapists three times before and knows the usual arrangements.

Therapist: You must have a reason for asking.

Patient: Well, I thought when you went away you didn't pay me, so why should I have to pay you when I go away? (Failure to differentiate blurs logic.)

Therapist: Does that feel the same to you?

Patient: Sure.

Therapist: (Stretching the capacity for reality testing.) You see no difference in our situations?

Patient: Yeah, I guess there are some. It still feels unfair, though. I'll be paying for all that time. (It succeeds.)

Therapist: What will I be doing with the time?

Patient: I never thought about that. (Therapist hasn't existed when not seen.)

Therapist: Can you imagine now? (Stretches object retention.)

Patient: You'll probably see someone else. (Objects are interchangeable to therapist as they are to patient because of the faulty differentiation.)

Therapist: Would you want me to do that?

Patient: No, I'd rather pay and know that the time is saved for me.

Therapist: You know, you have the right to telephone in that time if you'd like.

The patient does not telephone in the three missed sessions of the week-long vacation. But much inroad has been made. Beginning at his level of weak differentiation, the therapist has used the opportunity, while in the very process of evaluating it, to promote greater differentiation. There are patients who comply submissively with the regulations about fees and other arrangements. That is not necessarily indicative of a higher level of organization or of better self-object differentiation. It may be. But submission may also serve to obscure the problem and postpone treatment of it. There is usually not much we can do about that but await another opportunity which can emerge in any form around any issue.

The next case illustrates a problem in impulse control and split object images. A patient describes a diatribe against her husband. She reports that all the while she is berating him she thinks, "Why am I carrying on so? He hasn't really done anything. But I can't stop." Reality testing and judgment and cognition, the result of therapeutic repair of those functions earlier in the treatment, are overridden by failure of impulse control. Earlier, she had not been able to distinguish her husband from the primary object to whom she is bound by rage. Now she can appreciate that he loves her. But the "bad" object images have not yet combined with the "good" into representation of a whole person. This will be the task of ongoing treatment. The prognosis is now favorable because the ego functions that will be the ally of therapy have become more autonomous. The patient still experiences her object world within the frame of reference of all "for" or all "against," but she now *knows* better.

The following case illustrates low-level frustration tolerance and an apparent "resistance" or absence of motivation, faulty superego formation, failure in self-object differentiation and excessive rage:

The patient is a twenty-eight-year-old lawyer. He is the court-assigned advocate for juveniles who have committed serious crimes. He has good rapport with his clients because he merges with them in their rage and its quick translation into action. He wants to be treated because he is "in love" with a young woman who has had some therapy and has benefitted greatly. She urges him, and her former therapist makes the referral. He arrives. The challenge is immediate.

Patient: Well, she got me here. Now what?
Therapist: I don't know yet. I have to listen to whatever you may have to tell me.

This diffuses the challenge by not challenging in response. It proclaims a welcome regardless of the rage (and anxiety) beneath the bravado. It succeeds. Over a period of two or three sessions he tells the therapist much about his own concerns, about which his girlfriend does not know—near delinquent acts that, by inadequate differentiation, attract him to his clients. Such poor level of self-object differentiation is sometimes termed identification, but that is an error for it would imply a greater degree of differentiation. The layman refers to this phenomenon as vicarious.

Shortly after therapy begins, his hostility is attenuated enough so that the good object images come into ascendancy. He feels a surge of love which is welcomed but is examined with caution while there is not yet a whole object representation. Under its impetus, he plans a special evening with his girlfriend. He is able to be tender, to tell her that he loves her, and to propose marriage. Thus far, there appears to be a high level of anticipation, capacity to plan and to wait, and even capacity to love. The therapist begins to think that there had been a higher level of development reached and that the clinical picture is a regressive one.

In the next sentence, the therapist learns that the functioning collapsed rapidly. The young woman responded gently to the proposal, saying that much as she liked him, there were aspects of the relationship that she felt would impair a permanent one, and so she had to refuse. He reports that, before he could think, he exploded with, "What the hell do you mean you won't marry me?" Thus he produced a paradigm of exactly the behavior that had led her to decline his proposal.

The next case is illustrative of the developmental distortions created by a superior cognitive apparatus. Children need to discover, gradually, that the parents have human failings. This knowledge is best tolerated when it is attained at the phase-specific time, that is, when the organizing process has reached the point where it can encompass this event. We have said that the gifted overly hostile patient is adept at detecting the therapist's flaws. This can be turned to good advantage when the hostility subsides or where there is less at the outset. The gifted child may indeed experience a form of object loss with abrupt disillusionment. We have found it possible and therapeutically effective, with gifted adults, to use the good endowment to help the patients look back empathically at the children they were.

Patient: They were so rotten. I listened to my father talk about his shady business deals. They all laughed with so much pleasure when he got the better of someone. It frightened me.

Therapist: (With the immediate situation in mind, but also attempting to formulate a broad intervention that will open pathways for oedipal material to emerge in the future.) Were you afraid he'd get the better of you?

Patient: No. I knew I was smarter. I was more afraid of that.

Therapist: What was there to fear?

Patient: I could have shown him up.

Therapist: Why is that frightening?

Patient: I can outwit many people.

Therapist: (Brings it to the present) Does that include me?

Patient: You have no faults. You do everything right. (Defends the object.)

The therapist chose not to foreclose this theme too soon in the hope of being able to deal with it on many levels—optimally, but not always possible in severe borderline pathology, on the oedipal level as well. In order to keep the issue alive, it was approached with three possible steps in view:

1. To show the patient that he defends the object and that this was adaptive in childhood:

Therapist: You need a strong, powerful therapist and so you overlook my shortcomings. Surely you have noted them.

Patient: (With reluctance, many sessions later, after much persistence on the part of the therapist): You don't understand the fine points of my profession (music) very well. (The patient has chosen to mention a "flaw" that reveals obliquely his awareness that his endowment is superior to the therapist's, but places it in an area where the therapist's feelings will be least likely to be hurt.)

Very gradually, after many more sessions, the patient finds the courage to acknowledge, with the therapist's active assistance, that he has always known that he is unusually intelligent and gifted. (This results from competent reality testing and is not narcissistically unreal.) He gets so angry and impatient with the stupidity he sees all around him. The therapist affirms the reality of the endowment and tells the patient that he will always experience that those around him are less gifted. This would not be a problem in the present were it not burdened by the adaptation that was necessary in the past. He needed his parents as a child and therefore had to cloud his observations in order to preserve their omnipotence. Persistence of earlier needs makes for maladaptation in the present.

2. To help him practice his skills and vent his anger within the benign climate of the therapeutic situation. The therapist need not be brighter or more gifted than the patient in order to be able to function as a therapist. This case resembles that described in chapter 7, where that patient had become his mother's dolt because she needed to mold him in that direction. It is interest-

ing to discuss the organizational differences between these two cases in order to show that the technical approaches must be guided by those differences. In the first case, adaptation was to the mother's unconscious need for a dull child; in the second, the inborn apparatus was not suppressed by the environment. But it encountered conflict on the developmental levels of need for omnipotent parents, later of the need to protect the parents from excessive rage. These experiences in these first two levels so burden oedipal organization that, if that level is reached, the organization process is almost altogether unable to encompass it. This describes what we mean by inability to arrive at the oedipal position "with both feet."

3. One of the most difficult aspects of technique for the beginning therapist is to learn to plan ahead, to phrase an intervention with an eye to the future course of therapy even though the more immediate purpose is to deal with the problem where it presents itself at the moment. Taking the long view has many advantages. In *Ego Psychology: Theory and Practice* we describe the process of interpretation as a pyramid or broad-based triangle. The broadest interpretation is the last to be made, but the first and narrowest as well as those that follow include the last one in the therapist's mind and are phrased to encompass it. In the case described, the therapist had the levels of anxiety in mind. The patient was at the level of fear of loss of the object in the session detailed. But the intervention was phrased so as not to foreclose fear of loss of the object's love, fear of castration, and fear of the superego as these are condensed within the verbalization.

Kris said as long ago as 1956 that knowledge of childhood development helps the analyst of an adult to be keener about features of development that might have gone astray in the patient's childhood. That was the period when Spitz and Mahler had begun their pioneering investigations, but before knowledge about development reached the heights of Mahler's 1975 organizing principle. Ritvo (1974a) believes that it is useful for the analyst of adults to have been a child analyst as well. We do not regard that as an essential prerequisite, but we cannot imagine that adult psychotherapy or psychoanalysis can be conducted without developmental theory. The very cogent reason is that attunement in the therapist or analyst must be to organizational flaws resulting from interaction in the primary dyad. The therapist has to detect the very locus of the first and subsequent distortions in the organizing process. Spitz already knew this in 1959.

Can this be done at the present state of our technical knowledge? Not in every case. We are only now learning to be alert to the clues in adult behavior that help us to recognize inadequacies in organization. Some of these are to be found in:

1. The life history
2. Sometimes in the quality of sleep and dreaming
3. Object relatedness toward contemporaries
4. Behavior in the therapeutic situation; whether there is a tendency to search for replication of primary object experience
5. Tendency to split the object world into all "good " and all "bad"
6. Discrepancy between potential and performance; whether such discrepancy results from inhibition or from failure in quickening of the ego apparatuses

As to prognosis, we look for presence of hope that things will improve. This is not the same as "faith" in the therapeutic method. It informs us that there were positive affective experiences that may be revived in treatment.

Evaluation of the Reorganizing Capacity

In addition to clinical detection of flaws in the organization process, it is necessary to evaluate the potential for reorganization. In the very process of evaluating the organizing capacity, the therapist tests its limits by "stretching" it as illustrated in the preceding section. Thus, during the very process of evaluation, treatment begins to take place. Even if patients are to be referred, they may be prepared for treatment and will arrive there well ahead of where they were when they came for evaluation.

The organizing capacity appears to have the quality of an innate given. We know that some patients "use" therapy better than others. Perhaps, there, the reorganizing capacity is more efficient intrinsically. Often it is the less damaged patient who exhibits a better capacity. Is it because the innate endowment was such that severe damage was averted? Was the life experience better? We do not know; one sees patients who have suffered severely and yet make good progress, while others with equivalent or even less potentially traumatic environmental experience do not do as well in life or in treatment. Therapy cannot alter the innate endowment, nor do we know of other means of accomplishing such alteration. And so first we look for the most obvious. Probably intelligence is the most recognizable innate factor. Patients with low intelligence can be helped. The pace is often slower but that too varies, and there are always surprises. The more intelligent patients do have the capacity to get a better grasp of the treatment process. But as described earlier, they may also attempt to use their gift to defeat the treatment. We need not be more intelligent than they. We help them see how they use their gifts maladaptively in object relationships and help them alter that. We examine all apparatuses, where they are patent, to distinguish whether they are conflict free or conflict borne. If the former, they are presumably at maximum potential; if the latter, much can be done to help the patients approach their potential. In addition to distinction between endowment and whether ego functions are involved in conflict, also to be weighed is whether apparatuses do exist but have lain dormant for want of quickening. These are not easy distinctions to make. We do not have assured methods of evaluating them. Yet they have to be thought about among the matters that the therapist sifts in the continuing and ever-changing process of evaluation. That very process resembles the action-reaction-action cycle. Some of the illustrative dialogue we have presented shows that. In fact, the surest test of whether organizing capacity exists is whether action-reaction-action occurs. If it does, the organizing capacity is at work; therefore it exists.

The regressive potential is a determinant in evaluation of the organization capacity. In chapter 5 and in the preceding section of this chapter, we describe two patients whose regressions resembled plunging elevators as their behavior moved rapidly from rather high levels to low.

Another patient, a woman, has a disturbing dream. She dreams that her husband turned into a horse and flew away. The manifest content does not tell us why she found the dream so upsetting. After all, there are flying horses in myth, and a flying horse may be an appropriate symbol for an erection. The patient's interest in her husband's masculinity had not impressed the therapist as very great heretofore, nor does the affect match such an advanced dream thought. Matters become somewhat clearer as the patient describes the bas relief on a church she passes on the way to the therapist's office. The therapist is familiar with it and had thought of it as he listened to the dream. It depicts God's outstretched hands waiting to receive St. Paul as he ascends to heaven on a winged horse. This brings matters into the transference or object replication. We have an opportunity to distinguish if we use this material to that end. It takes precedence over dream interpretation. We are also searching out the patient's organizing potential by evaluating the depth of regression and capacity to recover, and especially by testing her ability to involve herself in an action-reaction-action cycle.

Patient: I found the dream so disturbing that after it awakened me I couldn't go back to sleep for hours. I feel a little shaky now even in telling you about it.

Therapist: Yes, I can see that.

(Therapist chooses to say *I* to put himself into the interchange rather than "Yes, you have made that clear," which contains less of the therapist. The question is whether the proffer to join in will be met and whether it will soothe.) Let us try to determine more precisely what it was that you found so troubling. (Again, an invitation, this time to work together.)

Patient: It's hard to say; it was all so nightmarish. (Patient persists in describing a global reaction, whereas therapist attempts to introduce thinking processes and a beginning movement away from overwhelming anxiety.)

Therapist: Yes, it's very clear that it was. I think, however, that if we can begin to look at it bit by bit it may help you feel less disturbed by it.

This appears like simple reassurance, but is designed to help the patient involve herself in the process and to test her reorganizing capacity. If she has to yield to this dream without being able to analyze it, she is more at the mercy of her anxiety, denoting a reduced capacity for self-soothing and possibly therefore for reorganization. That appears to be the case, but the therapist does not conclude that it is hopeless, only that his role has to be a more active one this time:[1] He awaits the next opportunity to try to lead her a step ahead. In such fashion the patient's capacity for reorganizing toward higher psychic structure is continuously and cautiously tested.

The organizing capacity of the intact, well-structured neurotic is by definition competent. Subphase flaws, by and large, would not be noticeable for they exist in the form of healed-over scar tissue rather than as malformations in organization. The unmodified ego of the analysand was always thought to be equal to the analytic tasks of regression in the service of the ego, interpretation of resistance, defense and unconscious fantasy, use of free association to loosen the cathexis of the secondary process thought. There, the analyst provided interpretation, while the task of working through was left to the patient's unmodified ego. Clinically, it has proven to be much more difficult to divide the therapeutic tasks so neatly, since, as we have said, many pre-

[1]This is another example of what we mean by avoiding external confrontation in order to determine whether the incident can be turned to therapeutic use by means of confrontation from within.

sumptively analyzable patients have been found to have residual lesions from subphase inadequate development. One of the more humorous descriptions of technique before the subphase tasks were defined and delineated was the oscillation from couch to chair as seemingly unanalyzable material was uncovered (Greenacre, 1959). More serious, however, was that some analysts dismissed from treatment those whose structures were found to be unanalyzable, even after many years of "analysis."

Many analysts now agree that psychic structure is not the closed system heretofore believed. Some interaction takes place even in the most classically arranged psychoanalysis. Identification processes inevitably and desirably occur. It is striking that this proposition was formulated by Loewald in 1956 in a paper given before the American Psychoanalytic Association, yet not published until 1960, and that it took almost two decades more before it attained wider acceptance. Loewald describes a differential that exists between analysand and patient, in some way analogous to the normal growth-promoting differential that should exist between parent and child to spur processes of identification. Current knowledge of subphase development confirms Loewald's observation. All the more, then, is it essential to determine, in the course of treatment, whether the patient is open to such an identification process when subphase experience has been such that neurotic structure is barely attained. One must determine how reparative experiences are to be provided and whether they can be put to use by the patient.

Reconsider now the patient who has difficulty with that part of the compact that holds the patient financially responsible for the sessions arranged if the patient cannot come. The subway train gets stuck, or the car breaks down, or the taxi is caught in a traffic jam. The patient rightfully protests that it was not his fault. It can be reasonably expected that the neurotically structured patient would, after some protest, be able to appreciate that the unfortunate event happened to him and that the therapist cannot take that upon himself, for they are different persons. The patient who understands that is reflecting a high level capacity for differentiation of self representations from object representations, an outcome of the organizing capacity. The patient who is confused by the therapeutic compact is presumptively on a lesser level. The patient may be willing to accept the therapist's or analyst's authority, and that may reflect either trust and confidence, or compliance, but without a grasp of the essential factor, differentiation of self and object representations. If such patients can become curious about such differentials, it is a more hopeful sign that the organizing process may be promoted. If they cannot, the therapist must try to determine whether their acceptance reflects simple compliance without regard for the object or whether some trust truly exists. Total compliance may reflect a more morbid level of identity formation and withheld rage, whereas trust is indicative that there were some benign experiences in the subphases during structure formation.

The patient who becomes angry about payments for missed sessions is not necessarily more disturbed. Anger may reflect defense of the patient's identity, in that he seeks to preserve what he thinks and feels to be his own. We do not arrange artificial situations but use what inevitably comes to hand to test organizing capacity. Much depends upon the patients' reactions in the ongoing discussion of such events. How disabling is their anger? Are they at all aware that the therapist may have a valid point? How long does it take them to recover? Do they try, in spite of their feelings, to continue the work, or do they feel so angry about it that they begin to move toward premature termination? These are samplings of reactions to issues which are indices for evaluation of the capacity for reorganization.

In common with working through, determination of the patient's reorganizing capacity involves the analyst in a process of learning how to slide, or roll, with the resistance. A fundamental premise is that patients are "entitled" to their resistance by virtue of their level of development. This is a technical corollary of the dictum that the therapist tunes in to the organizational flaw, not to consequences of the flaw, that is, the overt behavior. (We elaborate upon this in the following section.) With this technical tool the therapist can form some judgment about the patient's resistance which will enable him to evaluate the chances for working through. If they are slim, the organizing capacity is diminished and the therapist must fall back from the issue which has aroused the resistance. For example:

Therapist: Some time ago you asked whether your Monday session could be shifted. Then I was unable to do so. Now, however, it would be possible for me to see you at four o'clock as you requested. Would you want that?

Patient: Oh! I suppose someone else is asking for a change in hours! (This response introduces a new subject entirely, which now takes precedence.)

Therapist: As a matter of fact, that is precisely what makes it possible for me to offer you this shift now. But you are troubled by that?

Patient: Well, I don't like the idea that you would do this for someone else when you wouldn't do it for me.

Therapist: You're right, there is nothing to like about that, if that is what you think I was doing.

Patient: Well, weren't you?

Therapist: While I could answer that very simply, it might be more useful if we could try to understand what brought you to that conclusion.

Patient: Oh, you make me so angry that I feel like getting up and walking out. Why can't I get a simple answer to a simple question? (From past experience therapist suspects patient is at the end of his frustration tolerance.)

Therapist: In that event, let me tell you that I did inquire about the possibility of someone's changing the time with you, but no one could then. You have had such long experience with people being too busy to bother about you that your feelings follow that script automatically whenever something doesn't turn out as you would like. When I asked you to talk about it, I thought that you might be able to figure it out by yourself.

Patient: Well, even so, I still don't want to make the switch. They would not do it for me when I needed it, so why should I bother?

Therapist: You are certainly under no pressure to do so; if you feel it will inconvenience you, there is no reason for you to agree. (Therapist, aware of the shift in object replication from himself as depriver, to the other patient as sibling representative, affirms the patient's feelings, but at the same time establishes another differential, this time by suggesting that a reason for not agreeing to the change could be self regard instead of petulance. The issue, however, has to be dropped unless the patient returns to it.)

This case illustrates yet another area where one can test the patient's capacities, in this instance the capacity for positive investment. In a well-structured patient, positive transference counterbalances negative, and both are expected phenomena in the analytic procedure. As we go down the developmental ladder, however, hostility intervenes to disturb the balance and overthrows positive connection. Failures in the quickening of apparatuses such as memory, anticipation, and the like also retard affect differentiation and affect development (see case illustration, chapter 2). There does not develop sufficient affective interest to enable the patient to gratify libidinal need by means of a firm connection with the therapist in the therapeutic alliance. Such connection is essential to facilitate identification processes.

Not only does the organizing capacity depend upon the endowment and degree of structuralization that the patient brings to therapy, it also fluctuates from time to time, from session to session, and even during the same session. Our discussion artificially isolates techniques for evaluation of this capacity from other aspects of diagnosis and treatment. The case illustrations make clear that such isolation is hardly possible in practice. Detection of developmental malformations, evaluation of the reorganizing capacity, and ego-building interventions are all parts of the whole therapeutic engagement.

The Therapist as Catalyst of Reorganization

In the psychoanalytic tradition, the role of the therapist as interpreter has become so deeply engrained that it permeates not only psychoanalysis proper but also the psychoanalytically oriented psychotherapies—the so-called "expressive" or "insight" therapies. As we take into account that probably all levels of organization, including neurosis, are to some degree malformed as the result of less-than-adequate subphase interaction, we begin to question whether interpretation alone adequately captures the essence of therapeutic activity. True, as well noted in the standard texts on psychoanalysis, specific auxiliary techniques that pave the way for interpretation are clearly delineated—clarification, for example. But these are regarded still as subordinate to the main purpose. It is inconsistent, within the broad theory of psychoanalytic developmental psychology, to consider the roles of psychoanalyst and psychotherapist to be different except in quality and emphasis.

Two compelling reasons force us to reconsider the technical role in both forms of therapy: 1) psychic structure may no longer be regarded as a closed system, and, therefore, the analyst enters the system as something other than interpreter, and 2) organizational malformations enter most, if not all, neuroses and, of course, dominate the picture in the less-than-neurotic forms of organization. Therefore, while interpretation retains an important and even crucial position in the technical repertory, it is timely to think that, in many instances, it is subordinate to the principal role of catalyst of organization.

We describe the role of catalyst as that of a presence that does not participate in the action. That comparison with chemistry has to be modified somewhat, for the therapist does have to involve himself, minimally to be sure, in some form of interaction even in the psychoanalysis of neurosis. It is well known that the patient will notice and become familiar with the analyst's or therapist's specific personality—his appearance, clothing, office furnishings and especially his style of response to the patient's material. Beyond that inevitable minimum, we describe specific therapeutic interventions deliberately designed to enter the structure of neurotic patients and even to involve oneself in the immediacy of the interaction with patients whose lesser organization calls for such participation. These qualifications appear to vitiate the strict construction we have applied to the definition of catalyst. And yet we prefer to retain that construction because it provides a base for disciplined departure that will accord with the patient's organizational need; it guards against involvement that goes beyond that need. The analyst or therapist as catalyst of organization guides the reshaping of that organization where necessary, but minimizes the uniqueness of his own personality.

For purpose of fulfilling that role, we have stressed that which hardly needs so much emphasis—the consistently benign atmosphere[2]. Perhaps we are overly concerned to counteract the position taken by some that challenge is useful. In our view, the reliable benign atmosphere is essential because:

1. It provides consistency that the patient can count on as he begins to participate in reorganization.

2. It provides the positive valence often lacking even in the organization of neurotic patients whose self and object representations are of whole persons. Where there is greater malformation, in borderline and narcissistic organization, negative self-object experience is presumed to have dominated the primary interaction and it would be damaging to repeat that.

3. This brings into play the therapeutic differential—namely, the therapist's behavior and responses do not meet the patient's stereotyped object expectations.

Our position is guided by Mahler's organizing principle—that major aspects of psychic structuring take place around processes of separation-individuation—and includes also Jacobson's concept of selective identification as the paradigm of the process of development. These are the models which guide the therapist, also, in elaborating technical interventions to promote growth and expansion into the object world. They determine the essential features of the therapeutic experience and dictate the modality—psychoanalysis where optimal structuralization exists and psychotherapy for the infinite varieties and degrees of lesser levels of structuralization.

[2]"It is certainly possible to forfeit this first success [rapport] if from the start one takes up any standpoint other than one of sympathetic understanding . . ." (S. Freud, 1913, p. 140).

We have distinguished the role of the therapist from the role of the mother in primary dyadic affirmation of infantile developmental needs. The adult patient has internalized whatever was provided in the primary dyad and has proceeded in his organization according to his individual capacity. Included in that organization is processing of the malformations resulting from inadequate provision of phase appropriate affirmation. Obviously, to continue to promote organization that has proceeded in a distorted direction retains the malformation. We may compare this with weaving an intricate pattern. If there is a mistake and the weaving proceeds nevertheless, the flaw will be incorporated into the design. We do not, as does the weaver, rip out the ongoing organization to reduce it to the flaw, in order then to organize anew. The patient's organizing capacity has to be promoted to correct the malformation without destroying the organizational structure. A better analogy is the shoring that supports a building while flaws are under repair.

We propose, in what follows, to illustrate the techniques more sharply by focusing on some specific areas. A complete listing of an entire repertory of interventions is not possible and would even be limiting to the creative practitioner. It is our hope that presentation of sample interventions will demonstrate the nature of growth promotion as the therapist functions as catalyst.

OBJECT REPLICATION

Therapist: Good morning.
Patient: What's good about it? It was murder getting here today!
Therapist: I see that it doesn't feel like a good morning to you. Let's try to know how it does feel.

The therapist does not follow the "script" and avoids responding to challenge. The therapist attempts thereby to begin the long process of correcting distorted expectations, particularly the patient's anticipation of negative responses. By avoiding entering into the stereotopy of the patient's expectations the therapist creates a situation in which the patient must question his anticipation of object replication. Optimally, the patient continues to be "disappointed" by the therapist's responses. Resolution of this "disappointment" comes about by means of ongoing differentiation. First to be distinguished are present from past. This is invariably difficult. In a sense it is less than half the struggle for, to distinguish present from past requires also a greater degree of differentiation of self from object images, as well as some decathexis of the primary object, in order to be able to cathect the therapist.

Here is the first of many reflections in the therapy of the fact that, while the patient's responses are organized within the experiences and limitations of the primary experience and its resultant in organizational malformation, the therapist is playing in another ball park. Also illuminated is the use of the differential for growth promotion (Loewald, 1960). The therapist's capacity to retain positive affect through the storms of the patient's hostility highlights an affective gap, forcing contemplation by the patient's ego functions of cognition and reality testing. At some point, a "moment of truth" can be ventured. If the patient fails to comment, the therapist makes an observation about this discrepancy after it has been repeated enough times to make denial and negation difficult:

Therapist: You have affirmed many times that there are no good mornings for you, but the reasons for your feeling this way have not yet emerged, although obviously they are very real for you.

The repetition will continue, but an important issue has been raised. By failing to follow the antagonistic lines structured by the patient's negotiations with the primary object, the therapist has opened a pathway for reorganization, long and tortuous as that probably will be. There can be anxiety about object loss in the course of this therapeutic process. Because of this fact, the cure will often feel worse than the disease. Intense separation anxiety will ensue if the therapist's benign responses successfully create a differential that feels, to the patient, as though the patient has to abandon primary object cathexes. The patient is, of course, in error and this, too, has to be explained in some way. What he abandons is only the negatively cathected interaction, not the object qua object.

AFFECT DIFFERENTIATION

A patient in treatment for two years began to reach resolution of his impulsive outbursts of rage at the therapist. Better reality testing and a reasonably good cognitive capacity contributed to this progress within therapeutic absence of counterhostility. Yet, the patient persisted in dismissing all that the therapist said with, "It's all lies!" Even the recovery of memories of parental lying, which momentarily brought appreciation for the workings of therapy, became subsumed to the conviction that the therapist is not truthful. The patient did not feel anxiety, but only an overwhelming anger, now tempered. Recognition of anxiety (affect differentiation) had to await further growth. In the meantime the therapeutic work focused on attenuating the connection with the primary interaction so that the experience can cease to dominate present object relations. The therapist abides by the fundamental premise that the patient is "entitled" to his reactions by virtue of his primary experiences; this helps equip the therapist to cope with countertransference reactions.

As the patient becomes more adept at differentiating the experience of the therapeutic present from the past—in this case to develop greater conviction about the therapist's truthfulness—the next step may be taken. This is to try to put the patient's cognitive capacity to work on the blindly angry responses. The following is the next interchange:

Therapist: It's hard to tell what happens to you in these circumstances. Do you have any idea?

Patient: No, I don't. I just get terribly impatient with everything. I want to break things, but rather than do that I feel like walking out.

Therapist: So you are trying to find a way of coping with something—at least you try not to break things.

Patient: If you can call that coping. I just try to brush the whole thing off.

Therapist: And do you succeed?

Patient: (Laughs a bit.) No! Most of the time you're too mean to permit me.

Therapist: (Recognizes laughter as reflecting that the therapeutic alliance is operative and therefore tries to take another step.) No, you're begging the question. What does happen?

Patient: Of course something happens. But it's happening right now again, you bother me and I'm afraid that I will slip into that same feeling again.

Therapist: What does it feel like?

Patient: I get bothered and angry. The reasons don't seem clear.

Therapist: But do you notice the words you use; do they mean something?

Patient: No—I get too upset.

Therapist: Upset is a different word. You said you were impatient, you were afraid that you would slip back into being angry; but now you said "upset." Can you see how this more closely reflects anxiety and how that inevitably makes you upset and then angry?

Therapist has engaged the patient in an effort designed to enable the ego to exercise some lagging functions—self observation and particularly discrimination of affect. The therapist specifically avoids referring to the affects as anger because this would accept that the patient describes and expresses all affect in this one global form.

PROMOTION OF SELF-ESTEEM WITH AFFECT DIFFERENTIATION

Patient: I know that by now you meant what you just said and that it was a gentle and positive statement. Yet it made me so angry that I had to fight off an impulse to get up and get out of here, and that's really crazy!

Therapist: Wait a moment. It may have more of a rationale than either of us can see at the moment. We just need to know more of what went through your mind.

Patient: Nothing, just a wave of anger.

Therapist: Nothing is a good enough first answer. But as we think further we may be able to find the missing link that converted a gentle, positive statement into something to get angry about.

Patient: They always said I'm an angry person.

Therapist: Perhaps it wasn't what they said.

Patient: Well, I do have a vague idea that I felt other things. But they said it was anger and it feels that way now.

Therapist: It might have been an independent thought.

Patient: That feels right. I didn't agree with them and they said it was because I'm always so angry.

Therapist: But it was you.

Patient: You mean that when I'm being myself I'm not the same as others. They called it anger because they couldn't stand it.

LEADING THE PATIENT OUT OF THE IMMEDIACY OF THE PRIMARY DYADIC INTERACTION AND REPAIR OF SPLITTING

Patient: I look awful today.

Therapist: Then you are feeling bad about yourself.

Patient: My mother called me this morning and I just could not stand it. I'm in my middle forties and she's still telling me what to do every day. So I yelled at her and told her to leave me alone.

Therapist: And so you are now feeling so bad for having done that.

Patient: It's so confusing. She's a big pain in the neck and there is nothing to like about her behavior, yet it still makes me feel so bad, to be mean to her.

Therapist: Ah! Now you're getting close to what it is. You have trouble in understanding that you can dislike just that aspect of her behavior. When you yell at her and then feel bad, it's because instead of disliking this or that aspect, you dislike and want to discard all of her.

Patient: I see that. But why does she call me every day?

Therapist: Perhaps you both encourage that.

Patient: You mean she needs to do it?

Therapist: I mean that you need it too, and so you participate in it.

Patient: But I told you it makes me mad.

Therapist: That's because part of you wants to get out of it. But we have to deal with the part of you that still needs a mother.

Patient: Great! At my age I still need a mother. I suppose you're right. How do I get out of that? It feels so difficult.

Therapist: It feels that way because we haven't yet found what it is you need her for.

Patient: Maybe I like to have her tell me what to do but the adult in me can't stand it.

Therapist: That is one possibility. But I rather think that you don't feel comfortable about her need.

Patient: Oh. I get it. I'd push her away for good and then I'd have to be on my own.

Therapist: But I think you have additional worries—not that that one is so small.

Patient: Yes. What would become of her?

Therapist: So you have to remain a child so that your mother won't lose her "job" as mother. Otherwise she'd be unemployed.

Patient: She needs me, so I need her. We're in a vicious cycle.

Therapist: Now that you see that you may find a place where you can break into it without feeling that it will destroy her.

Patient: We'd be separate persons then.

Therapist: Might that feel good?

Patient: It feels terrific already. But can I do it?

Therapist: I believe now that gradually you will, as you see that it doesn't harm either of you.

Patient: But sometimes she is so good to me. I don't want to lose her. It makes me feel good, too—just as it makes me feel bad to yell at her when she encroaches too much.

Therapist: You experience her as sometimes good and sometimes bad. That's what makes you feel bad about yourself. You'd like to think of her as perfect so that you'll never get angry with her.

Patient: That's exactly what happens. One day we have a pleasant conversation. Sometimes in the same conversation I end up hating her.

Therapist: Because you are looking for a perfect mother and she disappoints you.

Patient: Everyone does. No one is perfect. But I can see that I want that.

We pause here, in describing the role of the therapist as catalyst of reorganization, to call attention to the consistent thread running through all case illustrations, demonstrating the technique of dealing with the organizational malformations whenever possible, not to their behavioral consequences. The patient's surly response to the therapist's greeting is perceived as the result of poor frustration tolerance, magical expectations of smoothness which, when disappointed, becomes something for which the therapist is blamed. By such understanding, the therapist eschews invitation to do battle.

The patient who consistently accuses the therapist of lying is seeking replication of the original object experience because of the threat of object loss implicit in cognition of a new positive object in a wider object world. This tempts to separation from the primary object and would bring on severe anxiety. The shadings of affect differentation—impatient, bothered, angry, anxious—become possible only if the therapist can see beyond the interpersonal provocation to the painful separation anxiety.

Self esteem can probably never be created by means of external confrontation. When the angry and provocative behavior can be understood and explained in its very formative processes, retrospective self empathy will produce a more positively cathected sense of self.

Similarly, healing of split representations, both of self and of object, requires a retrospectively empathic connection with the confusion and bewilderment of the child who had to organize structure around the infantile needs of her own mother. Such role confusion imposes age-inappropriate demands upon the child, leading to stresses which cannot be coped with in normal development. Thereby, malformations and distortions in self representations as well as object representations are formed and become involved in the ongoing organization. The behavioral manifestations caused by distorted early experiences produce frequent clashes and confrontations in ordinary living. It is most important that the therapist develop awareness of the many pitfalls in order not to follow the "script" of destructive primary interaction.

THE THERAPIST AS CATALYST OF DEVELOPMENT OF A CAPACITY FOR SELF-SOOTHING

While discussions of therapeutic methods of lowering anxiety levels abound, these are based mainly in terms of either understanding and resolving the causes of anxiety or in finding the most effective medication. The latter remains a palliative, while the former is a long-term goal. An interim goal of quickening or strengthening the capacity for self-soothing is useful. Especially is this true when capacity for signal anxiety has not been attained, or barely exists, as illustrated by the case in the second section—the patient who had a panic reaction when unexpectedly greeted by a friend in a restaurant. Perhaps more often than has been recognized heretofore, the problem lies in the organizational failure to develop past the fulcrum (Section G, chapter 5) from organismic distress, to external soothing, to self-soothing, and finally to signal anxiety. In such situations, the bottom line rests in the soothing qualities of the therapeutic interaction. Beyond this, the therapist provides, often with the patient's guidance, whatever interchanges can be used to promote soothing. Where the patient is invariably startled by the ringing of the bell announcing the arrival of the next patient, the patient can be asked whether he would prefer to be forewarned that the bell will ring shortly. Another patient found it soothing to have at least five minutes alone in the waiting room to help her make the transition to the consultation room even though it meant using up her own time for that purpose. A patient with markedly anally oriented problems "enjoys" the use of the toilet before each session. He expects "interpretation" (disapproval) but responds gratefully to the postponement of that aspect of the work in favor of accepting that this is the way he prepares himself for the session at that point in therapy.

Humor can be invaluable if it is not at the patient's expense:

Patient: I was mentally chasing all the other cars off the highway because I was so afraid of being late.
Therapist: Well, you made it, even with a few minutes to spare.
Patient: Yes, but barely.
Therapist: Since you are on time, perhaps we can talk about your fear that you would be late. What would happen, as you anticipate it?
Patient: I don't really know. I think you will be furious with me.
Therapist: Oh. Well, since you were almost late today, does it strike you that I am almost furious?
Patient: (Laughter.)

The fact that the therapist attempts to help the patient find soothing mechanisms, even when not always successful, contains the necessary experiential interaction which we expect will become internalized. This patient took a giant step in that direction as she responded to the therapist's efforts. She recounted a recent visit with her parents, an experience in which she demonstrated a marked improvement in her cognitive capacity and in objectivation. In a sense, she was able to describe the very process whereby progress toward signal anxiety had become fixated. Following her mother's greeting—"Darling, you're so thin and you don't look well"—she experienced a surge of memories, condensed in the reporting. "While I don't remember all the specifics, I can paraphrase my mother's behavior as follows: 'It's a nice day, but I must take Daddy to the doctor; it's a nice day, but I have indigestion from last night's dinner; you're looking well, dear, but your dress doesn't fit you; that's a lovely dress, but why do you look so bad?'" When every observation is leavened with a negative undoing, soothing is not available for acquisition of self-soothing mechanisms.

We summarize the technical measures designed to promote reorganization:

1. Provision of a reliable, consistently benign climate
2. Absence of counterhostility in the face of negative affect
3. Distinction between hostility as affect and separation-serving aggressive thrusts that are growth promoting rather than object directed
4. Maintenance of the therapeutic differential that will sooner or later force the patient's cognitive capacity to take into account that the wider object world represented by the therapist is different from the world of primary objects with whom the patient continues to interact as though they are still present
5. Designation of the malformations that have distorted organization in subphase interaction
6. Imposition of growth-promoting frustration that furthers the separation-individuation process
7. Explanation, a technique that precedes interpretation and is designed to help the patient understand where, in the subphase interaction, his organizational process began to include malformations because of inadequacy in subphase experience
8. Exposure of the manner in which replication of experiences in the dyad are continuously repeated for purpose of retention of the object connection, no matter how negative it was
9. "Tracking" the patient in attunement to the clinical expression of malformations and guiding their reorganization as described in chapter 11
10. Interpretation for those structures where a high degree of organization exists or where, by using growth promoting therapeutic measures, such organization has been attained.

It is not possible, nor have we tried, to isolate each aspect of therapeutic intervention and to list step by step how the therapy is to proceed. The matter is too complex. There are the multifaceted aspects of development and their potential for malformations in organization on the patient's side of the therapeutic encounter. On the therapist's side, we are groping with new theory and new extrapolations into technique. In the end psychotherapy will always remain an art. While psychoanalytic developmental psychology provides a firm basis for practice, there are as many styles of applying it as there are therapists. We are excited by the splendor of the theory which has hardly come to the end, as we must now. As Hartmann (1964) put it:

> But, as for the present, the concepts of developmental phase, conflict, trauma have become much more complex for us, and, I think, they will become ever more complex before we again reach that beautiful, peaceful state of affairs when both simple and general formulations become possible [p. 209].

Bibliography

Abelin, Ernest L. 1971. The role of the father in the separation-individuation process. In John B. McDevitt and Calvin F. Settlage, eds., *Separation-Individuation,* pp. 229–52. New York: International Universities Press.

—— 1975. Some further observations and comments on the earliest role of the father. *The International Journal of Psycho-Analysis* 56:293–302.

Alexander, Franz and Thomas M. French. 1946. *Psychoanalytic Therapy.* New York: Ronald Press.

Altman, Leon. 1977. Some vicissitudes of love. *Journal of the American Psychoanalytic Association* 25:35–52.

Apfelbaum, Bernard. 1965. Ego psychology, psychic energy, and the hazards of quantitative explanation in psychoanalytic theory. *The International Journal of Psycho-Analysis* 46:168–82.

Applegarth, Adrienne P. 1971. Comments on aspects of the theory of psychic energy. *Journal of the American Psychoanalytic Association* 19:379–416.

—— 1977. Psychic energy reconsidered. *Journal of the American Psychoanalytic Association* 25:599–602.

Arlow, Jacob A. 1961. Silence and the theory of technique. (*The Silent Patient.*) *Journal of the American Psychoanalytic Association* 9:44–55.

—— 1974. Panel on transference. (Arthur F. Valenstein, reporter.) *The International Journal of Psycho-Analysis* 55:311–21.

Benedek, Therese. 1959. Parenthood as a developmental phase. *Journal of the American Psychoanalytic Association* 7:389–417.

Benjamin, John. 1961. The innate and the experiential in child development. In H. Brosin, ed., *Lectures on Experimental Psychiatry,* pp. 19–42. Pittsburgh: University of Pittsburgh Press.

Bergmann, Martin S. 1971. Psychoanalytic observations on the capacity to love. In John B. McDevitt and Calvin F. Settlage, eds., *Separation-Individuation,* pp. 15–40. New York: International Universities Press.

Blanck, Gertrude. 1966. Some technical implications of ego psychology. *The International Journal of Psycho-Analysis* 47:6–13.

—— 1970. Crossroads in the technique of psychotherapy. *The Psychoanalytic Review* 16:498–510.

—— 1977. Towards the elaboration of practice theory. *Smith College Studies in Social Work,* pp. 104–11.

Blanck, Gertrude and Rubin Blanck. 1972. Toward a psychoanalytic development psychology. *Journal of the American Psychoanalytic Association* 20:668–710.

—— 1974. *Ego Psychology: Theory and Practice.* New York: Columbia University Press.

Blanck, Rubin. 1965. The case for individual treatment. *Social Casework,* Family Service Association of America 46:70–74.

—— 1967. Marriage as a phase of personality development. *Social Casework,* Family Service Association of America, 48:154–60.

—— 1973. Countertransference in treatment of the borderline patient. *Clinical Social Work Journal* 1:110–17.

—— 1977. Practice theory then and now. *Smith College Studies in Social Work,* pp. 95–103.

Blanck, Rubin and Gertrude Blanck. 1968. *Marriage and Personal Development.* New York: Columbia University Press.

—— 1977. The transference object and the real object. *The International Journal of Psycho-Analysis* 58:33–44.

Blos, Peter. 1962. *On Adolescence: A Psychoanalytic Interpretation.* New York: Free Press.

Brazelton, T. Berry et al. 1975. Early mother-infant reciprocity. *Ciba Symposium.* Amsterdam.

Brenner, Charles. 1971. The psycho-analytic concept of aggression. *The International Journal of Psycho-Analysis* 52:137–44.

Dewald, Paul A. 1976. Transference regression and real experience in the psychoanalytic process. *The Psychoanalytic Quarterly* 45:213–30.

Eissler, Kurt R. 1953. The effect of the structure of the ego on psychoanalytic technique. *Journal of the American Psychoanalytic Association* 1:104–43.

Erikson, Erik H. 1954. On the sense of inner identity. In Robert P. Knight and Cyrus R. Friedman, eds., *Psychoanalytic Psychiatry and Psychology,* pp. 351–64. New York: International Universities Press.

Escoll, Philip J. (reporter). 1977. The contribution of psychoanalytic developmental concepts to adult analysis. *Journal of the American Psychoanalytic Association* 25:215–34.

Fenichel, Otto. 1935. Concerning the theory of psychoanalytic technique. In Hanna Fenichel and David Rapaport, eds., *The Collected Papers of Otto Fenichel,* pp. 332–48. New York: Norton, 1953.

—— 1941a. The ego and the affects. In *The Collected Papers of Otto Fenichel,* pp. 215–27. 2d series. New York: Norton, 1954.

—— 1941b. *Problems of Psychoanalytic Technique.* New York: Psychoanalytic Quarterly.
—— 1945. *The Psychoanalytic Theory of Neurosis.* New York: Norton.
Fleming, Joan. 1975. Some observations on object constancy in the psychoanalysis of adults. *Journal of the American Psychoanalytic Association* 23:743–60.
—— 1977–78. Personal communication.
Freud, Anna. 1936. *The Ego and the Mechanisms of Defence.* In *The Writings of Anna Freud,* vol. 2. New York: International Universities Press, 1966.
—— 1963. The concept of developmental lines. *The Psychoanalytic Study of the Child* 18:245–65. New York: International Universities Press.
—— 1972. Comments on aggression. *The International Journal of Psycho-Analysis* 53:163–72.
—— 1966. Obsessional neurosis: a summary of psycho-analytic views. *The International Journal of Psycho-Analysis* 47:116–22.
Freud, Sigmund. *The Standard Edition of the Complete Psychological Works of Sigmund Freud.* 24 vols. James Strachey, ed. London: Hogarth Press, 1953–66.
—— 1895. Studies on hysteria. *The Standard Edition,* vol. 2. London: Hogarth Press, 1963.
—— 1900. The interpretation of dreams. *The Standard Edition,* vols. 4 and 5. London: Hogarth Press, 1955.
—— 1905a. Fragment of an analysis of a case of hysteria. *The Standard Edition,* 7:7–124. London: Hogarth Press, 1953.
—— 1905b. Three essays on the theory of sexuality. *The Standard Edition,* 7:125–221. London: Hogarth Press, 1953.
—— 1905c. Jokes and their relation to the unconscious. *The Standard Edition,* vol. 8. London: Hogarth Press, 1960.
—— 1909. Notes upon a case of obsessional neurosis. *The Standard Edition,* 10:153–318. London: Hogarth Press, 1955.
—— 1910. Observations on wild analysis. *The Standard Edition,* 11:219–30. London: Hogarth Press, 1957.
—— 1911. Psycho-analytic notes on an autobiographical account of a case of paranoia (dementia paranoides). *The Standard Edition,* 12:3–80. London: Hogarth Press, 1958.
—— 1912a. The dynamics of transference. *The Standard Edition,* 12:97–108. London: Hogarth Press, 1958.
—— 1912b. Recommendations to physicians practising psycho-analysis. *The Standard Edition,* 12:109–20. London: Hogarth Press, 1958.
—— 1913. On beginning the treatment. *The Standard Edition,* 12:121–44. London: Hogarth Press, 1958.
—— 1914a. On narcissism: an introduction. *The Standard Edition,* 14:67–102. London: Hogarth Press, 1957.

—— 1914b. Remembering, repeating and working through. *The Standard Edition,* 12:145–56. London: Hogarth Press, 1958.

—— 1916–17. Resistance and repression. Lecture XIX. *Introductory Lectures on Psycho-Analysis. The Standard Edition,* 16:286–302. London: Hogarth Press, 1963.

—— 1917a. The libido theory and narcissism. Lecture XXVI. *Introductory Lectures on Psycho-Analysis. The Standard Edition,* 16:412–30. London: Hogarth Press, 1963.

—— 1917b. Mourning and melancholia. *The Standard Edition,* 14:237–58. London: Hogarth Press, 1957.

—— 1917c. Transference. Lecture XXVII. *Introductory Lectures on Psycho-Analysis. The Standard Edition,* 16:431–47. London: Hogarth Press, 1963.

—— 1918. From the history of an infantile neurosis. *The Standard Edition,* 17:3–122. London: Hogarth Press, 1955.

—— 1920. Beyond the pleasure principle. *The Standard Edition,* 18:7–64. London: Hogarth Press, 1955.

—— 1923. The ego and the id. *The Standard Edition.* 19:12–68. London: Hogarth Press, 1961.

—— 1926. Inhibitions, symptoms and anxiety. *The Standard Edition,* 20:77–178. London: Hogarth Press, 1959.

—— 1930. Civilization and its discontents. *The Standard Edition,* 21:59–145. London: Hogarth Press, 1961.

—— 1933. Anxiety and instinctual life. Lecture XXXII. *New Introductory Lectures on Psycho-Analysis. The Standard Edition,* 22:81–184. London: Hogarth Press, 1964.

—— 1937. Analysis terminable and interminable. *The Standard Edition,* 23:209–54. London: Hogarth Press, 1964.

—— 1940. An outline of psycho-analysis. *The Standard Edition,* 23:141–208. London: Hogarth Press, 1964.

Friedman, Lawrence. 1969. The therapeutic alliance. *The International Journal of Psycho-Analysis* 50:139–53.

Furer, Manuel (panelist). 1976. Current concepts of the psychoanalytic process. Stephen A. Morgenstern (reporter). *Journal of the American Psychoanalytic Association* 24:181–95.

Galenson, Eleanor (reporter). 1978. The psychology of women. *Journal of the American Psychoanalytic Association* 26:163–77.

Garma, Angel. 1971. Within the realm of the death instinct. *The International Journal of Psycho-Analysis* 52:145–54.

Gill, Merton M. 1977. Psychic energy reconsidered. *Journal of the American Psychoanalytic Association* 25:581–97.

Gillespie, William H. 1971. Aggression and instinct theory. *The International Journal of Psycho-Analysis* 52:155–60.

Glover, Edward. 1939. The psycho-analysis of affects. *The International Journal of Psycho-Analysis* 20:299–307.

—— 1955. *The Technique of Psychoanalysis.* New York: International Universities Press.
—— 1956. *On the Early Development of the Mind.* New York: International Universities Press.
Greenacre, Phyllis. 1953a. Certain relationships between fetishism and the faulty development of the body image. *The Psychoanalytic Study of the Child* 8:79–97. New York: International Universities Press.
—— 1953b. *Trauma, Growth, and Personality.* London: Hogarth Press.
—— 1954. The role of transference. *Journal of the American Psychoanalytic Association* 2:671–84.
—— 1956. Re-evaluation of the process of working through. *The International Journal of Psycho-Analysis* 37:439–45.
—— 1957. The childhood of the artist. *The Psychoanalytic Study of the Child* 12:47–72. New York: International Universities Press.
—— 1959. Certain technical problems in the transference relationship. *Journal of the American Psychoanalytic Association* 7:484–502.
—— 1966. Problems of overidealization of the analyst and of analysis: their manifestations in the transference and countertransference relationship. *The Psychoanalytic Study of the Child* 21:209–19. New York: International Universities Press.
—— 1971. Notes on the influence and contribution of ego psychology to the practice of psychoanalysis. In John B. McDevitt and Calvin F. Settlage, eds., *Separation-Individuation,* pp. 171–200. New York: International Universities Press.
Greenson, Ralph R. 1961. On the silence and sounds of the analytic hour. (*The Silent Patient.*) *Journal of the American Psychoanalytic Association* 9:79–84.
—— 1965a. The problem of working through. In Max Schur, ed., *Drives, Affects, and Behavior,* pp. 277–313. New York: International Universities Press.
—— 1965b. The working alliance and the transference neurosis. *The Psychoanalytic Quarterly* 34:155–81.
—— 1967. *The Technique and Practice of Psychoanalysis.* New York: Hallmark Press.
Greenson, Ralph R. and Milton Wexler. 1969. The non-transference relationships in the psychoanalytic situation. *The International Journal of Psycho-Analysis* 50:27–39.
Hartmann, Heinz. 1939–1958. *Ego Psychology and the Problem of Adaptation.* New York: International Universities Press.
—— 1950a. Comments on the psychoanalytic theory of the ego. In Heinz Hartmann, *Essays on Ego Psychology,* pp. 113–41. New York: International Universities Press, 1964.
—— 1950b. Psychoanalysis and developmental psychology. In *Essays on Ego Psychology,* pp. 99–112. New York: International Universities Press, 1964.
—— 1956a. The development of the ego concept in Freud's work. In *Essays on*

Ego Psychology, pp. 268–96. New York: International Universities Press, 1964.

—— 1956b. Notes on the reality principle. In *Essays on Ego Psychology,* pp. 241–67. New York: International Universities Press, 1964.

—— 1964. *Essays on Ego Psychology.* New York: International Universities Press.

Hartmann, Heinz and Ernest Kris. 1945. The genetic approach in psychoanalysis. *The Psychoanalytic Study of the Child* 1:11–30. New York: International Universities Press.

Hartmann, Heinz, Ernest Kris, and Rudolph M. Loewenstein. 1946. Comments on the formation of psychic structure. *The Psychoanalytic Study of the Child* 2:11–38. New York: International Universities Press.

—— 1949. Notes on the theory of aggression. *The Psychoanalytic Study of the Child* 3/4:9–36. New York: International Universities Press.

Hartmann, Heinz and Rudolph M. Loewenstein. 1962. Notes on the superego. *The Psychoanalytic Study of the Child* 17:42–81. New York: International Universities Press.

Hartocollis, Peter. 1977. *Borderline Personality Disorders.* New York: International Universities Press.

Heiman, Paula and Arthur F. Valenstein. 1972. The psychoanalytic concept of aggression: an integrated summary. *The International Journal of Psycho-Analysis* 53:31–36.

Holt, Robert R. 1966. A critical examination of Freud's concept of bound vs. free cathexis. *Journal of the American Psychoanalytic Association* 10:475–525.

Horowitz, Milton H. 1977. The quantitative line of approach in psychoanalysis: a clinical assessment of its present status. *Journal of the American Psychoanalytic Association* 25:559–79.

Jacobson, Edith. 1954. The self and the object world: vicissitudes of their infantile cathexes and their influence on ideational and affective development. *The Psychoanalytic Study of the Child* 9:75–127. New York: International Universities Press.

—— 1964. *The Self and the Object World.* New York: International Universities Press.

—— 1966. Problems in the differentiation between schizophrenic and melancholic states. In Rudolph M. Loewenstein, Lottie M. Newman, Max Schur, and Albert J. Solnit, eds., *Psychoanalysis—A General Psychology,* pp. 499–520. New York: International Universities Press.

—— 1971. *Depression.* New York: International Universities Press.

Joffe, Walter G. and Joseph Sandler. 1968. Comments on the psychoanalytic psychology of adaptation with special reference to the role of affects and the representational world. *The International Journal of Psycho-Analysis* 49:445–54.

Kernberg, Otto F. 1974. Barriers to falling and remaining in love. *Journal of the American Psychoanalytic Association* 22:486–511.

—— 1975. *Borderline Conditions and Pathological Narcissism.* New York: Aronson.

—— 1976. *Object Relations Theory and Clinical Psychoanalysis.* New York: Aronson.

—— 1977. Boundaries and structure in love relations. *Journal of the American Psychoanalytic Association* 25:81–114.

Klein, Melanie. 1948. *Contributions to Psycho-Analysis, 1921–1945.* London: Hogarth Press.

Kohut, Heinz. 1971. *The Analysis of the Self.* New York: International Universities Press.

—— 1977. *The Restoration of the Self.* New York: International Universities Press.

Kris, Ernst. 1952. *Psychoanalytic Explorations in Art.* New York: International Universities Press.

—— 1956a. The recovery of childhood memories in psychoanalysis. *The Psychoanalytic Study of the Child* 11:54–88. New York: International Universities Press.

—— 1956b. On some vicissitudes of insight in psychoanalysis. *The International Journal of Psycho-Analysis* 37:445–55.

—— 1956c. The personal myth. *Journal of the American Psychoanalytic Association* 4:653–81.

Lewin, Bertram D. 1950. *The Psychoanalysis of Elation.* New York: Norton.

Lichtenberg, Joseph D. 1975. The development of the sense of self. *Journal of the American Psychoanalytic Association* 23:453–84.

Lipton, Samuel D. (discussant). 1976. Current concepts in the psychoanalytic process. Stephen A. Morgenstern (reporter). *Journal of the American Psychoanalytic Association* 24:181–95.

Loewald, Hans W. 1960. On the therapeutic action of psycho-analysis. *The International Journal of Psycho-Analysis* 41:16–33.

—— 1962. Internalization, separation, mourning, and the superego. *The Psychoanalytic Quarterly* 31:483–504.

—— 1972. Freud's conception of the negative therapeutic reaction with comments on instinct theory. *Journal of the American Psychoanalytic Association* 20:235–45.

—— 1974. Current status of the concept of infantile neurosis; discussion. *The Psychoanalytic Study of the Child* 29:183–88. New Haven: Yale University Press.

—— 1977. Instinct theory, object relations and psychic structure formation. Address at the Margaret S. Mahler Symposium. Philadelphia.

Loewenstein, Rudolph M. 1951. The problem of interpretation. *The Psychoanalytic Quarterly* 20:1–14.

Mahler, Margaret S. 1952. On child psychosis and schizophrenia: autistic and symbiotic infantile psychosis. *The Psychoanalytic Study of the Child* 7:286–305. New York: International Universities Press.

—— 1958. Autism and symbiosis, two extreme disturbances of identity. *The International Journal of Psycho-Analysis* 39:77–83.

—— 1961. On sadness and grief in infancy and childhood: loss and restoration of the symbiotic love object. *The Psychoanalytic Study of the Child* 16:332–51. New York: International Universities Press.

—— 1963. Thoughts about development and individuation. *The Psychoanalytic Study of the Child* 18:307–24. New York: International Universities Press.

—— 1965. On the significance of the normal separation-individuation phase. In Max Schur, ed., *Drives, Affects, and Behavior,* pp. 161–68. New York: International Universities Press.

—— 1966. Notes on the development of basic moods: the depressive affect in psychoanalysis. In Rudolph M. Loewenstein, Lottie M. Newman, Max Schur, and Albert J. Solnit, eds., *Psychoanalysis—A General Psychology,* pp. 152–68. New York: International Universities Press.

—— 1968. *On Human Symbiosis and the Vicissitudes of Individuation.* New York: International Universities Press.

—— 1971. A study of the separation-individuation process: and its possible application to borderline phenomena in the psychoanalytic situation. *The Psychoanalytic Study of the Child* 26:403–24. New York: Quadrangle Books.

—— 1972. On the first three subphases of the separation-individuation process. *The International Journal of Psycho-Analysis* 53:333–38.

—— 1973. Address at Association for Child Psychoanalysis. Paris.

—— 1974. Symbiosis and individuation: the psychological birth of the human infant. *The Psychoanalytic Study of the Child* 29:89–106. New Haven: Yale University Press.

—— 1976. Personal communication.

Mahler, Margaret S. and Paula Elkisch. 1953. Some observations on disturbances of the ego in a case of infantile psychosis. *The Psychoanalytic Study of the Child* 8:307–24. New York: International University Press.

Mahler, Margaret S. and Manuel Furer. 1963. Certain aspects of the separation-individuation phase. *The Psychoanalytic Quarterly* 32:1–14.

Mahler, Margaret S. and Bertram J. Gosliner. 1955. On symbiotic child psychosis: genetic, dynamic, and restitutive aspects. *The Psychoanalytic Study of the Child* 10:195–212. New York: International Universities Press.

Mahler, Margaret S. and Louise J. Kaplan. 1977. Developmental aspects in the assessment of narcissistic and so-called borderline personalities. In Peter Hartocollis, ed., *Borderline Personality Disorders,* pp. 71–85. New York: International Universities Press.

Mahler, Margaret S. and Kitty LaPerriere. 1965. Mother-child interaction during separation-individuation. *The Psychoanalytic Quarterly* 34:483–98.

Mahler, Margaret S., Fred Pine and Anni Bergman. 1975. *The Psychological Birth of the Human Infant.* New York: Basic Books.

Mendelson, Myer. 1974. *Psychoanalytic Concepts of Depression.* New York: Spectrum Publications.

Menninger, Karl. 1958. *Theory of Psychoanalytic Technique.* New York: Basic Books.

Milrod, David. 1977. The wished-for self image. Paper presented at the Rudolph M. Loewenstein Memorial Meeting of the New York Psychoanalytic Society and Institute, November 12, 1977.

Mitscherlich, Alexander. 1971. Psychoanalysis and the aggression of large groups. *The International Journal of Psycho-Analysis* 52:161–67.

Moore, Burness E., and Bernard D. Fine. 1967. *A Glossary of Psychoanalytic Terms and Concepts.* New York: American Psychoanalytic Association.

Nagera, Humberto. 1964. Autoerotism, autoerotic activities, and ego development. *The Psychoanalytic Study of the Child* 19:240–55. New York: International Universities Press.

—— 1966. *Early Childhood Disturbances, the Infantile Neuroses, and the Adult Disturbances.* New York: International Universities Press.

Novey, Samuel. 1962. The principle of "working through" in psychoanalysis. *Journal of the American Psychoanalytic Association* 10:658–76.

Nunberg, Herman. 1948. The synthetic function of the ego. In Herman Nunberg, *Practice and Theory of Psychoanalysis,* 1:120–36. New York: International Universities Press.

Orr, Douglass W. 1954. Transference and countertransference: a historical survey. *Journal of the American Psychoanalytic Association* 2:621–71.

Parens, Henri. 1973. Aggression: a reconsideration. *Journal of the American Psychoanalytic Association* 21:34–60.

Prall, Robert C. (reporter). 1978. The role of the father in the preoedipal years. *Journal of the American Psychoanalytic Association* 26:143–61.

Rangell, Leo (reporter). 1955. Panel: The borderline case. *Journal of the American Psychoanalytic Association* 3:285–98.

——1972. Aggression, oedipus, and historical perspective. Presidential address. *The International Journal of Psycho-Analysis* 53:3–12.

Rapaport, David. 1953. On the psychoanalytic theory of affects. *The International Journal of Psycho-Analysis* 34:177–98.

—— 1959. A historical survey of psychoanalytic ego psychology. Introduction to Erik H. Erikson, *Identity and the Life Cycle,* pp. 5–17. New York: International Universities Press.

Ritvo, Samuel. 1974a. Current status of the concept of infantile neurosis: implications for diagnosis and technique. *The Psychoanalytic Study of the Child* 29:159–81. New Haven: Yale University Press.

—— 1974b. Address at Margaret S. Mahler Symposium, Philadelphia.

Robbins, Fred (panelist). 1977. The contribution of psychoanalytic developmental concepts to adult analysis. Philip J. Escoll (reporter). *Journal of the American Psychoanalytic Association* 25:228–31.

Rosenblatt, Allen D. and James T. Thickstun. 1977. Energy, information, and motivation: a revision of psychoanalytic theory. *Journal of the American Psychoanalytic Association* 25:537–58.

Ross, John M. 1977. Towards fatherhood: the epigenesis of paternal identity during a boy's first decade. *The International Review of Psycho-Analysis* 4:327–47.

Ross, Manuel. 1976. The borderline diathesis. The *International Review of Psycho-Analysis* 3:305–21.

Ross, Nathaniel. 1968. Psychoanalysis and moral values. *Professional Digest* 5:2–5. New York Society of Clinical Psychologists.

—— 1975. Affect as cognition: with observations on the meanings of mystical states. *The International Review of Psycho-Analysis* 2:79–94.

Sandler, Joseph. 1976. Countertransference and role responsiveness. *The International Review of Psycho-Analysis* 3:43–47.

—— 1976. Dreams, unconscious fantasies, and "identity of perception." *The International Review of Psycho-Analysis* 3:33–42.

Sandler, Joseph and Walter G. Joffe. 1969. Towards a basic psychoanalytic model. *The International Journal of Psycho-Analysis* 50:79–90.

Sandler, Joseph and Bernard Rosenblatt. 1962. The concept of a representational world. *The Psychoanalytic Study of the Child* 17:128–45. New York: International Universities Press.

Schmale, Herbert T. (reporter). 1966. Working through. *Journal of the American Psychoanalytic Association* 14:172–82.

Schreber, Daniel P. 1955. *Memoirs of My Nervous Illness.* London: Dawson.

Schur, Max. 1955. Comments on the metapsychology of somatization. *The Psychoanalytic Study of the Child* 10:119–64. New York: International Universities Press.

—— 1966. *The Id and the Regulatory Principles of Mental Functioning.* New York: International Universities Press.

—— 1972. *Freud: Living and Dying.* New York: International Universities Press.

Schur, Max, ed. 1965. *Drives, Affects, Behavior,* vol. 2. New York: International Universities Press.

Settlage, Calvin F. 1977. The psychoanalytic understanding of narcisstic and borderline personality disorders: advances in developmental theory. *Journal of the American Psychoanalytic Association* 25:805–33.

Sharpe, Ella Freeman. 1950. *Collected Papers on Psycho-Analysis.* London: Hogarth Press.

—— 1930–50. The dynamics of the method—the transference. In *Collected Papers on Psycho-Analysis,* pp. 53–66. London: Hogarth Press.

Spitz, René A. 1945. Hospitalism. *The Psychoanalytic Study of the Child* 1:53–74. New York: International Universities Press.

—— 1946. Anaclitic depression. *The Psychoanalytic Study of the Child* 2:313–42. New York: International Universities Press.

——1957. *No and Yes.* New York: International Universities Press.

—— 1959. *A Genetic Field Theory of Ego Formation.* New York: International Universities Press.

—— 1965. *The First Year of Life.* New York: International Universities Press.
—— 1972. Bridges: on anticipation, duration and meaning. *Journal of the American Psychoanalytic Association* 20:721–35.
Stein, Martin H. (chairman). 1972. Panel on aggression. André Lussier (reporter). *The International Journal of Psycho-Analysis* 53:13–20.
Sterba, Richard F. 1934. The fate of the ego in analytic therapy. *The International Journal of Psycho-Analysis* 15:117–26.
Stone, Leo. 1975. Some problems and potentialities of present-day psychoanalysis. *The Psychoanalytic Quarterly* 44:331–70.
Storr, Anthony. 1968. *Human Aggression.* New York: Atheneum.
Strachey, James. 1957. Editor's note to instincts and their vicissitudes. *The Standard Edition of the Complete Psychological Works of Sigmund Freud,* 14:111–16. London: Hogarth Press.
Swanson, Don R. 1977. A critique of psychic energy as an exploratory concept. *Journal of the American Psychoanalytic Association* 25:603–33.
Tolpin, Marian. 1970. The infantile neurosis: a metapsychological concept and a paradigmatic case history. *The Psychoanalytic Study of the Child* 25:273–305. New York: International Universities Press.
—— 1971. On the beginnings of a cohesive self: an application of the concept of transmuting internalization to the study of the transitional object and signal anxiety. *The Psychoanalytic Study of the Child* 26:316–52. New York: Quadrangle Books.
Wallerstein, Robert S. 1977. Psychic energy reconsidered. *Journal of the American Psychoanalytic Association* 25:529–35.
Winnicott, D. W. 1953. Transitional objects and transitional phenomena. *The International Journal of Psycho-Analysis* 34:89–97.
Zeligs, Meyer. 1961. The psychology of silence: its role in transference, countertransference, and the psychoanalytic process. (*The Silent Patient.*) *Journal of the American Psychoanalytic Association* 9:7–43.
Zetzel, Elizabeth R. 1956. Current concepts of transference. *The International Journal of Psycho-Analysis* 37:369–75.
—— 1965. The theory of therapy in relation to a developmental model of the psychic apparatus. *The International Journal of Psycho-Analysis* 46:39–52.

Index of Subjects

Index of Names